Gilpin County Public Library
Box 551 15131 Hwy 119
Black Hawk, CO 80422

DEMCO

Citizen Soldiers
in the
War of 1812

Citizen Soldiers

in the

War of 1812

C. Edward Skeen

THE UNIVERSITY PRESS OF KENTUCKY

Publication of this volume was made possible in part
by a grant from the National Endowment for the Humanities.

Scholarly publisher for the Commonwealth,
serving Bellarmine College, Berea College, Centre
College of Kentucky, Eastern Kentucky University,
The Filson Club Historical Society, Georgetown College,
Kentucky Historical Society, Kentucky State University,
Morehead State University, Murray State University,
Northern Kentucky University, Transylvania University,
University of Kentucky, University of Louisville,
and Western Kentucky University.

Editorial and Sales Offices: The University Press of Kentucky
663 South Limestone Street, Lexington, Kentucky 40508-4008

03 02 01 00 99   5 4 3 2 1

Library of Congress Cataloging-in-Publication Data

Skeen, Carl Edward.
   Citizen soldiers in the war of 1812 / C. Edward Skeen.
      p.   cm.
   Includes bibliographical references and index.
   ISBN 0-8131-2089-6 (alk. paper)
   1. United States—History—War of 1812—Manpower.
2. United States—Militia—History—War of 1812.
3. United States. Army—Recruiting, enlistment, etc.—War
of 1812. 4. United States. Army—Mobilization—History—
19th century. 5. United States. Army—Military life—
History—19th century. I. Title.
E359.3.S48   1998
973.5'2—dc21   98-7953

Manufactured in the United States of America

To my wife,
Linda

Contents

Illustrations

Maps

Portraits and Wood Cuts

Acknowledgments

In the course of a study like this one, many individuals and institutions ultimately have a role in producing the finished product. The University of Memphis provided me with a semester's leave to work on the research for this study. I also gratefully acknowledge the assistance of the librarians in the microforms department of the Ned R. McWhirter Library of the University of Memphis, where the bulk of my research was done. I thank Dr. Devlin S. Fung and his students in the Department of Geography Laboratory for Remote Sensing and Geographic Information Systems, University of Memphis, for the maps in this book.

I am grateful to those who read chapters or the entire manuscript and gave advice, critical and encouraging, which was mostly accepted but on rare occasions rejected. I thank you all for allowing me to impose on your time. These people include my colleague and friend Major L. Wilson, whose judgment I always value. Donald R. Hickey graciously read my manuscript and gave me sound advice. My friend David N. Lumsden read and critiqued an early version. I owe my greatest debt of gratitude to Thomas H. Appleton, Jr., for his expert editorial talents. Finally, I had the support of my family. My daughters, Marianne Medlin and Laura Kuns, were unfailing in their interest and encouragement. My wife, Linda, to whom I dedicate this work, willingly endured long hours of hearing about the militia and no doubt learned a great deal more about militia than she ever wanted to know. She knows that she's "okay in my book."

Introduction

In a recent work, Donald Hickey enumerated more than a dozen topics on the War of 1812 needing further historical inquiry. One subject he did not mention was the militia. Nevertheless, the overwhelming majority of the soldiers employed during this war were militia, and their role and contribution during the War of 1812, surprisingly, has never been systematically studied or properly evaluated.[1]

Perhaps the reason for the neglect is the difficulty of preparing a comprehensive study of the various state militia encompassing all aspects of their participation in the War of 1812 (e.g., state-by-state accounts). Such an undertaking would be a daunting, perhaps impossible task, given the paucity of sources. I intend to pursue here only the modest objective of describing the federal utilization of militia to supplement the military forces during the War of 1812, surveying their performance in general, and reviewing the operational aspects of militia participation at the state level. For purposes of this work, I define "militia" to include drafted (or regular) militia plus volunteer militia companies (as distinguished from twelve-month volunteers in federal service). Finally, because the militia system obviously failed to provide an adequate force, particularly to prosecute the war vigorously, I will also attempt to explain the reasons for this failure.

The militia system broke down at the state level largely because the Constitution divided responsibility for the militia. While the federal government was empowered to use state militias to "execute the laws of the Union, suppress insurrections, and repel invasions," and to "provide for organizing, arming, and disciplining the militia," state governments had the right to appoint the officers and train the militia according to the discipline prescribed by the federal government.[2] There was, however, no coordination of training or organization of militia at the state level nor any clear definition of the proper relationship of state versus federal authority over the militia in wartime. Consequently, during the War of 1812 issues were raised concerning who was authorized to call militia into service; who paid them; who equipped and organized them; and how and where they were to be used. Obviously there were many other questions relating to the use of the militia during the War of 1812; I have noted only the most significant.

It is well known that the state militias were not prepared to fight a war in 1812. Long years of neglect by the states, or indifference on their part, meant that when Congress called on April 10, 1812, for 100,000 militia to be held in readiness for possible duty, many states were unprepared. State legislatures often passed elaborate militia laws, but public apathy, indifference, and even hostility led to a situation where there was no efficient, reliable militia force to prosecute the war. A congressional report in 1804 (still valid in 1812) asserted that there were few points on which any two militias were similar, "making impossible the interchangeability of units which was regarded as the essence of any national reserve force."[3] As late as 1812, despite the threat of war, which had been growing for several years, some states were effectively forced to organize their state militias from the ground up.

Ultimately, the problem with the utilization of militia was a question not of their willingness to fight but rather of their ability to fight. Incredible as it may seem, there were many reports that militia showed up not only without weapons but shoeless, barely clothed, and lacking blankets, camp equipment, or any of the articles necessary for a military camp. Also, perhaps equally incredible given our modern perceptions of frontiersmen, many militia not only had no musket but did not even know how to use weapons once they had been issued. Such raw militia could hardly be expected to master the twenty-three distinct motions required to prime, load, ram, and set a firelock in a flintlock musket in the brief time before they were marched off to engage the enemy. When properly organized, equipped, and capably led, the militia could be a formidable fighting force, as they showed at New Orleans. Militia were rarely properly trained or prepared to perform their military duties, however, and in numerous cases during the war militiamen broke and ran before the enemy had even engaged them in battle. Examples include one of the earliest battles at Brownstown and conduct by the militia on the west bank at the final Battle of New Orleans.

On several occasions during the war, state militia in federal service refused to enter Canada. While this was embarrassing to some state authorities, it accorded with the view of others that militia were to be used for the defense of the nation and not as an offensive force. Moreover, governors of several New England states refused to place their militia under federal control and supported their actions with a narrow, legalistic argument that certain federal constitutional requirements had not been met.

Other states were eager to call out their militia even when the national authorities had not asked them to do so, and they complained when the federal government refused compensation.[4] Understandably, the national government, with only limited financial means, could not permit unnecessary militia calls.

Perhaps the most damning indictment of the militia system, and an indication of its failure, was the establishment of state armies. Although the Constitution barred states from keeping troops in times of peace, it was silent on this subject during times of war. Undoubtedly, most state governors would have maintained that their state armies were just extensions of the militia system and were a way of organizing them for quick responses to federal requisitions, but in time such armies would acquire the attributes of a permanent force. Had the war continued another year, it seems certain that a significant majority of states would have had permanent state armies, with all the consequences implicit in such status, such as the need to withhold funds from the federal government to pay for the armies.

In fact, near the end of the war four states contemplated withholding a portion of their direct taxes to pay for defense costs. By 1815 ominous complaints were being heard from various parts of the country that many militiamen who had served in the war remained unpaid. As a result low morale made militiamen less willing to continue making sacrifices for the country.

Fortunately, the war ended before even more serious problems confronted the federal government. States quickly forgot their schemes to create efficient, standing military forces. Moreover, in the first flush of peace and the news of the victory at New Orleans, the militia was restored to its idealized status in the hearts of most Americans. Most responsible leaders of the federal government, however, understood the lesson of the War of 1812: the militia was an unreliable main defense force. Society at large continued to harbor a strong prejudice against a standing army, but the growing professionalism of the regular army after the War of 1812 portended increasing neglect of the militia by the federal government. Genuine reliance on the militia in the pre-War of 1812 era gave way to mere verbal reliance in the postwar era.

Chapter 1

The Militia before the War of 1812

Two of England's legacies for the American colonists were a fear of standing armies and a reliance upon citizen soldiers, or militiamen, for defense. The British generally left the local defense to the colonies, and they in turn placed responsibility for local defense on the colonial towns and the towns' militia. By regarding every man as a trained, armed soldier prepared to respond to any emergency, the colonists sustained a belief that there was no need for a professional, standing army. Consequently, there was no organized intercolonial militia system, no central command, and no permanent commissariat.[1]

During the Revolutionary War numerous problems arose in the use of militia. Short enlistments limited their availability; they lacked discipline and training; and they were poorly armed and led. Early in the war General George Washington confessed that he felt a "want of confidence, in the generality of the Troops." His experience confirmed him in his opinion, and his famous statement regarding the militiamen was often repeated: "[They] come in, you cannot tell how; go, you cannot tell when, and act, you cannot tell where, consume your provisions, exhaust your stores, and leave you at last in a critical moment." So many problems arose that the Continental Congress moved cautiously to create a regular army, which played an important role in winning independence. Nevertheless, of the 395,858 men who served during the American Revolution, 164,087 were militiamen.[2]

After the war, Washington and other military leaders recommended maintaining a small national force as well as proposing plans to improve and perfect the state militia forces to create, essentially, a national militia. A common feature of all these proposals by Washington, Baron Friedrich von Steuben, Henry Knox, and Alexander Hamilton was to make the state militia systems uniform and interchangeable when they were called into duty by the national government. In order to achieve the goal of uniformity and interchangeability, the training had to be carried out under the auspices of the national government, and militiamen were to be classed by age, with the youngest given more training and kept in a higher state of readiness; not all men were to be trained. These proposals, however, were met by two major objections: the cost of the training elicited criticism, and there were fears that such training would create an elite militia force equivalent to a standing army. State leaders opposed the plans, and nothing was done.[3]

The militia clause of the Articles of Confederation (Article 6) explicitly forbade the states to maintain an army in time of peace, but every state was to keep a "well-regulated and disciplined" militia, armed and equipped, and "constantly ready for use."[4] Without any central administrative supervision, however, little was done during the Confederation period beyond the maintenance of thirteen unrelated militia systems.

In the Constitutional Convention it was conceded that a national force could be maintained, but the country would rely chiefly on the militia for defense. It was also agreed that the national government must be able to use state militias or else it would have to rely on a standing army. The resulting compromise was shared authority over the militia, an experiment in federalism. The federal government was authorized to call upon state militias "to execute the laws of the Union, suppress insurrections, and repel invasions," and "to provide for organizing, arming, and disciplining the militia," but the states had the reserved right to appoint the officers and train the militiamen according to the discipline prescribed by the federal government.[5]

In the debate over ratification of the Constitution, many Anti-Federalists expressed fears, to be reiterated many times in the future, that congressional control over arming, training, and organizing the state militia would jeopardize the liberty of the people. Some Anti-Federalists, however, contended that Congress would fail to arm the militia and would leave the population disarmed or, even worse, that the citizens would react to the neglect of the government by shirking the burden of militia duties. Others argued that federal control over discipline and classification might create a select militia that would in actuality be a standing army. Without extensive training for the whole populace, it was argued, the large body of the population would be powerless against such a force. Still others believed that state militias would be forced to serve for long periods and would be marched to all parts of the union to maintain and enforce national laws.[6]

Congress displayed a timidity at the outset regarding its role in providing for a well-regulated militia. The need for a viable national defense force was painfully obvious in the first years of the republic. Many problems, for example, plagued commanders using state militias in the Indian disturbances in the early 1790s. The government employed a mix of state militiamen, regulars, and six-month volunteers. The difficulties of organizing and establishing lines of command can readily be imagined, and the poorly equipped and undisciplined troops, notably those under the command of Arthur St. Clair, governor of the Northwest Territory, suffered a terrible defeat on November 4, 1791. The Indian victory prompted Congress to increase the authorized strength of the regular army (from 900 to 5,373), and it also provided the impetus for an act to organize state militias.[7]

Secretary of War Henry Knox proposed a plan, dated January 18, 1790, for the uniform organization of all state militias. He proposed dividing militiamen into three classes: an advanced corps composed of eighteen-to-twenty-year-old men; a main corps of men twenty-one to forty-five years of age; and a reserved corps embracing men from forty-six to sixty years of age. He argued that an annual appropriation of about $385,000 would be sufficient for the federal government to train the advanced corps of approximately 32,500 men for thirty days, which was, he noted, less than one-eighth of a dollar per capita. The main corps was to be mustered and trained at state expense four days per year; the reserved corps was to be mustered for inspection two days per year. Knox's proposal was debated and tabled by Congress in both 1790 and 1791.[8]

In 1792, Congress finally produced a weakened version of Knox's proposal, the Uniform Militia Act. The final version was the result of intense debate, and the deletions made in the original bill were necessary to secure its passage. Although Federalists tended to support a stronger bill, the outcome was not a party or sectional measure. Rather, states' rights ideology, and not partisanship, apparently prevailed. Gone was Knox's classification scheme. Instead, all able-bodied white male citizens between eighteen and forty-five were required to enroll and to furnish their own stand of arms (a musket and accouterments: bayonet, cartridge box and pouch, cartridges, powder, lead, priming wire and brush, and flints). Thus a duty was laid upon a large body of citizens that entailed an additional expense; it was a form of tax imposed upon all militiamen, many of whom could not afford to arm and equip themselves. The federal government, in effect, shifted the responsibility for arming the militia to the individual and made the states responsible for enforcement. Instead of appropriating federal funds for training (the expense of Knox's plan may have been a factor for some congressmen), the law merely allowed states to organize their militia in their own fashion (which was a factor for congressmen concerned that states would lose control of their militia to the national government). Even worse from the standpoint of establishing a uniform militia, the law allowed state legislatures to form the divisions, brigades, and companies. For example, it recommended, rather than prescribed, that each brigade consist of four regiments "if the same be convenient." The only uniform feature specified was that each state would have an adjutant general and each brigade a brigade inspector. The next year, Knox cited several difficulties and inconveniences caused by the Uniform Militia Act. Beyond the failure of militiamen to arm themselves, he noted that the states were not imposing penalties to enforce the law. Again, he suggested that Congress establish a select corps of militia through classification.[9]

Based upon the experience of using militia in the St. Clair expedition, General Anthony Wayne made almost no use of militia in his campaign against the Indians in 1793-1794; his only concession was using mounted volunteers from Kentucky, who performed well for him. The first significant use of the militia after the Uniform Militia Act was the suppression of the Whiskey Rebellion in 1794. President Washington called out more than 12,000 militiamen from four states, New Jersey, Pennsylvania, Maryland, and Virginia. Numerous problems arose, not the least of which was raising the militia. There was widespread sympathy with the rebels among the lower class, and the militia force eventually raised was composed of draftees and substitutes. One historian has characterized the force as "the flotsam of early American society." The militiamen were unruly and destructive, and desertion rates were high. According to William Findley, who was a spokesman for moderate western Pennsylvanians during this crisis and later served as U.S. congressman, the conduct of the militiamen was such that they gave the militia a bad name. "In the late expedition," he said, "the name militia was understood to have the same idea fixed to it as *plebeian* or *lower order of citizens*." He added, "An army arranged in this manner never can have confidence within itself, nor embrace the confidence of their fellow citizens." Secretary Knox complained that the War Department had to issue 10,000 weapons to the 15,000 militiamen who served in the Whiskey Rebellion.[10]

Almost from the beginning, presidents and governors made proposals to reform and improve the state militias. It soon became evident, however, that Congress was reluctant to adopt any reform proposal, and governors were rarely successful in improving the organization and efficiency of their state militia. Obviously, since utilization of militia was a means of national defense, the initiative had to come from the national level, but given the reluctance of congressmen to confront the situation, it is not difficult to explain why such initiatives failed. The militia myth was deeply embedded in the psyche of the Americans, as well as the belief in states' rights and a distrust of the national government. Attempts to convert the militia into an efficient military force were met with deep suspicion.

State laws conforming to the Uniform Militia Act of May 8, 1792, restricted the national government's use of state militia in many ways. For example, provisions in some state constitutions restricted service to the state unless the legislature consented to allow the militia to be used elsewhere. Another problem was that militiamen called into national service were limited to three months' service in one year. Then, too, the states failed to eliminate perhaps the greatest defect of all, the use of substitutes to meet an individual's obligations. Knox, among others, lamented that the wealthy and middle classes escaped the burden of militia duty by procuring substitutes from "the most idle and worthless part of the community."[11]

The lack of preparedness and uniformity within the various state militias soon became evident. In his annual message of December 3, 1793, President Washington called upon Congress to correct the "imperfections" of the Uniform Militia Act. When nothing was done, he reminded Congress the next year of the "striking defects" in the militia law and suggested that "the devising and establishing of a well-regulated militia would be a genuine source of legislative honor and a perfect title to public gratitude." He renewed his call in 1795, and in his last annual message in 1796, Washington plaintively reiterated his appeal for militia reform: "My solicitude to see the militia of the United States placed on an efficient establishment has been so often and so ardently expressed that I shall but barely recall the subject to your view on the present occasion." One of Washington's last acts as president was to veto a bill passed on February 22, 1797, dismissing two companies of light dragoons. He agreed that some cavalry, either militia or regular, was needed, and it was his opinion "that the latter will be less expensive and more useful than the former in preserving peace between the frontier settlers and the Indians."[12]

Militia reform came before Congress in 1794, 1795, and 1796. David Cobb of Massachusetts, reporting for his House committee on the militia on March 24, 1794, concluded that "until further experience shall be had under the existing law, the committee are of [the] opinion that no amendment is necessary." In 1795, a House committee headed by William Branch Giles of Virginia reported a bill on February 12 that proposed a substantial reform of the militia. Included was a classification scheme similar to the plan advanced earlier by Baron von Steuben. Able-bodied white males between twenty and forty were to be divided into two classes: the select corps, those between twenty and twenty-five, and the reserve corps, comprising those between twenty-five and forty. This corps would be trained by the national government, although the amount of time and cost was not calculated by the committee. Concerns were raised in the ensuing debate about the great expense and the inconvenience to those called for training. The plan was declared unconstitutional and against the will of the people. Supporters of the proposal repeatedly pointed to the failures of the present system. Eventually, the measure was postponed, but a thousand copies of the proposal were printed and distributed to the states.[13]

In the next Congress, the bill was reintroduced in December 1796, but it immediately ran into trouble when a motion was made to strip out the classification scheme. Robert Goodloe Harper, a Federalist representative from South Carolina, cited President Washington's calls for militia reform and pointed to recent examples of raw and undisciplined militiamen incapable of performing their duties efficiently. "You must either give up the idea of an efficient military force, or you must adopt a mode similar to that now proposed," he declared. Thomas Henderson of New Jersey insisted, however, that the bill did not conform to the republican principle that "military service ought to be as equally divided among its citizens as possible." It was also unconstitutional, he argued, because the national government "had no power to call out people to train them for military service," and it was too expensive. Robert Rutherford of Virginia contended that the national government "had nothing to do with the Militia in the several sovereign States . . . for the Government to enact Militia laws is against the express decision of the Union."[14]

Harper, sensing the mood of the House, asked in exasperation, "Are we to let our Militia remain in its present situation, and throw our whole dependence on the Standing Army?" The question was referred to a committee headed by Henry Dearborn of Massachusetts. The House finally took up the militia reform bill on February 21. After perfunctory debate, the committee was discharged by a vote of 42-32, and militia reform in the Washington administration was dead.[15]

Despite the undoubted sincerity of many individuals on both sides of the militia reform issue, cynicism was developing about the militia. Charles Nisbet, president of Dickinson College in Carlisle, Pennsylvania, for example, wrote an English friend in 1792: "Our Leaders flatter the People by declaiming against standing Armies, and pretending to believe that the Militia is the best Security of a Nation." Republican party leaders alleged that the Federalists proposed a militia system so burdensome and frightening that Congress would strengthen the regular army instead. In fact, Federalists generally believed regulars were superior to militia. What they wanted was both an effective regular force and an efficient militia system.[16] On the other side, opponents of militia reform conceded weaknesses in the militia system but contended that if the federal government was truly to be a bulwark of liberty and preserve the people's rights, then it could not be allowed to appropriate the states' militia for its own use or to exercise control over the training of state militia. Classification raised the specter of professionalism. An efficient elite militia force might pose as much of a threat to the nation as a standing army.

The unreliability of the militia caused the Federalists to turn to other expedients during the crisis of 1798 when war with France loomed. President John Adams invited Congress on May 16, 1797, to consider revision of the militia laws, but he undoubtedly knew that little was likely to happen. Instead, the Federalists, especially the Hamiltonian wing of the party, pushed not only for an increase in the regular force but also for a volunteer force and a provisional army in lieu of dependence on the militia. Although a provisional army was authorized, President Adams could activate it only if war was declared or in case of invasion or the imminent threat of invasion.[17]

The crisis passed, and the provisional army was never activated. But it was clear that the Federalists had lost faith in the militia even as a reserve force. In fact, Secretary of War James McHenry asserted, justifying the creation of a military academy in a message to Congress in 1800, that "even in times of the greatest danger, we cannot give to our militia that degree of discipline, or to their officers that degree of military science, upon which a nation may safely hazard its fate."[18] Had the Federalists remained in office, it is likely that in any future crisis they would again have turned to volunteers or provisional forces controlled by the federal government to supplement regulars. In fact, the states were very remiss in forwarding to the federal government the annual reports on the status of their militia. When the Republicans came into office in 1801, only six states and one territory reported, and this number was more than had ever done so before.

It was party dogma for the Republicans that state militias were the bulwark of liberty and the main support for national defense. President Thomas Jefferson, however, modified that position somewhat in his inaugural address. He declared his faith in "a well-disciplined militia, our best reliance in peace and for the first moments of war, till regulars may relieve them." In his first annual message on December 8, 1801, he reiterated this idea and asked Congress "to amend the defects which from time to time shew themselves in the laws for regulating the militia until they are sufficiently perfect."[19]

Like his predecessors, Jefferson urged militia reform in every annual message but one. In his fifth message on December 3, 1805, Jefferson proposed a specific mode of reform for the militia: the old Federalist scheme of classification. He suggested that Congress should "organize or class the militia as would enable us on any sudden emergency to call for the services of the younger portions, unencumbered with the old and those having families." The census, he argued, showed that there were upwards of 300,000 men between the ages of eighteen and twenty-six years of age, "a competent number for offense or defense in any point where they may be wanted, and will give time for raising regular forces after the necessity of them shall become certain." He claimed classification would reduce active service "to the early period of life" and allow in "advanced age a quiet and undisturbed repose in the bosom of their families."[20]

Congress responded to Jefferson's calls for reductions in the regular force. His partisans sought to carry out a "chaste reformation" of the army, namely, to "republicanize" it and make it responsive to the Republicans, and in 1802 they reduced the regular army to approximately 3,000. Despite the obvious intention of the Jefferson administration to continue to rely on the militia for national defense, Congress remained reluctant to make changes in the system. For example, a House committee headed by Joseph Varnum of Massachusetts reported on February 7, 1803, that there was no need to amend the Uniform Militia Act because any deficiency in the system was not "in that part of the system which is under the control of Congress, but from omission on the part of the State Governments." The committee consequently proposed a resolution urging the president to write a letter to the state governors "to carry into effect the militia system adopted by the national legislature."[21]

Varnum was also the chairman of the House committee that reported on Jefferson's classification scheme proposed in December 1805. The committee raised numerous objections, including the point that classification and reorganization of the militia would violate the constitutions of several states and derange existing systems. Contrary to all evidence, the committee asserted that "military discipline is rapidly progressing . . . and it cannot with propriety be doubted, that the militia of the United States, under the existing organization, are amply competent to a defence against the intrusion of any invading enemy."[22] Clearly, for a variety of reasons, Congress did not want to tamper with the militia.

The stubborn refusal of Congress to make any alterations in a militia system so obviously disorganized and so poorly prepared to fulfill the role expected of it forced the Jefferson administration to rely on volunteers for national defense just as the Adams administration had earlier. An act of February 24, 1807, authorized the president to accept 30,000 volunteers. It was stipulated that if they were called into service, the volunteers would be commanded by their own officers. The volunteers were to be on call for two years, and they were obligated for one year's service if they were called to duty. Ironically, Republican support for volunteers may have been influenced by the fact that the officers of the militia, for the most part, were Federalists.[23] In April 1808, because of the war in Europe and problems with England, Congress at Jefferson's urging increased the size of the regular force to approximately 10,000, although the actual level never exceeded 6,000 before 1812.[24]

Congress did take one step forward in militia reform when it passed a law on April 22, 1808, providing $200,000 annually for the distribution of arms to the militia. The arms would be distributed and apportioned on the basis of the returns of the states. The lack of arms among the militias, particularly in the South and West, was a national disgrace. It was a good estimate that perhaps fewer than one-third of the militiamen were armed according to the law. One committee of Congress calculated in 1806 that there were about 250,000 arms in the hands of militiamen, but very likely many of the arms were unfit for use. Militia returns are incomplete, but the number of enrolled militiamen was somewhere between 650,000 and 700,000. The sum allocated would not procure much over 14,000 arms per year, hardly enough to keep up with the natural increase each year in the newly enrolled militiamen.[25]

President Jefferson called out militiamen and volunteers in 1808 to enforce the embargo policy, but the exercise confirmed the disorganization of the state militias. Half of the states failed to render inspection returns, an indication that they probably had little or no idea of the number of militiamen organized or available for duty. Five governors failed to acknowledge the president's request at all, and many of those who did complained about the difficulty of mobilizing their militiamen, warning that they could give no guarantees about the condition of the troops or the arms.[26]

Militia reform thus eluded the Jefferson administration, and Congress thwarted or evaded recommendations from the administration to render the militia more useful to the government as a national defense force. Undaunted, Jefferson's successor, James Madison, renewed the requests for militia reform, including classification. There was little like-lihood that Congress would act. As Senator Samuel Smith of Maryland reported for his committee on March 6, 1810: "The prejudices against such a mode of organization in many parts of the Union, and the diffi-culties to be surmounted, at a moment like the present, have deterred the committee from submitting such a project." Smith concluded, "If the States are anxious for an effective militia, to them belong the power, and to them too belong the means of rendering the militia truly our bulwark in war, and our safeguard in peace."[27]

An acrimonious debate arose in Congress in 1810 during the sec-ond session of the Eleventh Congress as to whether state militias could be used in an offensive war beyond the border of the United States. Surely arguments used in this debate, which gained wide circulation, served some militiamen during the War of 1812 in their refusal to cross into Canada.

President Madison asked Congress on January 3, 1810, to renew the act authorizing 100,000 militiamen, due to expire on March 30, and requested a volunteer force of 20,000 "for a short period." He also urged that the militiamen be classified and organized to ensure their prompt aid when needed. In the House of Representatives, Samuel W. Dana (Conn.) raised objections on January 10 to the way in which the detach-ment of 100,000 militiamen had been allocated among the states. He asserted that the allocation should reflect state population and not mi-litia returns. Otherwise, he argued, states could exempt more of their citizens and reduce "their proportion of the public burden." Southern states, whose representation was based in part on their slave popula-tion, objected, and it was also noted that some western states had nearly doubled their population and, until the next reapportionment, would fall quite short of their just proportion. Eventually, the question was committed to a select committee.[28]

The committee reported a bill on March 1. The president was authorized to require state executives to hold in readiness 100,000 mi-litiamen, basing allocations on militia returns or, where they were not current, "by such other rule as he shall judge equitable." Other provi-sions authorized volunteers to serve six-month tours under their own officers and, if called to duty, to serve "any place, not beyond the sea, out of the jurisdiction of the United States." After a brief debate about the equity of basing the allocation on militia returns, Archibald Van Horne (Md.) moved to strike the words "not beyond the sea," because he did not believe the militia could be marched anywhere outside the United States. A desultory debate ensued over what sort of troops these were and the meaning of the term "volunteer."[29]

Erastus Root (N.Y.) acknowledged that the Constitution was silent on whether the militia could be sent out of the jurisdiction of the United States, but he argued that the expression "repel invasion" could never have been intended to stop the militia at an arbitrary line. He asserted that militiamen when called into service became regular troops. Van Horne, in reply, stubbornly insisted that he could find no constitutional authorization to use the militia to invade a foreign territory, and he asked why, if they were regular troops, the officers were appointed by the state.[30]

Ezekiel Bacon (Mass.) declared that militiamen as volunteers could give their "free consent to go out of the limits of the United States." Philip Key called this force a provisional army to invade Canada and argued that such troops could not "act under officers deriving their commissions from the several states." Matthew Lyon (Ky.) declared that the bill had all the constitutional objections voiced against Mr. Adams's volunteers "save that they are to be commissioned by the State authorities."[31]

John Ross (Pa.), for the committee, responded that they had wanted to raise a force to meet current exigencies that would "not be a moth in the finances, and yet . . . effectual when it is requisite to call it into action." The "not beyond the sea" clause was to address a contingency that might happen. States were to commission the officers because it might have excited jealousy if the United States had undertaken to commission them. Opposing the bill, he said, was "to impede the Administration of the Government." Supporters argued that it provided a force for defense, and it was cheap. The volunteers received no pay unless called into service, and the only expense would be arming the force and providing for ten days of training a year.[32]

By this time, it was generally conceded that the militia constituted a military force that might be used in case of war, but it was also believed the militiamen must voluntarily consent to cross a territorial border. Federalists threw up numerous amendments clearly designed to defeat the bill. Republicans beat back the amendments, usually by substantial margins of thirty to forty votes. One motion made by Jacob Hufty (N.J.), a Republican, was accepted: the quotas for states whose returns had not been regularly received were to be apportioned according to the number of free white males between sixteen and forty-five in the last census. Near the end, Jonathan O. Moseley (Conn.) reiterated a point made by many, that militias were never intended "to be permanently relied upon in case of actual warfare." If it was necessary to raise a regular army, he argued that it should be done openly.[33]

Federalists charged the bill would raise taxes and would lead to a standing army and military despotism. It was acknowledged, however, that danger would arise from a president with "more martial ambition than the present." The bill passed 70-47. The Senate, however, postponed action on the House bill on April 28 and did not take it up again.[34]

Following the debate, on March 22, 1810, John Randolph of Roanoke introduced a resolution to reduce the military and navy establishment. When the resolution was taken up on April 16, Nathaniel Macon (N.C.) moved to amend the resolution to read "that the whole Army ought to be disbanded." Macon was probably acting from a belief that the regular army was too demoralized to be effective. In any event, his motion created an uproar. Roger Nelson (Md.) expressed his astonishment; he doubted that anyone but the mover would vote for the resolution. Alexander McKim (Md.) pronounced it "the most extraordinary proposition ever made to a deliberative body." But there were supporters of the resolution. Samuel McKee (Ky.) maintained that even if war was certain, it was still unnecessary to keep a large regular army. He preferred to rely on "the hardy sons of the country for defence" rather than on those who had "loitered out their days in camp" and were taken "from the very dregs of society." If the war came, he assured the House, the people would "rally around the standard of the country." Samuel Dana argued that Macon's motion, if passed, would require militiamen to serve in garrisons to preserve the public stores, an action that would be "extremely vexatious" to citizens. "We would spoil one very good cultivator of the soil to make one very bad soldier," he declared.[35]

Erastus Root amended Macon's bill to read that the military and naval establishment ought to be reduced; the amended bill passed and was referred to two committees. John Smilie was assigned to chair the military reduction committee, while John Randolph chaired the naval reduction committee. On April 24, Smilie reported a bill to reduce the army to one regiment of light artillery, two regular regiments, and one company of bombardiers (roughly 3,000), but the bill was apparently never taken up, no doubt because of concern that it might never pass. Randolph's committee called for the reduction of the navy by half, to three ships, but after lengthy debate, the bill was ordered to lie on the table.[36]

It is unclear whether this debate was a delicate game of bluff, designed for constituent consumption, or a sincere effort by some members to abolish or drastically to reduce the regular military establishment during a relatively dangerous period. Those who supported reduction appeared to place great faith in the militia. The assumption seemed to be that if war came, U.S. forces would be involved only in defensive operations.

When the Eleventh Congress reconvened for its third session in December 1810, Madison's annual message advocated training "at the public expense . . . certain portions of the commissioned and non-commissioned officers." He argued that "the instruction and discipline thus acquired would gradually diffuse through the entire body of the militia." Also, Secretary of War William Eustis, responding to a Senate resolution of April 7, proposed new regulations to improve the discipline of the militia. While the modern French system "would claim preference," he asserted that it would require an entirely new organization of companies, battalions, and regiments, and it was "doubtful whether the officers of the militia would bestow, gratuitously, the time and attention necessary for their own, and the instruction of the men under their command." He recommended continuing the regulations prepared by Baron von Steuben in 1779.[37] Aside from the fact that inertia and apathy probably made it impossible to reorganize the state militias on the French system—a point that Eustis made—it was inappropriate to tinker with militia reorganization on the eve of a possible war.

Little was done in the third session to meet Madison's call for a volunteer force. The Senate authorized a number of volunteer companies on February 28, 1811, "not exceeding fifty thousand men." The House, however, decided that it was too late in the session to attempt to remodel the law, and the bill was indefinitely postponed.[38]

The Eleventh Congress, true to its reputation, weak and divided, did virtually nothing to prepare the country's defenses in the face of a looming crisis with Great Britain. Neither the army nor the militia was measurably strengthened. This task remained for the Twelfth Congress, which at least had a clearer idea of what it wanted to do.

Chapter 2

Congress and Military Mobilization

On the eve of war with Great Britain in 1812 it was clear to many that Congress had failed to provide for a uniform militia. North Carolina's legislature passed a resolution in December 1811 complaining that state militias were disciplined "according to the notions that prevail in different parts thereof; thereby tending to create disorder, rather than an uniformity of Discipline." Its representatives in Congress were instructed to work to establish "one detailed and general system . . . to make an improved uniform organization in Military Tactics throughout the United States." Kentucky's legislature suggested classification in a resolution of February 8, 1812, as a measure that would save "more than a million dollars" annually just in labor for those "excused from uselessly attending musters." Kentucky and North Carolina, at least, believed that the solution to the militia problem lay with the federal government.[1]

Congress, notwithstanding, apparently believed the militia could be used primarily as an auxiliary force without extensive reform. The early military failures in 1812, however, which were largely attributable to the militia, quickly disabused Congress of the assumption that the militia would be adequate even as an auxiliary force. Despite their natural inclinations to favor militias and their generally penurious ways, Republicans in Congress gradually moved to increase the regular force and raise volunteers. Still, the obstructionist tactics of the Federalist minority and dissident Republicans limited the success of these efforts to raise a force to prosecute the war and raised questions about their loyalty to the Union. The government also faced a shortage of money to wage the war. Not just Federalists but even many Republicans were too parsimonious to raise the taxes necessary to fund the government adequately during the war.

Madison's third annual message of November 5, 1811, as the crisis with Great Britain grew, clearly showed a move toward reliance upon volunteers rather than drafted militia. In the new Twelfth Congress a debate quickly arose over the correct proportion of regulars versus volunteers. In the Senate, William Branch Giles (Va.) addressed a proposal to enlist 25,000 additional regulars. Although Giles was not persuaded that militias could not be used beyond the limits of the United States, he asserted that this view precluded Congress from including the militia in the estimate. Giles did not believe a volunteer force would be suited to an offensive war, because "it was always found to be the most expensive and least efficient force." Joseph Anderson (Tenn.), on the other hand, argued that 25,000 additional regulars would be impracticable. Newly raised troops would be little better than volunteers, and the latter would be "more acceptable to the nation." After further debate, the bill passed and was sent to the House.[2]

In the House, Henry Clay supported a 25,000 increase in the regular army. It was better, he argued, "to err on the side of the largest force." Volunteers, he declared, might be suited for "the first operations of the war," but they would be unfitted for siege operations or for the manning and garrisoning of forts. William Widgery (Mass.) insisted that there was no need to raise a regular force to take Canada. "The Militia of New England States only wanted authority to do the business," he said, ignoring the fact that Federalist leaders would oppose such an action. John C. Calhoun also supported the proposed increase in the regular army. "We ought either to submit," he stated, "or make an energetic defence." After lengthy debate, during which members mostly explained their vote, the House passed the Senate bill, with slight modifications, by a three-to-one margin. President Madison signed the bill into law on January 11, 1812.[3]

The measure to raise 50,000 volunteers, which had been separated from the regular army bill and passed by the House, came to the Senate in late January. Giles again spoke against relying upon volunteers, declaring that the 30,000 authorized during Jefferson's presidency had been merely a paper army, so why should they rely on one now in the face of the threat of actual war? He "disliked to vote for nominal, when the country required actual measures." Nevertheless, the bill passed and authorized the president to accept and organize a volunteer military corps not exceeding 50,000 men, committed for two years but to serve for only twelve months. The volunteers had the same status as the militia, for the presumption was that they were not to be used for foreign service without their consent. Militia companies who volunteered would be allowed to keep the same officers.[4]

Peter B. Porter (N.Y.) introduced a resolution on February 18 to authorize the president to engage, commission, and organize an additional 20,000-man provisional army of short-term volunteers that could be used while the 25,000 regular army was being raised. Militiamen who would "not submit to the drudgery of a camp for five years" might volunteer to attack Canada while there was no one to oppose them but militia "inferior to our own." If an attack on Canada was delayed a year to raise a regular force, he warned, they would be met by regulars "superior to our own." Although many of his fellow New Yorkers were ready to do service, "they will not become slaves to the Army for five years." As Porter noted, approval of 25,000 regulars and 50,000 volunteers had not given the president a single man. "Should they insult the President by telling him to go to war, when he had not a man to fight with?" Porter's resolution, however, was defeated.[5]

On January 28, David R. Williams, chairman of the Committee on the Militia, introduced a proposal to divide the militiamen into three classes: a minor class (eighteen to twenty-one) to do duty only in the state and serve up to three months; a junior class (twenty-one to thirty-one) to serve in any part of the United States for not more than twelve months; and a senior class (thirty-one to forty-five) to serve in the state or adjoining states and territories for no longer than twelve months. Also, the bill proposed to give each militiaman a stand of arms when he reached eighteen years of age and enrolled in the militia. An additional $400,000 annual appropriation was proposed to purchase such arms.[6]

Classification was always a sectional issue. Southerners generally favored classification; Northerners opposed the innovation. Motions to strike out classification, to alter the way the arms were distributed, to recommit, and to postpone indefinitely were all defeated. A motion to lower the additional sum for arms to $200,000 passed.

Ebenezer Huntington, who served as a colonel in the Revolutionary Army and as a congressman from Connecticut in the third session of the Eleventh Congress, expressed the northern point of view regarding classification. The militia, he wrote early in 1810, generated "enormous waste and expense attending their every movement." He added, "Too much has already been done with the militia, if they are not to be a substitute for standing troops, and too little will *always* be done if they are made a substitute." Whatever was done, he declared, would "make them food for powder on the day of battle." There were good reasons for opposing classification. Even in Connecticut, Huntington noted, the limits of military company districts often had to be spread wide to obtain sixty-four men; if classing was used, the districts would have to be inconveniently large to embrace men of a certain age group. It would be even more of a problem in the sparsely settled South and West. Huntington doubted that militias would ever be made efficient. "It is our parsimony which makes us too highly estimate militia; if the militia were more expensive than enlisted troops, there is not an American but would reprobate the idea."[7]

Benjamin Tallmadge, perhaps remembering this correspondence with Huntington, now asked what urgent occasion there was for this bill. Militias in the northern states, he asserted with considerable exaggeration on February 2, 1812, had become "formidable armies." Classing would cause great inconvenience. It would "introduce novel distinctions" and "smells too strong of the detestable conscription of the French Emperor." An army formed from such conscripts, "called out under the imposing title of classified militia . . . , would be an army unknown to the Constitution." He reiterated a point made by many speakers on this subject: the militias belonged to the several states and were not militias of the United States.[8]

During the debate there was an effort to separate the issues of classing and arming the militia. Some speakers favored arming but opposed classing. After lengthy debate, the bill was engrossed for a third reading by only three votes (62-59). On February 4, the bill was defeated by three votes, 55 to 58. Obviously, supporters of the bill were unable to keep the coalition together. One member who voted for the original bill changed to the opposition, but the most critical factor was that nine of the bill's supporters, including several southern members, were absent for the final vote.[9]

A few days later, Williams introduced a separate bill to arm the militia. When Jonathan Roberts (Pa.) moved to give the state legislature the discretion on distribution of arms, supporters of the bill responded that the amendment would arm the state government and not the people. In rebuttal it was argued that the legislature could be trusted and could better distribute the arms. Eventually, Roberts's motion and all other efforts to alter the bill were defeated, and the bill passed and was sent to the Senate. The upper chamber amended the House bill, but the nature and extent of the amendments were not reported. The only alteration noted was that the appropriation was set at $300,000. The House received the Senate amendments, and then the bill was laid on the table, and it was apparently never taken up again.[10] Perhaps the Senate amendments were of such a nature that the House believed attempts to reconcile the differences would be futile. More likely, the House itself was so divided (the bill had passed by a margin of only five votes) that a bill satisfactory to all proponents was unlikely to be obtained.

On paper, Congress had created a formidable force. It had approved a regular army of 35,000 and an additional 50,000 volunteers, presumably men coming from existing militia companies. On April 10, Congress authorized 100,000 militiamen in the states to be detached for call for a two-year period. The militiamen called into service, however, were to serve up to six months instead of the usual three.[11]

In all of the years from the passage of the Uniform Militia Act in 1792 to the Civil War, Congress came closer in the first session of the Twelfth Congress to amending and reforming the militia law than it ever did. In the end, Congress made a fateful decision to keep the militia system in place rather than try to reorganize it significantly on the eve of the War of 1812. All things considered, the decision was probably wise, but Congress and the nation were soon to learn that the nation's defense could not safely be entrusted to the militia.

Congress's failure to address the militia problem adequately during the war is unsurprising, given its failure to reform the militia in the years prior to the War of 1812. In fact, after the military defeats in 1812, which were generally blamed on the militia, Congress sought to increase the regular force and raise volunteers. But partisan politics divided the Congress. The government also faced a shortage of money to wage the war. Even Republicans were too parsimonious to raise the taxes necessary to fund the war effort adequately.

The failures at Detroit and along the Niagara frontier, the experiences of calling out militiamen either poorly equipped or not at all, and the myriad problems of organization, training, and discipline, not to mention refusals to cross international borders, convinced many observers that militias were too unreliable and too expensive. Consequently, when the Twelfth Congress reconvened for its second session on November 2, 1812, reassessment of the role of the militia in the war effort was on its agenda.

Secretary Eustis resigned in December, and James Monroe became the acting secretary of war. Monroe proposed to the chairmen of the two military affairs committees that the militia should be reserved primarily for defensive operations and should be supported at critical points by regulars. Monroe called for an additional 20,000 regulars for one year. Monroe conceded, however, that recruitment of the force already authorized had been slow.[12]

In the House, David R. Williams introduced a bill on December 29, 1812, to raise an additional force of 20,000 regulars deemed necessary because the militia was unreliable. Experience had shown that when militiamen were called out, the number of officers were proportionately greater than needed, while the number of privates was less than needed, so that the government was compelled "to pay nearly double the force necessary to maintain any one point." Congress should not deceive themselves that they could rely on volunteers. "It is a miserable contrivance," he asserted, "perfectly nugatory, except to accomplish disappointment."[13]

The debate in the House lasted for more than two weeks and occasionally degenerated into nasty and acrimonious exchanges. Many supporters of the bill candidly assessed the failures of the militias as justification for this bill. Jonathan Moseley, a Federalist from Connecticut, mocked supporters of the bill, who had assured the House in the last session that in a few months militiamen with a few regulars would conquer all of Canada except Quebec. But "disasters and disgrace" resulted from the military operations. Now it was being said that 20,000 men raised for one year would be adequate. Moseley wondered whether the raw troops to be raised would be any better than ordinary militia. Such a force, he asserted, would be "totally inadequate."[14]

According to Lyman Law, another Federalist from Connecticut, the proposed bill said to the militiamen, "You are useless, you are no longer to be trusted—they are despised, degraded, and neglected." He predicted that the militia would "dwindle into insignificance." John Rhea (Tenn.) disputed Law's statement. The bill's object, he maintained, was to preserve the militias within the limits of their respective states, so that the militias "may be less frequently taken off from their rural and other occupations." Rhea added cynically, "it is well known how careful the Governors of some States are of the militia." Lest his listeners miss his point, which was that some New England governors had withheld their militias from the federal government, he added that the proposed bill would give the president a force that would "not be controlled by any novel constructions of the Constitution."[15]

Felix Grundy (Tenn.) argued that the force was not wanted, as some Federalists alleged, to put down insurrection at home. The opposition denounced militiamen and volunteers as "inefficient" and "a useless waste of the public treasure," but they also opposed this force. They seemed to want to carry on a war "without an army." George M. Troup (Ga.) agreed that the war must be conducted with either regulars or militiamen, but when militias were asked for, the opposition said no: "they are constitutionally under the control of the State authorities for local defence." When regular troops were asked for, the opposition argued that "regular armies are dangerous to Republics; they confer too much patronage." The opposition really wanted to repeal the declaration of war and have the United States "lay down our arms, and throw ourselves upon the generosity of the enemy."[16]

Attempts to amend the bill, including extending the period of service from one year to three, were defeated. Harmanus Bleecker, a Federalist (N.Y.), maintained that the failures of the militia should not be attributed to the governors of Massachusetts, Connecticut, or Rhode Island for withholding their militias. It was not because the war was unpopular that the ranks of the army had not been filled; the reason was simply that the people were more comfortable at home and preferred to stay there. The militias had rendered no efficient service, and he quoted George Washington that they were no better than "armed mobs." The war, he avowed, was destroying the illusion so long "kept up in the country by the many strange and absurd things which have been said of the importance and efficiency of the militia. Sir, it is all idle—the militiaman is best employed at his plough." If the regular army was to be filled, he concluded, it "must be composed of idle, dissolute, and disorderly persons."[17]

As the bill moved to the third reading and virtually every debating point possible had been made, many were reiterated. John Randolph, near the end of the debate, renewed the charge that the bill degraded the militia and raised in its place "a great standing, military, mercenary force." The militia, he argued, was the army of every free country and "that country in which they are not honored . . . is at the brink of that abyss," in other words, on the verge of despotism.[18]

Joseph Desha of Kentucky chided the Federalist opposition that their long-winded speeches (no doubt antiwar speeches not delivered in June 1812) would not change the vote of the "substantial part of this house," and they did not. The bill passed easily, 77 to 42, on January 14, 1813. In the Senate, the bill, with amendments, was accepted. It was then signed into law on January 29.[19]

Joseph Gales supported the measure in the *National Intelligencer.* "It is supposed, that in the neighborhood of the enemy, large bodies of respectable citizens will turn out to serve for one campaign, who would not engage to serve for five, or even more than one year." Undoubtedly, he said, it would be better to raise men for five years, "if they were to be had." He noted that whenever it was proposed to the militia corps, "to pass the line [the Canadian border], the constitutional objection is raised, which creates division, and reduces the number for service." He added, "The absurdity of having a force in the field, to march to a certain line and halt there, must be evident to every one. The only force to be relied on must be one, willing to go any where, and every where . . . , completely trained and well-disciplined."[20]

The question of arming the militia was again raised in the second session of the Twelfth Congress. In the House, a bill was proposed from the Committee on the Military by David Williams to appropriate

$400,000 for arms, which also included a section for classification of militia. Benjamin Tallmadge (Conn.) opposed, arguing that the bill would punish those who had complied with the law by arming themselves and would reward those who had not. About $1 million had accrued to the fund since the law of 1808 passed, he observed, but apparently less than $100,000 had been expended for arms, and another $100,000 had passed to the credit of the sinking fund "because it had not been drawn for within the time limited by law." Either the executive department "has been guilty of gross neglect in the non-execution of the law of April, 1808," he declared, "or else that the money could not be judiciously expended." In any event, with ample money on hand, the extra sum did not seem necessary. The true problem, he continued, was that in the United States there was a "want of artisans, who shall be capable of doing the business in a workmanlike manner." He noted that an army officer who had recently inspected the arms at the public armory at Springfield reported "that out of fifty or sixty thousand stands . . . he could not select one thousand fit for use." Tallmadge did not suppose private factories could do much better. If they could deliver 20,000 stands a year, the appropriation under the law of 1808 would still be adequate. He noted that at that moment—five years later—many states still had not received a single stand of arms (weapon and accouterments).[21]

William Ely (Mass.) doubted that the current arms were as defective as Tallmadge suggested. Yet he conceded that mistakes had been made in the past, as when bayonets had been soldered to the barrels of 15,000 muskets. Many of these, he observed, might still be made into good muskets. Ely acknowledged that skilled artificers were scarce and that experience had shown that arms procured under contract "were very poor." Such arrangements, he asserted, should not be made without good reason to believe that they could be fulfilled competently. He cited a case in Pennsylvania where a contract for rifles had been let to a manufacturer reputed to produce them "more perfect than in any other part of the Union." Two thousand were inspected, received, and paid for. Although the inspectors had been highly recommended, complaints were made later, and upon reinspection, "not one rifle of the whole number was found to be fit for use, or good for anything."[22]

Ely also opposed classification "pressed upon us year to year, by gentlemen from the Southern section of the Union, he knew not why." Southern militia, he claimed, were imperfect because of neglect, and "if the States would not enforce those laws, he had no idea they would enforce this." If the South wanted classification, then they should adopt it rather than press for a measure that would injure the militias in one part of the Union more than it would benefit those in the other. Indeed, classification probably would not have helped the South. Classification might have inconvenienced fewer men, and in an agricultural region this point might have carried some weight, but the greater dispersion of population in the South would have made it very difficult to form, organize, and train militia.[23]

Josiah Quincy saw something darker in the effort to establish classification. The Massachusetts congressman believed the object was to place "all the youth of the nation at the command of the Executive, as a disposable force, to march anywhere, and do anything for which any Congress may pass a law." Despite these and other objections, supporters of the bill prevailed by a vote of sixty-seven to forty-eight. In the Senate, however, Joseph Varnum (Mass.), after reporting the House bill without amendment, moved to postpone further consideration. As Joseph Gales reported in the *Daily National Intelligencer,* the militia bill was "suffered to die a natural death, not having been taken up in the Senate."[24] No further measures affecting the militia were introduced in the Twelfth Congress.

In the first session of the Thirteenth Congress, the touchy issue of compensating states for militia drafts not authorized by the federal government was raised. Solomon Sharp (Ky.) moved on June 4, 1813, to study what compensation ought to be made for mounted riflemen called into service from Kentucky in 1812 to defend Forts Wayne and Harrison. Felix Grundy (Tenn.) noted that many states had incurred expenses for defense "not authorized by law," and he asked that this matter be referred to a committee. Charles Goldsborough (Md.) agreed. Citing his state's grievance against the national government for uncompensated militia costs, he said that all expenses of the militiamen "called out by the State authorities for the defence of the soil, ought to be defrayed by the General Government." Sharp declined to make his motion general, but Goldsborough moved to broaden the study for paying militia expenses called out under state authority in 1812.[25]

Samuel McKee (Ky.) argued that Goldsborough's amendment altered the nature of the original motion, which dealt with a special case where the Kentucky militiamen had been called out and not to defend their particular state. Goldsborough's amendment, nevertheless, received solid support and was passed, with the stipulation that territorial governments be included upon the motion of Jonathan Jennings of the Indiana Territory. Troup of Georgia reported for his committee on the resolution in the second session of the Thirteenth Congress. They recommended that individuals who lost property be compensated, but the committee did not recommend any increased compensation for "extraordinary military services."[26]

The subject of the distribution of arms under the law of 1808 was raised again during this session. Timothy Pitkin, a Federalist from Connecticut, observed that documents placed before the House showed that approximately 16,000 of 31,000 arms procured under the appropriations of the 1808 law had been distributed to only eleven states and territories. He offered a resolution to inquire why some states had received a distribution and others had not. Troup responded that the resolution might "excite distrust and jealousy between the General and State governments." If the distribution was examined, he argued, "we shall find that nothing like political prejudice has operated, as the gentleman has seemed to insinuate." Three New England states (New Hampshire, Rhode Island, and Vermont) had gotten 4,500 of the 16,000, and although Connecticut and Massachusetts had received none, neither had Pennsylvania, New York, or Virginia. Pitkin denied that he sought to introduce political considerations; the construction placed on the law, he argued, differed from that which had been intended. Apparently, he added, the secretary of war could give arms to "particular favorite States . . . whilst to others not a single musket would be given." He claimed "each State, whether well or ill-armed previously, ought to have its proportion of arms."[27]

James Fisk (Vt.) moved successfully to refer the resolution to the Committee on Military Affairs. He opposed the resolution, he said, because it implied "a censure on the Executive." He thought that the arms had been distributed where they were most needed and that the Executive had "proceeded on perfectly just grounds." First-term congressman Daniel Webster (N.H.) entered the debate, arguing that the Act of 1808 was a peace measure, not a war measure, and contained no provisions for making distinctions. John C. Calhoun (S.C.) observed that the law's object was the defense of the country. Even the peace establishment had for its ultimate object a state of war. Eventually, the resolution was adopted "with very few dissenting votes." On July 8, however, Troup reported the opinion of the Committee on Military Affairs that it would be "inexpedient" to make any changes in the law, and the report was ordered to lie on the table.[28]

The Committee on Military Affairs in the Senate also took up amending the militia law pertaining to responsibility for militia drafts. The War Department had recently announced rules for calling out militia, placing that responsibility with the commanding general of each of the military districts. The bill now pending allowed state governors that authority. Senator Samuel Smith (Md.) consulted Secretary John Armstrong on the proposed bill. Armstrong offered several objections. He explained that the War Department rules were made to operate on individuals and not on companies, regiments, or brigades. Prior to the establishment of rules for drafts, there was often "a great deficiency in the rank & file, and a great redundancy in the commissioned part of the Corps." Some brigades called out had a full complement of staff and platoon officers that did not contain a thousand privates. The War Department rule was designed to establish a balance in the grades. Under the proposed bill, Armstrong continued, a governor would presumably "take them as he finds them, already organized into Companies and Regiments; and will, by doing so, perpetuate the evil."[29]

Armstrong further observed that the bill did not provide for muster or inspection by an officer of the United States prior to acceptance, which was "indispensable with regard to militia detachments." The bill also gave governors power to exhaust the military arsenals of the United States and made no provision for the safekeeping or return of arms drawn from the arsenals. Finally, he questioned the principle embodied in the bill enabling states or territories to defend themselves at the expense of the United States. "The expenditures made at different points during the last year," he noted, "carry in them an admonition against the employment of militia, under calls not immediately authorized by the Executive of the Union."[30] As far as can be determined, the bill never emerged from committee.

As the year 1813 drew to a close, the government could point to mixed results in its conduct of the war. Some successes were intermingled with continued failures. In the West, Tecumseh was dead and his Indian confederacy broken. The British had been defeated at the Battle of the Thames, and the West and Lake Erie were safely in American hands. The militiamen deserved part of the credit, particularly volunteer militiamen under Col. Richard M. Johnson. Along the Niagara frontier, early successes were marred by devastation and defeat at the end of the year, and along the St. Lawrence virtually nothing had been accomplished even to threaten this vital waterway. Large numbers of militiamen still refused to cross the international boundary, and they continued to display a lack of discipline by retreating before the enemy. Congress seemed incapable of providing an alternative, and the country faced the next campaign still relying on militias to bear a large part of the burden of military action.

In the second session of the Thirteenth Congress, which met in December 1813, compensation for militiamen called out under state authority was brought up again. In this case the issue was pay to Tennessee militiamen engaged against hostile Indians. John W. Taylor (N.Y.) reported for the House Committee on Militia that no legislative provision was necessary. The proper procedure, he said, was to apply to the federal government for sanction to use militia, and the committee had no knowledge of any cases where sanction had been refused. There had to be controls, he said; otherwise the United States would be charged with the "expenses of militia detachments, ordered into service, perhaps, without necessity, and possibly for objects inconsistent with the public welfare."[31]

After returning from the northern front in late 1813, Secretary of War Armstrong proposed on January 1, 1814, that Congress fill the ranks of the regular army by conscription. An adequate regular force, he argued, would "enable us to finish the war (without again calling on Militia) in one Campaign." Armstrong considered the militia wasteful, poorly trained, and unreliable. His plan would have classed "the whole body of militia into as many classes as there were soldiers wanting, and to make every class furnish one during the war, or to have one draughted from each of them." Elisha Potter (R.I.) thought it more equitable to raise soldiers by enlisting and giving large bounties to induce them to enlist voluntarily than by adopting the conscription plan proposed by Secretary Armstrong. This would have compelled "the young and very poor men," he said, "to do all the duty and bear the burdens of the war, while the rich, and those who are excused from doing duty in the militia, would be excused." Potter also bitterly criticized the refusal of the New York and Pennsylvania militiamen to cross into Canada in the Niagara campaign. He presumed some were men who approved the conduct of the administration and were "willing to support the war by voting, when it costs neither blood nor money." The militias of both states, he declared, had proven "a dead weight on the Administration . . . , and although much fault had been found with the Administration about the prosecution of the war, for his part, with such help as they had, he felt more to pity than to find fault with them."[32]

Jonathan Fisk (N.Y.) defended his state's militia from the charge of cowardice. He insisted that insufficient boats were available to comply with Gen. Stephen Van Rensselaer's order to cross at Queenston in November 1812, and Gen. Alexander Smyth "refused to lead them over." In fact, Fisk said, some militia "broke in pieces the arms they could not be permitted to measure with the enemy . . . , yet they are charged with refusing to do their duty!" Morris S. Miller (N.Y.) gave a very different assessment of his state's militia. He defended Van Rensselaer, but the state militiamen "were lost to every generous and manly feeling" and were "guilty of a shameful desertion of the standard of their country, and a cruel and cowardly abandonment of their commander in the hour of danger."[33]

On February 3, 1814, Troup introduced a bill to allow the president to retain in service certain volunteer corps. Under the 1812 law authorizing 50,000 volunteers, six regiments had been called into service: one from New Hampshire and Maine; two in New York; one in Virginia; and two in Louisiana and the Mississippi Territory. Their terms were now expiring, but about 1,000 were willing to serve during the war, provided they serve under their own officers. Even this seemingly innocuous bill met stiff opposition because it was feared that more than 1,000 would offer their services. Ultimately, the bill passed.[34]

Finally, the second session attempted to revise the militia law. The bill was introduced by John W. Taylor on March 28, 1814. The opposition objected particularly to provisions that strengthened the powers of courts-martial to proceed against militiamen in their absence, to punish individuals for contempt of court by word or gesture, and to compel witnesses to attend. Taylor defended the bill, arguing that the objective was "to prevent the requisitions of militia by the President from being disregarded by the Governors of States, or rendered inefficient by the contumacy of subordinate officers or privates." Despite criticisms of the powers given to courts-martial, the measure made its way through both houses and became law on April 18. In addition to strengthening the courts-martial, militiamen were compelled to serve six months after arriving at the place of rendezvous. (They were to be paid, however, for expenses incurred in marching to the rendezvous.)[35]

Congress did not lack for advice. Many proposals were put forth during the war to resolve the manpower problem. One proposal for militia reform was put before the country early in 1813 by Col. Edmund Pendleton Gaines. Adj. Gen. Thomas Cushing inquired whether any elementary treatise might be adapted to the discipline of militia. Gaines responded in a long letter dated January 2, 1813, that was published in March in the *Daily National Intelligencer.* He called for "a radical change in the militia laws." The militia system, he asserted, "must be improved, or it must be laid aside altogether." Discipline could not be learned "in the sweet social walks of domestic life." Gaines proposed that young, unmarried men be organized and marched to military posts on the frontier and seacoast, placed under discipline from regular army officers, and asked to "serve as regulars or *regular militia* for two or three years." New militiamen would rotate in as the old went out. If this plan was adopted on a small scale, he said, it would soon be seen as "the most economical and efficient system of defence that can be devised" and would in a few years gain the approbation of 90 percent of the people. He denied that his scheme would be tantamount to establishing a standing army. "Who can for a moment believe that such an army of regular militia, alternately going from and returning to the bosom of their friends in every part of the union, can be considered as dangerous to our happy republic?"[36]

Near the end of the war, Andrew Jackson gave Tennessee congressman John Rhea advice about militia reform. "I hope Congress will see the necessity of placing the militia in a state [condition]," he wrote, "that when called for, they can be relied on." He proposed two specific reforms. First, the length of service should be extended "at least to one year." Short enlistments, he argued, were "the greatest curse to a nation in a state of war—and such army can never be in a state to operate." Second, any militiaman called into service who left it "without a regular discharge should be apprehended, and transferred to the regular service and compelled to serve during the present war." He added, "This will alone put down the spirit of mutiny and desertion that pervade our militia."[37]

Jackson also expressed to Acting Secretary of War Monroe in November 1814 a plan to reduce expenses entailed in the frequent calls for militia. Basically, after the government had determined the number of militiamen needed for the war (Jackson supposed about 150,000) and the apportionment of each state, they should be called out for the duration of the war. The quotas would, Jackson argued, be filled immediately if these militiamen were given the premiums and bounties currently offered by the government. Placing these troops under selected and experienced officers for training, the force would "present an effective army in every quarter, sufficient to drive all enemies from your shores, and to reduce Canada."[38] In effect, Jackson proposed to conscript the militiamen into the regular army. He perhaps did not appreciate the political difficulties of carrying out on the national level a scheme that turned the state militia into a standing army. Jackson's proposal would also have been strongly opposed by many state leaders.

The *Daily National Intelligencer* published several similar proposals in late 1814. One was a series of essays signed "Spirit of the Times," who criticized individuals who opposed improving the militias by citing the cost and inconvenience of placing citizens in camps for training and discipline. As a consequence, the writer averred, the nation had paid dearly for want of such training. Citizens must "yield a portion of his personal ease and comforts" and go into camps and submit themselves to training. A second essay chastised Congress for not making the militia more efficient. The new system must provide for classing the militia; "it will be in vain to alter the old [system]." A third essay advised Congress to limit exemptions to those "really disabled, or *conscientiously* scrupulous of bearing arms," but they should pay a pecuniary compensation in lieu of service. Also, younger men should be placed in military schools and should be educated at public expense.[39]

Another writer, "Jackson," declared that Congress should compel every eighth or tenth person to provide an able-bodied person, which would raise a force of 140,000 to 160,000. "Jackson" also questioned exempting persons over forty-five during wartime. Such people, he argued, generally had more to defend, and many would be willing to serve.[40]

Another anonymous writer argued that temporary forces raised for an emergency and disbanded after the crisis were inadequate. As a substitute for the current inadequate enlistment system, he proposed that "every seven, ten, or twelve men . . . find one person to serve for one, two, or three years or during the war." Since some substitutes were paid as much as $100, he argued that if ten men united to pay $50 each, the total of $500 plus the present inducements for enlistment—$124 bounty, 160 acres of land, and the pay of $8 per month—would supply "thousands who would cheerfully accept the above sum of near *one thousand dollars* . . . ." (The average unskilled worker earned about $10 per month.) A regular force would more effectively impress the enemy, he argued. "It is well known they estimate our militia very lightly, and that they dread our regulars."[41]

The Thirteenth Congress reconvened for the third session on September 19 in an atmosphere of crisis. Washington had been burned, the peace negotiations at Ghent had apparently broken down, and the prospects were that the British would prosecute the war even more vigorously. Worse, recruitment in the regular army lagged, and the strength of the army was only about half the authorized strength of 62,000. It was imperative that Congress devise ways of mobilizing American manpower. Madison not only asked Congress to fill the regular army and to encourage volunteers but also renewed his request for classification to give the militia greater energy and efficiency.[42]

James Monroe, who took over the War Department after Armstrong's resignation in early September, submitted a bewildering array of options to the House Military Affairs Committee on October 17. One possibility was to classify the free male population (ages eighteen to forty-five) into groups of 100. Each group would provide four men; failing to do so, the men would be raised by a draft on the whole class and would be paid by a tax upon the inhabitants of that class. A second option was to class the whole militia into three groups (eighteen to twenty five, twenty-five to thirty-two, and thirty-two to forty-five) that might be called upon as necessary by the president for service of up to two years. A third proposal was to offer exemption from militia service to every five men who provided one to serve for the war. The final choice was to continue the present policy of raising troops but to increase the land bounty. Senator Obadiah German of New York complicated matters by offering yet another plan that would divide the militia into classes of ten, with each class to provide one man for one year. German would have these men serve "in a corps of local militia, to be organized in each State for the defence thereof," while Monroe's idea had obviously been to use the force not for defense but for offensive purposes.[43]

These preliminary proposals at length gave rise to two bills introduced in the Senate on November 5. One legalized the enlistment of men eighteen to twenty-one years old without the consent of parents or guardian, and it doubled the land grant to 320 acres. Despite considerable opposition, this bill passed the Senate on November 12. The House took up the bill on December 2 and debated it over the next four days. Cyrus King (Mass.) denounced the measure as "calculated to destroy the militia system, and . . . the sovereignty of the States." Ignoring the fact that eighteen-year-olds served in the militia, King termed the bill a minor conscription bill, "the most inhuman, immoral, and oppressive, that ever was attempted to be established by this, and, of course, by any other assembly, called deliberative." He declared melodramatically, "I beseech you, as friends of humanity, to spare the tears which the passage of this law will cause to flow; I appeal to you as fathers, by every endearing tie which binds you to your children, not to deprive the aged parent of the child of his youth, the support and solace of his declining years, lest you bring his gray hairs with sorrow to the grave." King asserted that the administration had first tried patriotism to raise troops. When that failed, it attempted to buy soldiers with bounties, land, and wages, and, still baffled, they were now turning to conscription, "to kidnap the people, as you would slaves; and," he added, "they will deserve this fate, if they tamely submit to such oppression." Thomas P. Grosvenor, a Federalist from New York, thought that the bill might add perhaps 1,000 recruits to the army. It was, he said, "a measure combining strong characters of weakness and violence, of folly and madness," and he cited his agreement with Daniel Webster's argument that if apprentices could be enlisted in defiance of their masters, then why not enlist slaves?[44]

One change to the Senate bill was made when the House accepted a motion by John W. Taylor to allow recruits a four-day period to change their minds. All Federalist attempts to amend or weaken the measure were defeated decisively. The bill passed the House on December 6 by a vote of 95 to 52, and it was signed into law four days later.[45]

The second measure, dubbed a conscription bill by the Federalists, engendered a vast amount of acrimonious debate. The bill provided that the whole body of the militia would raise 80,430 men to serve for two years. Each state was to fill its quota, based on its ratio of representation in Congress. The militia of each state was to be divided into as many classes as were required to provide men, and each class was obliged to furnish a man, either by contract or draft..Any two classes who provided two soldiers for the regular army were to be exempted from the operation of the act. Denunciations of the bill quickly followed. Joseph Varnum, a Republican from Massachusetts, declared that the bill was "unnecessary, unequal, and unjust." Varnum was possibly trying to head off a Federalist assault on the bill, but he had always been sensitive to any tampering with the militia system. He subjected the bill to a devastating critique and concluded that it violated correct military procedure and all pretense at fairness between rich and poor. In the end, he charged, it would fail to produce the number of soldiers wanted.[46]

David Daggett (Conn.), a Federalist, asserted that in Connecticut, five-sixths of the property was possessed by exempts. This bill unjustly placed the burden upon the least affluent. Moreover, as the bill depended upon state governments to carry the law into effect, he doubted that many state governors would consent "to annihilate the power of the State over its militia." In New England, he noted ominously, "They too well know and too highly appreciate the privileges of free men to approve a conscription, however disguised."[47]

Beyond converting all the state militias into a regular army, Jeremiah Mason (N.H.) saw another insidious purpose in Monroe's proposal, namely to levy a tax on the free male population and to relieve "the slaveholding States from the increased tax." He calculated this would mean a difference of $400,000 between Virginia and Massachusetts. Another New England Federalist, Christopher Gore (Mass.), contended that the militia was never intended to be used to prosecute an offensive war or even to be relied upon as a permanent defense force. Classing was the "first step on the odious ground of conscription. . . . The honey on the edges of the cup will not disguise the bitterness of the venomous drug at its bottom." Gore's motion to reduce the term of service to nine months was defeated by six votes.[48]

Similar denunciations followed. Robert Goldsborough, a Maryland Federalist, lamented "that blood-stained plea of tyrants, which has served every scheme of usurpation to sacrifice the lives and liberties of men." Eventually, the bill was passed on November 22 by a seven-vote margin and sent to the House.[49]

"Americanus" decried in the pages of the *Daily National Intelligencer* the "heedless clamor against the bill" and asked why it was called conscription. Under the old system, if 100 men were wanted, then each regiment had to furnish by lot 50 men who were obliged to go or find a substitute. In the new system every 25 men furnished 1, thus exempting 24 men, and if each class had one willing to serve, the force was raised voluntarily. Furthermore, the old system took poor men who could not afford a substitute as well as poor men who served as substitutes, a "manifest inequality." Under the new system the rich participated, at least in contribution. The author also questioned the reasoning that "it is more just to *force* a man to serve six months, contrary to his will, than for him *voluntarily* to agree to serve as many years."[50]

It is often difficult to separate political rhetoric and genuine statements of principle, but in this debate the concern expressed by the Federalists appears to have been real. No doubt the characterization of this measure as a "conscription" bill served as an emotional rallying point for the opposition. Federalist orators repeatedly alluded to the French conscription. Joseph Pearson, a Federalist congressman from North Carolina, in a letter to his constituents, characterized the bill as one that threatened "the horrors of *conscription and impressment*, under the disguise of militia draft." Even in the privacy of his room, Timothy Pickering, the Federalist congressman from Massachusetts, confided in a private memorandum that the country seemed to be heading toward a military dictatorship. "The French revolutionary scenes will be acted over again," he wrote, "conscription, forced loans, military tribunate, and the guillotine." Pickering contended that the people never contemplated "vesting Congress with a general power to *impress* the men requisite to compose an *army*."[51]

The House took up the Senate bill on December 2. George Troup criticized the Senate measure because it placed reliance for the prosecution of the war on irregular militia, and he predicted that "defeat, disaster, and disgrace must follow." The country needed a regular force. Volunteers and state troops should be raised to serve in lieu of militia. A regular force would be not only more efficient but more economical as well. John C. Calhoun responded that the reason for preferring the Senate bill was obvious. It had already been passed by the Senate, and if the House passed it, it would become law.[52]

A select committee of the House offered several amendments, which were debated at length. One, easily passed, authorized the president, whenever the governor of a state failed to comply with the requisition, "to call directly on the officers of the militia." Another based apportionment of the militia on free population in the last census rather than on representation. John W. Eppes (Va.), perhaps to make the bill more palatable to Republicans, moved to reduce the term of service from two years to one year; the motion passed by twenty votes.[53]

Morris Miller (N.Y.) cited a case in New York where the governor had pardoned a horse thief "on condition that he should enlist, and serve in the Army." He warned that if the majority persisted in attempts to raise a force for conquest, "the States must and will take care of themselves; and they will preserve the resources of the States for the defense of the States." He added that some states "may consider themselves bound by duty and interest to withdraw from this Confederacy."[54] No doubt Miller's speech, delivered only a week before the antiwar meeting of the New England states at Hartford (see Chapter 9), had a sobering effect on the House, but it may also have served to keep the administration supporters together despite the obvious distaste that many Republicans felt for the bill.

Daniel Webster also raised his mighty voice against the conscription bill. On December 9, he depicted a desperate government trying to raise a standing army from the militia; a government "more tyrannical, more arbitrary, more dangerous, more allied to blood & murder, more full of every form of mischief, more productive of every sort & degree of misery, than has been exercised by any civilized Government, with a single exception, in modern times." Conscription would mean death to half of those chosen. "They will perish of disease & pestilence," he said, "or they will leave their bones to whiten in fields beyond the frontier." He predicted that the states would interpose their authority "between their citizens & arbitrary power." If the administration could not form an army without conscription, it would find that "it can not enforce conscription without an army." He ridiculed charges that New Englanders were trying to dissolve the union. Rather, "Those who cry out that the Union is in danger are themselves the author of that danger."[55]

Charles J. Ingersoll (Pa.) dismissed the "pathetic threats" of the Federalists, but he feared this opposition would deter supporters from any action. Experience had shown that neither militia nor voluntary enlistments could be relied upon. "The fatal doctrine of citizen soldier," he said, ". . . has cost us more money, more blood, more mourning, in six months, than a war of six years should or would cost under proper military organization." He added, "No rational, no feeling man can doubt as to the shocking inexpediency of such a system." Militia classification and draft was obviously the best and fairest way to raise a force. He concluded, "Dismemberment would be but a little misfortune, contrasted with what may be our lot, unless we rise up to the exigency. . . . Convulsion is no more to be dreaded than paralysis."[56]

Richard Stockton (N.J.) declared that the bill "reverses everything." The militia, he argued, "is converted into the regular force, the regulars into the auxiliary!" William Irving (N.Y.), in defense of the bill, asserted that it was "impossible to fill the ranks of the Army" because of "various and unjustifiable means that have been resorted to, for the purpose of impeding or discouraging enlistments." "What are we to do," he asked, "but try more efficient means, or surrender the honor, and barter the interests of the country for imaginary Constitutional scruples?"[57]

Several efforts were made to weaken the bill, without success. A motion by Webster to reduce the term of service to six months, however, failed by only one vote. After an unsuccessful attempt to recommit the bill, it was engrossed and ordered to a third reading by a margin of twenty votes.[58]

By now it was clear there were enough supporters to pass the bill. All the opposition could do was to make dire predictions about the consequences of passage. Artemas Ward, Jr. (Mass.), declared that no government had the right "to compel the citizens of our country to enter the regular Army," and he added, "resistance is not only lawful . . . ; it is a duty."[59]

A call for the previous question finally shut down the debate by a twelve-vote margin. The bill was passed by the same margin and sent to the Senate. The close margin reflected, perhaps, that some Republicans defected when they believed it safe to do so. The major changes made in the Senate bill reduced the term of service from two years to one; the president was allowed to bypass state governors who refused to act by using militia officers to requisition troops; and the force could be used beyond the limits of the state or contiguous state. The Senate accepted the latter amendment, but it refused to accept the two former amendments. The House refused to yield on its amendments and called for a conference committee. The House conferees recommended eighteen months' service as a compromise and receded on the amendment authorizing the president to call directly on militia officers for troops. The House, however, refused to yield on either point and demanded another conference. In the Senate, on December 28, Rufus King (N.Y.), taking advantage of the fortuitous absence of some of the bill's supporters, moved to postpone the bill to the end of the session, and his motion passed by 14-13. This step effectively killed the bill for the session. Daniel Webster wrote his brother that King's motion was "accidental— unpremeditated . . . Mr. King made the motion—some members happened to be out—it was immediately put & carried."[60]

After three months of discussion, Congress still had not provided a means of raising additional troops. "Franklin" argued in the *National Intelligencer* on October 25, 1814, that Congress by raising bounties and paying beforehand was doing it wrong. He recommended raising

150,000 volunteers who would serve six months and would be given liberal pay and allowances. They would "answer all needs and would be cheaper."[61]

Perhaps reflecting this attitude, George M. Troup, for the House Military Affairs Committee, on October 27 reported a bill to authorize the president to accept the services of volunteers. On November 2, Troup proposed an amendment to raise the term of service from nine months to twelve. The three additional months, he explained, were for discipline and instruction, leaving nine months for actual service. The motion passed by two votes. Troup admitted in debate that the volunteers were not intended to substitute for the kind of force needed to prosecute the war.[62]

The bill generated considerable debate and several amendments. Richard M. Johnson (Ky.), a member of the Military Affairs Committee, commented on November 7 that the committee had decided to call up the bill in the belief that "it would meet with little or no discussion or diversity of opinion." It had been so amended, however, that some provisions of the bill were inconsistent, and he moved to lay it on the table. Nearly a month later, on December 2, Johnson moved to amend the bill "to reinstate it precisely in the form in which it stood before it underwent amendment by the House." The bill was ordered engrossed, was read a third time, and passed on December 6.[63]

The Senate did not act on the volunteer bill until the failure of the conscription bill. Now the volunteer bill stood as the only viable option. The House bill was amended by the Senate, the most important change being to authorize the president to accept state troops to meet the militia quota of the state. The House accepted some amendments and disagreed on others. After going to a conference committee, the bill finally passed and was signed into law on January 27, 1815. The president was authorized to accept up to 40,000 state troops (apportioned by states). If the number of state troops did not reach 40,000, additional volunteers were authorized up to a total of 80,000. The officers would be commissioned by the president, subject to Senate approval. The term of service was twelve months.[64]

Early in February 1815 yet another idea for raising troops was broached by Charles Rich (Vt.), who proposed instructing the Committee on Military Affairs to study arranging into classes citizens owing direct taxes of $400 to $800; each class would then be allowed to furnish one man for the army in lieu of taxes. "Every taxable citizen," he believed, "would in a degree voluntarily become a recruiting officer." Webster declared the plan would "seriously obstruct the recruiting service" and would "produce no good." Furthermore, the direct tax had already been pledged, and an additional tax was not practicable. Thomas Grosvenor (N.Y.) characterized the plan as a "wild project," but the proposal gained some support. James Fisk, Rich's colleague from Vermont, declared that "some efficient and certain measures to fill the ranks of the regular army" had to be taken. "What answer," he asked, "could they give to their constituents, if they returned home and left the country comparatively defenseless?" Troup noted that his committee had endeavored to ascertain the opinion of both houses on the different modes of raising men and had found "no efficacious measure, calculated certainly and promptly to fill the regular army." Certain measures were not pushed on the House because there was no disposition to act on them. The committee had tried instead to improve the recruiting service and to gain acceptance of volunteers and state troops. The 80,000 authorized, with the 60,000 regular troops already approved, gave a possible force of 140,000, and it "might reasonably be expected to produce one hundred thousand; as great a number, perhaps, as, under the circumstances, the finances of the country would bear." Despite opposition, the resolution was referred to the Committee of the Whole by a six-vote margin. A little over a week later, however, the matter was postponed indefinitely following news of the end of the war.[65]

Thus after three years of conflict, Congress still had not provided the country with an adequate force to prosecute the war. The effort was flawed from the beginning. Assumptions about the utility of the militia were difficult to overcome, and even at the war's end some congressmen maintained that the militia was a competent force to prosecute the war. Always lurking in the background was the fear of a standing army. No doubt, many Federalists were being hypocritical when they wrung their hands about the classification of militia, about conscription as an alternative to militia, and about the use of volunteers in lieu of militia. On the other hand, many Republicans had to overcome deeply ingrained prejudices to support party measures that proposed the various plans that have been enumerated. In the end, Congress was too divided and too indecisive to provide the manpower to prosecute the war.

Chapter 3

Militia Organization

Federal utilization of militia was based upon the idea that each state militia was organized, armed and equipped, and capable of turning out quickly for duty upon the call of the government. Sadly, this was rarely the case in any state. The disorganized state of the militia was not unknown when war was declared on June 18, 1812, but no doubt few understood or anticipated the myriad problems that would be encountered in using militias to prosecute the war. Senator Obadiah German (N.Y.) was one who pointed out that those who counted upon using the militia to prosecute the war would be disappointed. On June 13 he observed that the 1,600 militiamen from New York called into service exhibited "a spectacle that would wound the feelings of the most callous man." They were without hats, blankets, camp kettles, or any necessary camp equipage. It was with utmost difficulty that their officers prevented them from marching back home. He predicted, correctly, that the militia would not perform well in the campaign of 1812: "the evils attending upon calling a large portion of the militia into actual service for any considerable time, is almost incalculable. After a short time, sickness, death, and many other evils will teach you the impropriety of relying on them for carrying on the war."[1]

Indeed, frontier militia units were so poorly organized that when state militiamen were drafted, it was difficult to determine who belonged to which militia company, because many units had never been mustered. Although state laws prescribed fines for failure to join a militia unit, many eligible men never enrolled. Ohio Governor Return J. Meigs, ignoring the fact that states were ultimately responsible for militia organization, lamented to his legislature in December 1812 that Congress had not provided "a more efficacious system of militia organization, discipline and duty." He complained particularly that so much time was consumed in collecting and organizing militiamen that it was often too late to meet an emergency.[2] Meigs's statement reflected the situation in Ohio and generally throughout the West and South.

The lowest level of organization for militias was the company. Typically, a company had sixty-four privates, but it varied from forty to eighty on the frontier, where the population was scattered and it was not always convenient to form companies according to the prescribed numbers. Militia districts might have to be spread out too far to reach the prescribed numbers, or the number of eligible men in a district might not be enough to form two companies. A typical company had one captain, two lieutenants (first and second), an ensign, four sergeants, four corporals, and a drummer. A fifer and a clerk were often added as well. Captains and subordinate officers were elected by the company. The captain then typically chose the sergeants and corporals and ranked them.

The situation became more complicated when Adj. Gen. Thomas H. Cushing issued new rules on March 19, 1813, for militia drafts. All requisitions had to be made by an officer of the United States authorized to make such calls on the executive of the state or territory; calls would be explicit as to the number of privates, noncommissioned officers, and commissioned officers required (the previous method of calling for regiments or brigades was thereby discontinued); companies called into service should have 100 privates, eight noncommissioned officers, and five commissioned officers; and payment would be made by the regimental paymaster or the paymaster accompanying the army or the division to which it belonged.[3]

When the federal government issued the new rules for drafted militias, state governors were confronted by the fact that the companies of their state militias usually had only about two-thirds the number of privates called for by the national government, so that to meet the quota it was necessary to merge companies. Some officers had to be left home, and men were forced to serve under unfamiliar officers. Consequently, governors urged their legislatures to improve and revise state militia laws to meet the new situation. Governor Joseph Alston of South Carolina, for example, recommended in November 1813 that the legislature increase the number of divisions. Otherwise, if South Carolina troops acted with U.S. forces or troops of sister states, "our general officers must always invariably be outranked." Governor James Barbour also noted to the Virginia legislature in December 1813 that the state militia system did not comply with the regulations of the War Department, so that some officers had been excluded from service. Pennsylvania governor Simon Snyder also pointed out to his legislature "the discordance between our militia system and that of the United States." Conforming with the rules and regulations of the United States would hasten de-

taching militiamen to service and would prevent "those contests between corps and officers for rank and precedence which have too frequently tended to injure the reputation of our citizen soldiers and the
public service."[4]

In his annual message in October 1814, Georgia governor Peter
Early called for consideration of abolishing the cavalry because the war
had offered "little use for this species of troops." They were "for the
most part exempt from the public service." Early recommended "radical changes" in the militia system, "calculated for a peace Establishment." Specifically, he wanted to change the law that prescribed election of officers after the militia had marched to rendezvous, because it
left no means to organize and march them there. He also called for
revising the Georgia militia organization, which varied from those prescribed by the federal government and created problems when they
were to be received into the service of the United States.[5]

It was notorious that most states never solved the problem of militia requisitions. Governor Isaac Shelby of Kentucky, for example, called
upon his legislature in December 1815, after the war was over, to revise
militia laws to "prevent in future those evasions and delays in complying with executive requisitions for militia which were so severely felt
during the last war."[6]

The next level above the company was the battalion, composed of
four to eight companies (again, the number varied on the frontier) with
approximately 500 men. Two battalions formed a regiment (roughly
1,000 men). The next higher level of organization was the brigade, con-
sisting of two to four regiments, and finally the division was the highest
level, formed out of two to four brigades. The officers above the rank of
captain, filling the positions in battalions and regiments, were elected
by the commissioned officers, and the highest levels (brigadier and major
generals) were usually appointed by the governors of the states, approved by the legislature.

One of the most vexing problems in using the militia related to
disputes over time in service. Congress extended the tour of duty for
militiamen in federal service from three months to six months in April
1812. Several states passed similar laws, but others retained the three-
month tour for state service. Sometimes, however, militiamen were not
retained for the full term. Problems arose when the same militiamen
were summoned for a second tour. When a call for militiamen was made
on May 17, 1814, for example, Georgia militiamen who had already
completed a term of service, even those who had served for only sixty
days, resisted the new draft. Governor Early issued a general order on
June 3, 1814, that those who had served for sixty days on the frontier

the previous winter, as well as those who had served with General John Floyd, were exempt from this call. It also became an issue whether volunteer cavalrymen were liable to do duty as classed militia. A general order of June 25 declared that "whenever any militia man has been drafted into the first class, but has since joined a troop of cavalry, he is nevertheless to do duty in the line." Governor Early cited the problem to one cavalry officer in September 1814: "I have for months past felt such great inconvenience from the existence of a number of half filled volunteer companies through the State, that I consider it adviseable [sic] to commission no more of them." He added, "We cannot get them received into the United States service with their present numbers, and notwithstanding the willing spirit which prevails among them, they become exempts from service."[7]

Early's point was well taken. When Capt. Jack Cocke's volunteer rifle corps appeared at rendezvous in October 1814 with sixty men—rather than the ninety-six promised—Early ordered Col. Jett Thomas, the regimental commander, and General Floyd, the brigade commander, to merge Cocke's company and added that if he gave any trouble he should be arrested. Nevertheless, Cocke's company resisted being merged, and Thomas and Floyd did not act as the governor ordered, probably from doubts about their authority to do so. Governor Early, in fact, in his message to the legislature on October 18, requested power to consolidate volunteer companies. On November 17, Early informed Floyd that a law providing for the consolidation of volunteer companies was about to pass and that he would order a sufficient number to join Cocke's company to complete it. On December 1, he wrote Floyd that the law had passed and that he would order troops from a recently commissioned rifle company commanded by Captain Henry Buford to choose by lot enough troops to complete Cocke's company. Buford and his other officers promptly submitted their resignations, but Early refused to accept them, noting, "You ought to be aware that an officer cannot resign whilst under orders." Nonetheless, Buford and his company were not forced to merge with Cocke's. Early informed Floyd on February 1, 1815, that while he had the power under the law to consolidate the volunteer companies, they were officered under the old state regulations, and he added that it was "impracticable unless I were present, to exercise this power with any advantage. Perhaps under all the circumstances," he concluded, "it would be best, if General [Thomas] Pinckney will sanction it, to let them remain as they are, provided the number of officers shall bear a proper proportion to the number of privates in each company."[8]

Normally, when the federal government issued a call for militia, state governors first appealed for volunteers. Many who joined were from organized volunteer units. Presumably they were more willing to serve and were better trained and disciplined than ordinary drafted militia. Most of those who were ultimately raised, however, came from the regular militia companies, and their training was often either indifferent or nonexistent. When the troops were being recruited for volunteer units, the recruiter frequently turned to the organized militiamen and appealed to their patriotism. If this did not raise sufficient troops, then the recruiter might threaten a militia draft. If a draft was used, militiamen might have to serve under officers who were strangers. The argument was made that if the recruits formed a volunteer company they would serve under officers of their own choosing. On occasions, prospective volunteers were plied with alcoholic beverages, liberally distributed, and then signed up. Such tactics often bred bitter resentment and lowered the morale of the troops thus raised.[9]

Because of the lax organization of the militia, and despite the fact that all able-bodied men between the ages of eighteen and forty-five, by law, had to join a militia company, there were many who were able to slip through the cracks and never had to perform militia duty. Others who belonged to militia units often did everything they could to avoid military duty. During peacetime many individuals never attended muster and paid fines for their nonattendance. When war was declared they remained nonparticipants.

For those individuals who were opposed to militia duty, or for whatever reason, even merely because it was inconvenient, every state authorized the hiring of substitutes. Maryland, for example, allowed Quakers and other "conscientiously scrupulous" men to pay a three-dollar exemption fee during peacetime to avoid militia duty, but it was stipulated that in wartime they must either meet the draft or procure a substitute. If they did not, the regiment commander was authorized to hire a substitute, chargeable to the individual drafted and, if necessary, to recover the costs by a distress action and sale of property. Judging from the frequent references to their ill-kempt appearance, those hired as substitutes were desperately poor men who were enticed to accept service by offers of substantial sums. Many were physically or mentally incapable, which accounts for laws in several states that the substitutes had to be able-bodied and acceptable to a company commander. State laws also included provisions that a person acting as a substitute must stand his own term, but if he was drafted while serving a term for another, the individual hiring the substitute must either do the service of the substitute or hire another.[10]

Substitutes could make their best deal with any individual, but in the states where fines could be used to hire substitutes, the laws often established maximum amounts that could be paid to a substitute. If state laws are any guide, the average fee was around $20 a month (as in Ohio and Indiana Territory) or $100 for a tour of six months (Kentucky). New Jersey authorized a fee of $50 for an unspecified period of time.[11]

State laws reflected a great concern to ensure equity in militia service. States defined, often in elaborate ways, the procedure for calling out militia. Vermont was one of the first to elaborate a procedure in November 1812. Two boxes were used, one with the names of those eligible, and the other with either a blank card or one that said "drafted." Names were drawn until the required number was reached. In several states, a classing system was used, although methods for choosing men varied. Pennsylvania and Maryland broke their militiamen into ten classes (or groups) by lot. Each class rotated into service until everyone had served. Ohio divided each infantry company into eight classes, and each class served in succession. Kentucky and New Jersey were like Ohio, except that they created as many classes by lot as were required for the draft, and each class provided one individual for service. New Jersey imposed a $50 fine on any class that failed to designate an individual to serve; the fine was used to procure a substitute. A Virginia law of January 18, 1815, devised the most elaborate and complex classification procedure of all. It would group militiamen according to property values as nearly equal as the proximity of the individuals would allow. Each class furnishing a man for the draft exempted the entire class, but failure to provide a soldier resulted in a fine of $0.50 for every $100 of value of property in the class. The war ended before the law was implemented.[12]

Although there were severe penalties for desertion, including death, many militiamen, coerced into service, refused to do their duty and returned to their homes. No doubt they did not consider their action to be desertion. On one occasion in the fall of 1812, Ensign William Holton and twenty-five Kentucky militia, rather than obey an order from Gen. William Henry Harrison of which they disapproved, returned to their homes in Kentucky. However desertion was defined—whether it was failure to appear for duty or absence without leave—it was a serious problem throughout the war. The most common causes cited by militia deserters were poor health, substandard food, no pay, lack of proper clothing, bad leadership, and morale problems among the militia. No doubt fear of death in battle also played a part in desertions.[13]

In the early months of the war, desertion was dealt with by appeals to patriotism and condemnation in public newspapers. Also, rewards were advertised in newspapers, usually for ten dollars, for the apprehension of deserters. Nearly every newspaper issue in the early months of the war carried such advertisements. In October 1812, President Madison issued a proclamation offering a full pardon to all deserters who surrendered to the commanding officer of any military post.[14]

Failure to rendezvous was dealt with in much the same way as desertion. Kentucky, for example, lumped the two together. An individual failing to rendezvous or to provide a substitute was considered a deserter, and a law of February 3, 1813, declared that a person taking a deserter would be rewarded with "a credit for a tour or tours of duty for the length of time such deserter was bound to serve." The receipt entitled the bearer to exemption from a tour of duty (the receipt was assignable). The deserter was required to serve the next tour or to complete his present tour. Mississippi Territory and Virginia also gave persons apprehending deserters credit for a six-month tour. In Mississippi the deserter had to serve the term of the person apprehending him. Many states treated desertion as just another offense subject to fines and/or imprisonment punishable by court-martial. North Carolina, however, was more drastic than most. A law in 1813 stipulated that deserters could be fined $20 to $50, could be required to forfeit their pay, and could be imprisoned from one to six months. At the discretion of the court-martial, the deserter could also be turned over to serve as a private in the regular army of the United States not exceeding double the time of the term called out for state service.[15]

Some states were more zealous than others in enforcing fines for failing to appear for tours of duty. Governor Meigs called upon his Ohio legislature on December 7, 1813, to review the state militia law, citing "various and contradictory constructions by the militia Boards of Inquiry." He noted that "the merits or demerits of the delinquent, in regard to neglect or refusal, seem, in many instances, not to have been considered; but the highest possible penalties have been adjudged." Such penalties pressed heavily upon "those whose circumstances are unprosperous or unfortunate." He called for a more uniform rule, but he added that they should not move from one of "too much rigor" to one of "too great relaxation of the principle of duty."[16]

States adopted still other approaches to deal with individuals failing to perform militia duty. Maryland considered empowering militia officers to force recalcitrant militiamen into service, but instead it passed a law providing that an individual failing to serve in person or to provide a substitute (approved by the company commander) would be fined up to fifty dollars. A Georgia law in 1814, passed because of the frustrations caused by the failure of militiamen to show up at a rendezvous, declared that the company commander was "invested with full and ample power to coerce the attendance of any defaulter." The law also stipulated that any person moving to another area had ten days to report with a certificate from the captain of his former district stating the class he belonged to; failure to do so would cause him to be assigned to the class next called into service. In the Mississippi Territory, Governor David Holmes, without the benefit of law, but drawing on the opinion of his attorney general and "gentlemen learned in the law," determined that militia officers had the power to compel obedience. Holmes directed that the duty be performed by an officer of discretion and moderation who would not allow the men under his command "to insult the person whom they may be about to apprehend, or to use towards him any personal violence except that which is absolutely necessary." In no event were they to "fire upon a person resisting the order, or suffer any act that may hazard the life of such person, unless the detachment should be assailed in a manner that made self-defence necessary to their own preservation."[17]

Obviously, most states settled on less drastic remedies. Most imposed large fines and, in some cases, imprisonment. South Carolina established the most extreme penalties for failure to rendezvous: a fine (imposed by a court-martial) of up to $500, plus the amount of taxes last paid to the state, and imprisonment for up to three months. The most common rate was $20 per month which, with a six-month tour, came to $120, still very harsh, considering that this was a sum equal to a year's wages for the average unskilled worker. States also mandated imprisonment along with fines. The average period of incarceration was three months, although some states tied the length to the amount of the fine, usually one month for every $5 of fine. Fines and/or imprisonment did not deter Rhode Island and Virginia from also compelling a militiaman to serve the next tour of duty.[18]

Courts-martial, which were authorized to levy these penalties, did not always give out maximum sentences. In the Mississippi Territory, for example, when a volunteer cavalry unit failed to obey a callout, the court was very lenient. Capt. James K. Cook, the commander, was court-martialed for disobeying the order of his commander-in-chief by refusing to repair to the place of rendezvous. The court found Cook guilty, but he was sentenced only to pay a forty-dollar fine and to be publicly reprimanded; thereafter he would be restored to his command. Governor Holmes expressed his "astonishment at the inadequacy of the punishment." He asserted that this was "the first and only instance" in which an officer refused to obey an order and to appear at the place of rendezvous with his command. "No punishment that could have been legally inflicted upon the accused," he declared, "would have been disproportionate to his offence." Holmes remitted the part of the sentence that publicly reprimanded Cook, deeming such reprimands applicable only to minor offenses, but decreed that the fine would be executed. Holmes then revoked Cook's commission, as well as his two subalterns, dissolved the volunteer company, and required the individuals in it to enroll in infantry companies.[19]

At least three states passed laws against encouraging desertion. Vermont decreed in 1812 that any person who might "flatter or menace" a militiaman from doing his duty or induce him to desert could be fined from $20 to $500 plus costs of prosecution. Virginia stipulated in 1813 that those who encouraged desertion could be fined up to $300 and imprisoned up to one year. Ohio provided that persons dissuading militiamen from marching were subject to a fine of up to $150.[20]

At the beginning of the war in 1812 the situation was often too chaotic to enforce military discipline by courts-martial. In time, the organizational structure was better formed, and courts-martial to enforce discipline were more effectively applied. Desertion and numerous other infractions, such as sleeping on guard duty, insubordination, and striking a superior officer were among the offenses punishable by courts-martial. Generally, soldiers in the regular army were held to a stricter code of conduct than members of the militia. Militia courts-martial usually punished men who deserted by applying some physical punishment. Prisoners were typically paraded before the entire unit, which witnessed the punishment. Whipping was abolished in the army in May 1812, but other cruel expedients were used, such as to "ride the wooden horse," a narrow pole or sharpened block of wood. Courts-martial sometimes prescribed that weights be attached to the feet of those riding the wooden horse. They might have their hands and feet tied together and be carried around the camp suspended from a rail. Prisoners were also stripped to the waist, daubed with tar, and labeled with a paper attached to the tar stating the nature of their crime in large lettering. Also, mutilations were employed, including cropping of ears and branding (usually on the cheeks). Other humiliations forced upon these unfortunates included having one eyebrow shaved or half of the head. William Thackara, a private in a Pennsylvania volunteer unit, noted in his diary that one soldier "was drummed out of camp, to the tune of the Rogue's March, with a bottle around his neck and a label on his back for drunkenness."[21]

Perhaps the most common punishments were fines, hard labor with a ball and chain, and reduced rations (such as bread and water, or whiskey). Capital punishment was also employed, of course, sometimes as an object lesson. One unfortunate Ohio soldier, William Fish, was executed for desertion and for threatening the life of his commander.

Three other privates were condemned to death by the same court-martial, but they were pardoned by Gen. William Henry Harrison. One soldier, however, was placed beside his coffin with a cap over his head. He remained there while Fish was shot and then heard his reprieve announced. Such affairs obviously had a sobering effect on the assembled troops.[22]

Although the soldiers were infused with a sense of deference for their officers, those officers who failed to gain the confidence of their men could sometimes be cruelly victimized by pranks. One such officer was Brig. Gen. James Winchester, a man who had served with credit in the Revolutionary War but who was from Tennessee and was distrusted by the Kentucky militia. Private Elias Darnall recorded in his journal that Winchester, "being a stranger and having the appearance of a supercilious officer," was "generally disliked." Private William Northcutt related two pranks played on Winchester. On one occasion a porcupine was killed and skinned. The skin was stretched "over a pole that he used for a particular purpose in the night, and he went and sat down on it, and it like to have ruined him." Winchester's dignity was also assaulted when troops "sawed his pole that he had for the same purpose nearly in two, so that when he went to use it in the night it broke into and let his generalship, Uniform and all fall Backwards in no very decent place, for I have seen his Rigementals hanging high upon a place the next day taking the fresh air."[23]

Offenses of disobedience, drunkenness, neglect of duty, incompetence, and general bad conduct were of course not limited to the rank and file. Officers found guilty of such offenses, however, were usually cashiered or were given the opportunity to resign, although lesser offenses were punished by suspension from service for a period of time, fines, or reprimands, which were sometimes read before the assembled regiment.[24]

Early in the war, governors were flooded with requests for deferments. Militiamen on the frontier cited the danger of Indians and of leaving their homes unprotected or the need to plant their crops. Still others cited the press of their business and the financial hardship that would result from their absence. States varied on how they handled the matter of exemptions. The 1792 militia law allowed states to add individuals or groups to those exempted in the law by Congress, and the list grew over the years to the point where it could be called an abuse in many states. In Massachusetts, which was not necessarily the worst example, a legislative committee estimated early in 1813 that there were at least 120,000 able-bodied males in the state but only 70,530 enrolled in the militia.[25] For those unable to squeeze through the legislative loophole of a legal exemption from militia training, others simply paid the relatively modest fines levied by the state militia laws.

When the war came, however, the situation changed. Some state laws stipulated that the exemptions applied only in peacetime, and some states amended their laws to reduce the number of exemptions and to enroll many who had heretofore not been a part of the system. Maryland, for example, in a law of January 7, 1812, set out an extensive list of exempts: judges, registers, clerks, teachers, customhouse officers and clerks, mail carriers, ferrymen, pilots, inspectors of imports, treasurers, ministers of the gospel, Quakers, Menonists (Mennonites), Tunkers (Dunkers), and others conscientiously scrupulous against bearing arms. On June 18, 1812, the day the war was declared, a law stipulated that only ministers of the gospel and those exempted by Congress were not liable for service. All certificates of disability were even declared null and void, and surgeons were required to take an oath to grant none but to those justly entitled to them.[26]

Governor William Plumer pointed out to the New Hampshire legislature early in the war that many men procured exemptions from militia service from surgeons "without sufficient cause." The effect created "a spirit of murmuring and complaint in those soldiers who were equally entitled to certificates, but who disdaining to apply for them, performed their duty."[27]

Kentucky also drastically revised its list of exemptions. An Act of January 29, 1812, included most occupations noted above for Maryland, plus new ones such as keepers of jails and guards, the public printer and his employees, and the president, cashier, and clerks of the Bank of Kentucky. Still, conscientiously scrupulous individuals were required to pay for their exemption at the rate of one dollar per muster, with six musters mandated by the law. An act of February 3, 1813, decreed, however, that all previously exempt had to stand for duty except ministers of the gospel. The law authorized a commanding officer of a company to hire a substitute if a conscientiously scrupulous individual refused to perform his duty or failed to secure a substitute. Whatever was paid to the substitute, up to $100, must be borne by that individual. If the delinquent belonged to a society, such as the Quakers, the law provided that the sheriff might bring a debt action against the community property and sell some of the property to satisfy the fine. Some states did not alter their lists of exemptions, but they encouraged the body of exempts to organize volunteer groups. Among these states were Connecticut and Vermont, as well as the Mississippi Territory.[28]

In some cases, states went beyond bringing exempts back on the rolls. Tennessee authorized the governor to enroll volunteer companies of old men, presumably those over forty-five. While service under Tennessee's law was optional for those over forty-five, Rhode Island organized able-bodied individuals over that age into a "senior class." This force, which was to be organized for the duration of the war, was in all respects under the same rules as the regular militia. Only ministers of the gospel and the conscientiously scrupulous were to be excused.[29]

In North Carolina, the question was raised whether exempts must serve during emergencies. When the British invaded the state in the summer of 1813, Col. Nathan Tisdale wrote to Governor William Hawkins from New Bern of a problem: "There are in this town," he wrote, "a number of persons who are exempt by law from ordinary militia duty and who now (I am sorry to say) hold back on that ground and I am in some doubt whether I can compel them or not." Hawkins responded that "although their conduct in availing themselves of this exemption at this period cannot be considered very exemplary, yet I do not think you have the power to compel their attendance under the present alarm." This incident may have been a factor in the passage of a North Carolina law in 1814 limiting exemptions only to judges of the Superior Court and ministers of the gospel. Even free blacks were required to enroll, although the law, perhaps for reporting purposes, required captains of companies to designate the free blacks in a separate column from the rest of the militia.[30]

In one notable case, in Louisiana, with New Orleans facing imminent invasion in late 1814, a traditionally exempt class was conscripted for duty during an emergency situation. On December 16 the legislature, no doubt aware that exemption as a seafaring person was a traditional refuge for many men wishing to escape militia duty, passed a law requiring all seafaring men in Louisiana not currently in the United States service to report within twenty-four hours to be enrolled in militia companies. Those who refused to comply were subject to arrest.[31]

In Louisiana and also in the Mississippi Territory, the question was raised about individuals residing in those areas who claimed to be French citizens and therefore exempt from the militia service. In October 1812, Governor William C.C. Claiborne of Louisiana informed the French consul at New Orleans that every individual residing in Louisiana at the time of its admission into the Union who was not exempted by law "was subject to the operation of the militia laws & must conform to the same." Governor Holmes took much the same position in the Mississippi Territory in 1814, when the French inhabitants of Hancock County refused to obey a general order calling men in the area into service. Holmes characterized these Frenchmen as "deluded," but he informed his militia officer, Lieutenant Colonel Morgan, that he had decided to proceed with "mildness." He instructed Morgan to notify those legally drafted to appear at the rendezvous or to furnish a substitute, and he was to inform them of the consequences of disobedience. Morgan was to use a force sufficient to compel obedience and, if necessary, to bring them to trial. "No portion of the community," Holmes asserted, "must be permitted to prostrate the laws which are made for the security and benefit of the whole, and which are equally binding upon every citizen of the Territory."[32]

While stiff punishments were often prescribed for militiamen who refused to participate, states frequently provided incentives to those who did by giving additional pay beyond the nominal pay and allowances given to the militiamen while in United States service (for privates eight dollars a month). Four New England states authorized extra pay. Rhode Island allowed two dollars per month above the normal pay, while in Massachusetts a militia private who furnished his own blanket and uniform was allowed $3.75 per month and $2.50 per month if not. Vermont paid an extra $3.34 per month, and in New Hampshire the monthly bonus was two dollars, plus one ration per day (fixed at the rate of twenty cents). New Jersey also allowed its militiamen $3 per month above the pay and emoluments allowed by the United States, and Pennsylvania lavished $10 a month extra on their privates, $11 on corporals, and $12 on sergeants.[33]

Bounties were also offered on occasion to induce militiamen to extend their service. Pennsylvania, Kentucky, and Ohio all responded to the crisis of the Northwest army during the winter of 1812-1813 by offering their militiamen an incentive to stay beyond their normal terms. Pennsylvania and Ohio offered twelve dollars to militiamen who volunteered to serve two months beyond their present term. Kentucky authorized a bounty of seven dollars to its militiamen to extend service for an unspecified period of time. The number of volunteers was limited to 1,500. At this same time, some Pennsylvania legislators, apparently deeply ashamed of the conduct of some of the state's militiamen in the Northwest under Gen. William Hull and on the Niagara frontier under Gen. Stephen Van Rensselaer and Gen. Alexander Smyth who balked at crossing over the international border, introduced a measure early in 1813 to punish militiamen who refused to march to "any place or places whatsoever within or without the United States." The motion was defeated 52-34, apparently because of doubts whether a state could punish militiamen by court-martial for disobedience of orders while in the service of the United States.[34]

When the draft was resorted to, these troops were always of low quality, ill disciplined, and ill equipped. Drafted militiamen seldom had uniforms (in fact, they wore all kinds of clothing), although many of their officers did. The general impression presented by the militiamen when they rendezvoused must have mortified veteran soldiers. States had laws imposing fines on militiamen who appeared at musters without proper equipment, but the reality was that very few had arms. In North Carolina, Maj. Gen. William Lenoir informed Governor William Hawkins in May 1812 regarding the 7,000 militiamen who met the state's quota that "a considerable part of the detachment from the militia of this State will be unarmed. . . . how they are to be furnished with arms after they are embodied I know not." Fortunately, Hawkins arranged to obtain from Secretary of War Eustis over 2,000 stand of arms, which were counted against North Carolina's quota of arms under the Act of 1808; no arms had previously been forwarded to the state under the law.[35] Even so, the arms were not accompanied by powder, ball, or cartridge boxes.

Lack of equipment remained a vexing problem. Militiamen lacked virtually every item necessary to conduct a war. At almost every rendezvous, a majority of militiamen could be expected to show up without arms or equipment of any kind: no rifles, no muskets, not to mention powder, balls, cartridge boxes, rifle flints, blankets, camp kettles, artificer tools, knapsacks, and so on. Making matters worse, such supplies were hard to find, and commanders pleaded with their governors and the federal government to make up the shortage. Some state governors undertook to secure weapons from private sources. In the fall of 1814, for example, Georgia governor Peter Early contracted with Adam Carruth, a gunmaker from Greenville, South Carolina, to provide 500 rifles for the Georgia militia at twenty-two dollars each. Later, when the weapons were not delivered, Early wrote Carruth on March 3, 1815, that the conclusion of peace ended the need for the guns and canceled the order. Carruth objected that this was breaking a contract, but Early contended that Carruth himself had conceded he could not deliver the arms because of another contract with the state of South Carolina. As this account suggests, weapons and accoutrements were, because of the demand, expensive. Shopkeepers and businessmen soon refused to forward supplies on credit to federal or state governments. Consequently, funds authorized to compensate the militia were often diverted to pay for supplies, which led to dissatisfaction among the troops. The shortage of supplies had unfortunate consequences. It was reported in the winter of 1812 that over 300 militiamen in the Northwestern Army were suffering from frostbite.[36]

Supplies also included food to feed the army. The federal government preferred to rely on contractors to provide food, presumably because Congress believed that this method was the cheapest. Contractors, however, after winning a bid, were sometimes unable to find food at the price they had bid and consequently failed to fulfill their contracts, particularly if doing so would cause them to lose money. Throughout the war there were complaints that contractors either failed to provide food for the troops or delivered substandard food, such as rancid flour and spoiled beef. The daily fare of the troops was spelled out in one contract. It specified "a daily ration of 1¼ pounds of beef or ¾ pounds of salted pork, 18 ounces of flour or bread, one gill of whiskey, rum or brandy. For every one hundred rations, there were to be distributed two quarts of salt, four quarts of vinegar, four pounds of soap, and 1¼ pounds of candles." Contracts usually called for sugar and other spices. While there was usually a shortage of food, at least one group of Ohio militiamen was sent home by General Harrison in 1813 because they were consuming too much of the food being collected for the invasion of Canada.[37]

Once the militiamen had rendezvoused and were organized, camps had to be set up and order established. Sanitation and maintaining clean camp grounds was essential, and troops were assigned to police the camps. Guard duty was crucial, especially on the frontiers, and militiamen were sternly punished for failure to perform the duty properly. Officers were compelled to drill their troops in military exercises. Daily fatigue duties were ordered to keep the men active, which included working on breastworks, digging trenches, building blockhouses, and other activities to keep the camp habitable for large groups of soldiers. A typical day began very early, sometimes as early as four in the morning. The men were assembled and often drilled for an hour before breakfast. Mornings were spent on fatigue duties, while the officers received orders of the day and training for drills under brigade majors. Following lunch, details continued until four in the afternoon, when those not on guard duty, sick, or otherwise assigned were assembled in a body for perhaps another two hours of drill. The evening meal was served between seven and eight, and the men retired at nine.[38]

Unfortunately, deaths in camps due to disease took many more lives than the battlefield. Samuel R. Brown wrote in 1814, "For every soldier killed, three die of disease." The most fatal disease was dysentery or "flux, or *camp distemper*," which, he declared, was a disease that "every old woman in the country would cure in three days with a decoction of milk, pine bark and spikenard root." Among the New York militia camped at Buffalo in the fall of 1812 there were many deaths, a problem compounded by the lack of proper medical attention. One report said that an average of eight to nine men died each day. Two to three graves were dug daily, with two to four men placed in each, and the graves covered two acres. The deaths were attributed to maladies such as "fever," pleurisy, dysentery, and measles.[39]

In the fall of 1812, the troops of the Northwest Army under Gen. James Winchester suffered severely due to a shortage of food and supplies. Private Elias Darnall complained in his journal on December 24, 1812, that the troops were "deprived of the common necessaries of life," and he related that 100 lives had already been lost. "The sufferings of about 800 sick at this time, who are exposed to the cold ground, and deprived of every nourishment," he continued, "are sufficient proofs of our wretched condition!" Typhus hit the camp and killed an average of three or four men a day. More than 300 remained on the sick list daily. Many soldiers were practically without shoes and had only skimpy clothing; frostbite was a common affliction.[40]

Capt. Eleazer D. Wood, who shared many of the rigors of the Northwest Army, complained about the lack of proper medical treatment. There was, he noted, no head of the Hospital Department at Fort Meigs in northwest Ohio during the winter and spring of 1812-1813. "Those to whom the important duties of that department had been committed were but a young, inexperienced set of men," he wrote, "with nothing but the title of Surgeon to recommend them, or to give them the claim to employment, and the principal part of whom had been picked up here and there among the militia wherever a person could be found with a lancet in his pocket, or who had by some means or other *obtained the title of doctor.*" He added, "Such were the persons whose duty it became, to say whether the limb of a gallant officer or brave young soldier should be lopped off, or preserved."[41]

Capt. Robert B. McAfee, a member of Col. Richard M. Johnson's mounted regiment of Kentucky volunteers observed that when Johnson's troops were at Fort Meigs during June and into July 1813, "a most fatal epidemic prevailed in the camp, which carried off from three to five, and sometimes as many as ten in a day. It was computed that near 200 fell a sacrifice to it, within the space of six weeks." McAfee laid most of the blame on "bad water" and "the flat, marshy, putrescent condition of all that region of country, [which] was well calculated to destroy an army of men, who were alike unused to such a climate, and to the life of a soldier."[42]

Another tragic example occurred after the British departed the North Carolina coast in late summer 1813. Governor William Hawkins assigned four companies of militia at Fort Johnston, near Wilmington, and two companies at Fort Hampton, near Beaufort, to work on the fortifications, which he contended were, "not long since, mere apologies for forts." Maj. John A. Cameron, in fact, wrote from Fort Johnston on August 21 that his troops were destitute of all kinds of supplies, including medicine, that an average of thirty a day were in the hospital, and that there was growing discontent in camp. A month later, W.R. King, following his return from the camp at Fort Johnston, wrote Hawkins that the troops lacked even the most common conveniences. A "malignant fever" had killed many, and the morale of those who remained was very low. In their present condition, King declared, the men were worse than useless; detaining them any longer at the post "would be a sacrafice [sic] of life without any prospect of benefit to the country."[43]

Such suffering was not an isolated event. Shortages of supplies, accompanied no doubt by a rudimentary knowledge of sanitation and medicine, killed many more soldiers. During the winter of 1814-1815, the death rate among the troops encamped reached new highs. At Wilmington, Maj. Edward B. Dudley wrote the new governor of North Carolina, William Miller, that militiamen who had thought their terms were three months were threatening mutiny and general desertion. Gen. William Croom also informed the governor in December 1814 that the detached militiamen in the service of the United States at Beacon Island on the North Carolina coast were in a deplorable state. One-third were sick and had thin clothes and no blankets. Miller maintained that because the troops were in federal service there was nothing he could do. Those called into active service, he said, "must expect to endure some privations." On January 24, 1815, Maj. Thomas Blount reported to Miller that among the men in the camp at Beacon Island there were 180 effective, 214 sick, and fifty-seven on leave due to serious illness.[44]

Miller may have taken solace in the fact that reports of militiamen dying in camps in Virginia exceeded even those in North Carolina. On January 16, 1815, Col. Duncan McDonald wrote to Miller from Camp Peach Orchard near Norfolk, Virginia, where he was purchasing supplies for his brigade. The suffering of the troops there was "almost incredible": "about 160" had died since his arrival. Col. Richard Atkinson echoed McDonald's report in a February 1 letter to Miller, from Camp Defiance, also near Norfolk. Twenty had died since he arrived, and over 200 had died since their arrival in camp. That day 282 were reported sick, with 40 in the hospital. Measles seemed to be the scourge.[45]

Near the end of the war, Thomas Ritchie, editor of the *Richmond Enquirer,* commented on the disparity in health between militiamen and regulars. If there were any yet so "completely wedded to the *present* Militia System, as to be opposed to the substitution of a more permanent and regular force," he wrote, "we beg leave to submit to them the following abstract from the official returns of the state of our troops at Norfolk . . . and see how much *fewer lives* are wasted in the more regular service, than under the militia system." The abstract showed that 250 of 1,660 regulars were sick; another 21 had died. Of 4,590 the militiamen had 2,012 sick, 160 deaths, and 290 discharged for "inability"; 691 having served a tour of duty, were discharged that month, "half sick."[46]

When militiamen were healthy, the key to using them was giving them training and instilling some form of discipline. Even General Harrison, a strong advocate of the militia, declared to the secretary of war in late August 1812, "The troops which I have with me and those which are coming from Kentucky are perhaps the best material for forming an army that the world has produced. But no equal number of men was ever collected who know so little of military discipline." Most of the militiamen were entirely ignorant of the manual of exercise, such as marching in time, facing, wheeling, and so forth. On the other hand, competence in the military fundamentals was a mixed blessing, as one private confided in his diary. His Pennsylvania volunteer militia unit, he noted, "received very flattering praise . . . , and we were informed that we were to be the *advance* of the army in case of an engagement: thus to have the first chance of being shot, which is surely a remarkable privilege."[47]

The officers were often little better than their men. Maj. William A. Trimble complained to Ohio governor Thomas Worthington that "seven tenths of the militia officers are entirely ignorant of military discipline and some of them are calculated to promote insubordination and mutiny than to instruct and discipline the men under their command." Trimble asserted that many officers were elected because of their "jovial, indulgent, disposition" and consequently were "men who would exercise no authority but suffer everyone to do as he pleased." There were reports that some militia officers even believed that sergeants in the regular army outranked them. Generally speaking, the officers were wealthy and prominent members of their community. Quite naturally, given the deferential character of American society at that time, such men would be chosen for high-ranking militia positions. Wealth, of course, did not necessarily equate with military leadership abilities. Micah Taul, a future Kentucky congressman, was elected captain of his militia company even though he completely lacked military training. He admitted his name had never been on a militia muster roll. In fact, it was not his political prominence that won him the position; instead it was his ability to best his opponent in a no-holds-barred brawl. According to Taul's account, "After a hard fight, fist and skull, biting, gouging, etc., I came off victorious."[48]

Militia officers were frequently as undependable as their men. One reason General Hull gave for his surrender at Detroit was that he could not count on his officers to obey his orders. Gen. Andrew Jackson had little use for officers who did not set an example for their men. He court-martialed two officers when the militia they commanded broke and fled before a charge by Creek Indians on January 24, 1814. One officer was acquitted, but the other was cashiered.[49]

In fairness, many militia officers would not give some orders because they knew that their troops would not obey them and that desertion might ensue. Stern disciplinarians were not popular with their men. Private William Thackara, a volunteer in the Pennsylvania militia, was critical of Maj. Charles W. Hunter, the adjutant general of the First Division of the Pennsylvania militia. Hunter, Thackara wrote in his diary, "makes everything uncomfortable for us, throws as much trouble as possible on the volunteers." Another officer, however, a colonel, was characterized as "a *great officer*, breaks through all rules and despises discipline." It should be noted, however, that Thackara later altered his opinion of the colonel: "Weak, imbecile, and good natured, though easily excited, he is entirely unfit to be lieutenant, let alone a field officer."[50]

Militiamen were far more apt to perform creditably when they trusted and believed in their commanding officer. They were much more unpredictable when they doubted the fighting quality of their superior officers. A good example of the unreliability of the militia was the expedition of Maj. Gen. Samuel Hopkins, who led about 1,250 mounted riflemen from Kentucky in the fall of 1812 against the Kickapoo and Peoria Indians in the Indiana Territory. From the beginning, some officers expressed doubts about the expedition, but they agreed to go on. By the time the men reached Vincennes, the "discontents and murmurings" increased, but they abated when the force arrived at Fort Harrison and supplies and provisions were freshened. Still, Hopkins reported that many troops deserted at this point. Proceeding into Indian country, about four days out, the "spirit of discontent" returned. The next day, a prairie fire set by the Indians further upset the troops, and Hopkins, fearing that his troops were about to desert, called a council of his officers and asked them to take the sense of the army. He declared that if 500 would stay with him he would continue the expedition. The report came back that the troops preferred almost unanimously to return. Hopkins asked his officers to march to cover the reconnoitering parties rather than take a direct return. When the troops were paraded and Hopkins called upon them to follow him, however, they marched off in the opposite direction. Hopkins sent his officers to turn the troops, but the officers reported that they could not get them to turn, that "the army had taken their course and would pursue it." Hopkins had no choice but to follow his troops back home. He had failed to engage the enemy, despite coming, as he related to Governor Isaac Shelby, within twenty miles of the Indian villages before he was forced back.[51]

There were numerous other problems related to the use of the militia, including rivalries between militia officers and regular army officers. Governor Levin Winder of Maryland wrote to Secretary of War John Armstrong in August 1813, for example, about a misunderstanding with Col. Henry Carberry of the Thirty-sixth Regiment, U.S. Infantry. Some of Carberry's officers, according to Winder, had "taken up an opinion that an officer of the army of the United States cannot be commanded by a militia officer of any rank." Winder declared, "In vain I have referred them to the information I possessed on the subject and amongst others to the ninety eighth article of war which is as explicit, I conceive, as language can be."[52]

Military rules called for rank to take precedence, and militia officers often outranked far more competent and experienced regular officers. One example was Lt. Col. James Miller, Sixth Regiment, U.S. Infantry, who marched with General Hull. Upset that Colonels Samuel Findley, Lewis Cass, and Duncan McArthur all outranked him, Miller told Hull that he "would not consent to be commanded" by them. Hull informed Miller that he was outranked. Miller denied later that the dispute hurt the service. He stated that with Cass "sometimes he commanded; at others I did." He continued, "I was on good terms with all the colonels. I thought I ought to rank above them."[53]

The most notable dispute between a regular and a militia officer concerned Brig. Gen. James Winchester and Governor William Henry Harrison. After Hull's surrender, Winchester, the ranking officer in the regular army in the West, assumed command of the Northwest Army. The state of Kentucky, however, reacting to public clamor, gave Harrison a commission of major general, a higher rank than Winchester's. Yet Winchester retained the command because Harrison's commission was only a brevet rank. Also, there were legal questions raised by Kentucky's appointment of Harrison. Its state law required one year's residence for such an appointment, and the one major general's position authorized was already filled. Harrison, perhaps acknowledging the illegality of his appointment, deferred to Winchester as the commanding officer of the Northwestern Army. At about this time, however, Harrison was given a regular commission of brigadier general by the federal government. At first he refused the appointment, because by the date of rank he would still be outranked by Winchester. Finally, he agreed to accept the appointment if he was placed in command of the Northwestern Army. Despite this extraordinary condition, the government agreed and gave Harrison the command of the army over Winchester. To his credit, Winchester, recognizing that Harrison was the popular favorite of the government and the people of the West, consented to an arrangement generously proposed by Harrison whereby the two men would share the command. Winchester's capture by the British at the River Raisin on January 22, 1813, technically ended the problem of rank, and the appointment of Harrison as a major general on March 2, 1813, officially terminated the problem.[54]

William Thackara gave an example of the sort of division that occurred between regulars and militia. When Brig. Gen. Thomas Cadwalader, a militiaman, reached his camp, he was "received with cheers to the mortification of U.S. officers who have taken great airs of late." There were even tensions between volunteers and drafted militia. Thackara wrote in his diary that the volunteers "form an elegant line and have a good band of music," and "the militia do not parade with us." One day the volunteers were given orders "to prime and load as quick as possible." Several companies hurriedly gathered, and it was supposed that the enemy had landed. Instead they were marched to surround the militia encampment, which was in "a mutinous state, owing to the inattention of the quarter master, who had not furnished their rations for 48 hours. Having nothing to eat, they refused to do their duty." Fortunately, General Cadwalader was able to placate the militiamen and avoid violence.[55]

There were occasions when the militia of one state refused to serve under an officer from another state. Kentuckians in the fall of 1812 refused to march under Ohio militia general Edward Tupper. Charges were subsequently brought against Tupper for refusing to obey orders, but he was acquitted because the militiamen had refused to march.[56]

Perhaps the most serious problem with using militiamen was the brevity of their terms. Congress extended the term of militia service from three months to six months, but even that time was too short to muster, organize, equip, train, and employ in the field before the men's terms were up. Brig. Gen. Robert Taylor of Virginia, who commanded the militia at Norfolk, expressed his frustration. He resigned early in 1814, stating, "I have lost all hope of being useful in an army, where the officers as well as men, are constantly changed. To introduce skill, order and economy into troops thus composed, will require more energy and intellect, than have fallen my lot."[57]

Nor could the militiamen be expected to remain on duty even a day longer than their terms, even in critical circumstances. Capt. Eleazer

D. Wood, for example, complained bitterly in his journal about Virginia militiamen who left Fort Meigs in 1813 when it was in imminent danger of attack. "The 2d of April arrived," he wrote, "and away went every Virginian belonging to the drafted militia, without the least concern as to what became of those left behind, or caring whether the enemy or ourselves were in possession of the camp, so long as they could escape from the defense of it." Wood did note, however, that 150 Pennsylvania militiamen agreed to stay another fifteen to twenty days.[58]

Brig. Gen. George McClure was left with only about 100 troops to defend Fort George on the Niagara peninsula in December 1813 when his militiamen departed as soon as their terms expired, despite his pleas to stay longer. McClure noted that "having to live in tents at this inclement season, added to that [circumstance] of the pay-master coming on only prepared to furnish them with *one* out of *three* month's pay has had all the bad effects that can be imagined." He noted that his militiamen, "finding that their wages were not ready for them, became with some meritorious exceptions, a disaffected and ungovernable multitude."[59]

Andrew Jackson experienced the same difficulties in keeping a force in the field. After his victories against the Creeks at Tallushatchee and Talladega in November 1813, he was confronted with a lack of troops to maintain his momentum against the Indians. His force was composed of one brigade of militiamen and another of one-year volunteers. The volunteers, raised in 1812 and marched to Natchez, commanded by Brig. Gen. William Hall, argued that their time spent at home counted toward their period of service, which was up on December 10, and they intended to go home. As for the militia, part of the problem arose from confusion over the terms of service, namely, whether the militiamen under his command were state troops (with three-month terms) or federal militiamen (with six-month terms). Jackson insisted that they were six-month troops, but the militiamen, including their commander, Brig. Gen. Isaac Roberts, maintained that their term of service was three months. On one occasion when the militiamen tried to leave camp, Jackson used the volunteers to block them and force them to return to camp. Later, the militiamen were deployed to block the departure of the volunteers. Hall's volunteers were the first to leave for home. Although Jackson, complaining about the "disorder, mutiny, and delay of the expedition, so disgraceful to the state of Tennessee," ordered the inspector general of the militia not to muster out the militia, he was not supported by the Tennessee governor, Willie Blount, and the militiamen went home. Jackson wrote to his friend Hugh Lawson White that on January 4, 1814, the whole brigade of militia, except one small company, left him. Worse, the men detached to replace them turned around and returned home, "notwithstanding I had condescended to send them written assurance . . . that their services would be thankfully recd., for the term which the[y] had been tendered, viz. 3 months."[60]

Jackson court-martialed the officers of the latter group of militia. In a letter written jointly by three of these officers, Captains Samuel B. Patton, James Harris, and James Pickens, they justified their actions by arguing that they had bargained with General Roberts to volunteer for a three-month tour and that Roberts had agreed to release them from their obligation if Jackson did not accept those terms. When they were within three miles of Jackson's camp, they learned that Jackson would not agree to their conditions, and so they went home. On February 15, 1814, a court-martial found the three captains and one other officer guilty of "desertion, mutiny, and other crimes." Their sentences were light, however, because General Roberts was believed to be primarily responsible for the situation. General Roberts was shortly thereafter cashiered for his conduct.[61]

Jackson's problems mirrored those of many militia leaders. Getting the militiamen into the field and keeping them there was a difficulty that vexed and troubled state leaders throughout the war. The quality of the force was another concern of the officers. The lack of professionalism, a hallmark of the militia system, far from being a virtue, proved to be a curse during the War of 1812.

Chapter 4

The States and Militia Mobilization

Problems relating to the utilization of state militias by the federal government caused state leaders many frustrations during the War of 1812. State governors had to cope with the innumerable details of organizing, equipping, and arming their militia—problems compounded by a lack of assistance from the federal government. Militiamen called out had to be mustered, reorganized, and inspected by a regular officer to ensure that they conformed with federal requirements. Often the federal government could offer little in the way of arms or equipment to meet militia needs and even lacked money to pay those called out. Although state cooperation sometimes fell short of what was required by the federal government, it was still a remarkable testimony to the goodwill of the states that they bore the burden of federal demands and performed as creditably as they did. Although often woefully inadequate, militias were put into the field.

Newspaper accounts immediately after the declaration of war in June 1812 indicate that there was an enthusiastic response to militia callouts and to recruiters for the regular army. The war was greeted with particular enthusiasm in the western country. Kentucky held more than one-third of the Americans in this region, and its influence on the conduct of the war in the West was great. By the fall of 1812, six Kentucky congressmen had donned uniforms, including Samuel Hopkins, who served as the major general of the Kentucky militia. More than 2,000 Kentuckians enlisted in the regular army for five-year terms, and perhaps 9,000 more eventually served in militia or volunteer units. Ohio's response was nearly as enthusiastic. Governor Return J. Meigs's call in June 1812 for 1,200 militiamen to march to Detroit was met promptly.[1]

Reports from Virginia and New Jersey stated that volunteers more than met the state quota for militiamen. Even in New England there were favorable reports. In Concord, Massachusetts, fifty-eight out of sixty men in a militia company volunteered to serve. In Vermont, three times as many men volunteered for service as were needed to meet the state's quota. In New London, Connecticut, three companies were called to fill their quota, and all but three men volunteered. Pennsylvania's allotment was made up entirely of volunteers, and the same was true for Ohio. In Charleston, South Carolina, the share was met by volunteers. It was also related that companies were being formed of men over the age of forty-five, who were by law exempt from militia duty. Hezekiah Niles enthused in his Baltimore-based *Weekly Register,* "In many parts of the United States they are drafting militia—not for service, but to ascertain *who is to stay at home,* many more than is required offering themselves." Reports about recruiting were optimistic. Joseph Gales bragged in the *National Intelligencer* on June 2 that recruiting "has succeeded beyond the most sanguine expectations."[2]

As many congressmen predicted, however, raising the regular force took a long time. On June 6, only twelve days before the declaration of war against Great Britain, the adjutant and inspector general, A.Y. Nicoll, informed Secretary of War William Eustis that only 1,125 recruits had enlisted between January 1 and April 30, but 1,000 had been recruited in May. On June 8, Eustis generously estimated to Joseph Anderson, chairman of the Senate Military Affairs Committee, that 5,000 had been recruited. Two days earlier, Eustis directed the governors of the states under the act of April 10 (which called upon the states to make available 100,000 militia) to furnish detachments of militiamen on the requisitions of the generals charged with the defense of the maritime frontier. Most of the militia, as noted earlier, were poorly organized and were unable to provide any immediate assistance.[3] Thus, on the eve of the war, the nation was woefully unprepared to wage war unless it used the obviously unreliable state militias.

As might be expected, with the call for such large numbers of militiamen and regulars, problems arose. One complaint by militia officers was that army recruiters were enlisting and taking away their men at critical times after a callout, thereby deranging their companies. In New York, Maj. James R. Mullany, commander of the fourth recruiting district, defended his recruiters early in the war by stating that they were acting upon orders from Col. Alexander Smyth, acting inspector general. He asserted on July 12, 1812, that while it may be unpleasant for a militia officer to have his men enlisted in the U.S. service, "he certainly cannot prevent it, and further he is accountable for every man enlisted which he refuses to deliver the United States."[4]

An example of a problem created by aggressive recruiters occurred while the Mississippi Volunteers were in Camp Armstrong near Baton Rouge, Louisiana, in June 1813, awaiting assignment. Two officers protested to their commander, Gen. Ferdinand Claiborne, that recruiting parties were active in their camp. "Large sums of money have been furnished them and almost every seductive means used to decoy our volunteers from us," they wrote. "Good order prevailed previous to the arrival of these parties," they continued. "The scene is changed into riot, intoxication & *disorder*. In short the honor of the corps is completely destroyed and we feel disgusted with our situations, being daily liable to insults and those kinds of disorders."[5]

Another question raised was the status of apprentices and minors. Several habeas corpus proceedings during the war produced conflicting results. In Richmond, Virginia, in early June 1812, militia captain Samuel G. Adams was called into court because he had accepted two apprentices as volunteers in order to meet the state's quota. Adams argued that he was authorized to receive apprentices, but he would abide by the court, which subsequently ruled that he could not. In October 1812 there was a habeas corpus case in the District Court of Pennsylvania involving a J. Shorner, a minor who had enlisted without his mother's approval. The law required parental consent, and Shorner's counsel argued that the approval of both parents was required; as Shorner's father was dead, he was thus unable to give his consent. Judge Richard Peters, a Federalist, ruled that the enlistment was invalid.[6]

In Baltimore, Maryland, in August 1813, writs of habeas corpus were brought on behalf of two apprentices who had been taken into custody for failing to obey a militia callout. Capt. John Kennedy, the arresting officer, was compelled to appear before Judge Theodoric Bland, associate judge of the Sixth Judicial District. Essentially, the question was whether a state could infringe on the rights of masters and compel apprentices to perform militia duty. Bland observed that the militia laws did not exempt apprentices above the age of eighteen. Masters, he said, had the right to the service of their apprentices according to the laws of the state, but he added, "There was a period at which *the state* had also a right to his services, and that right was paramount to that of the master." He then asked, in times of crisis, "could any reasonable man suppose that the legislature intended that judges and courts of justice should be employed in uselessly issuing writs of Habeas Corpus when the enemy might be at our doors?" Bland remanded both apprentices to the custody of Captain Kennedy.[7]

There were undoubtedly numerous other habeas corpus cases during the war that went unreported in the newspapers. It is also very likely that there were more in New England than in other sections. Of the cases that were reported, one involved a Mr. Lamb in Charleston, South Carolina, who refused to perform militia service and was arrested. He applied for a writ of habeas corpus to be discharged from arrest on the ground that under the militia laws he was punishable by a simple fine and not confinement. The judge ruled in favor of Lamb. Another case in March 1814 involved William Bull, who enlisted at the age of nineteen without a guardian's consent (both parents being dead). He subsequently deserted and was arrested, court-martialed, and sentenced. Ann Powell, his sister, applied for a writ of habeas corpus before the Supreme Judicial Court of Massachusetts on the ground that his enlistment was invalid. The court ruled that Bull, being less than twenty-one, was an infant and could not bind himself and ordered his discharge from the service.[8]

At least two court cases arose involving the act of Congress of December 10, 1814, authorizing the enlistment of minors (eighteen to twenty-one) without the consent of parents, masters, or guardians. One occurred in Pennsylvania, where Jonas Roop, an apprentice of Abraham Polinger, enlisted. Polinger obtained a writ of habeas corpus to secure the services of his apprentice. Judge C.J. Tilghman, for the Pennsylvania Supreme Court, declined to act, since personal liberty was not involved, because Roop wanted to remain in the army. Tilghman also noted that if Polinger wished to challenge the validity of the law of Congress, he should appeal it to the Supreme Court of the United States.[9]

The act of December 10, 1814, was also challenged by a Connecticut law that authorized judges to issue writs of habeas corpus to release from military duty minors or apprentices enlisted without the consent of parents, masters, or guardians. Hezekiah Niles noted, "The United States officers had determined to treat this law with the contempt it so richly deserved, but the intervention of peace prevented the consummation of the folly of the fools (or something worse) who made it." Niles also cited a Hartford city ordinance, obviously designed to discourage army recruiters, that any person carrying a flag or colors, drumming or playing any martial instruments within the limits of the city, could be fined thirty-four dollars.[10]

The Madison administration's intention to rely on volunteers and state militiamen to prosecute the war met with a setback in New England almost immediately. At issue was not just how the militia was to be used, at least in the early months; it was also whether the national government could use them at all. The Act of April 10, 1812, gave New England as a quota 20,000 of the 100,000 militiamen called for by Congress. Secretary of War Eustis alerted Connecticut governor Roger

Griswold on June 12, that his militia might be ordered into service for coastal defense on the call of Gen. Henry Dearborn. Griswold replied that such a call would be executed "without delay." When Dearborn, however, called for two companies each of artillery and infantry on June 22, "to be placed under the command of the commanding officer at Fort Trumbull, near New London; and one company of Artillery, to be stationed at the battery, at the entrance of the harbour at New Haven," Griswold balked. He queried his Council of State whether militias could be legally demanded "until one of the contingencies enumerated in the Constitution shall have arisen," and "whether a requisition, to place any portion of the militia under the command of a continental officer can be executed." The Council predictably replied that none of the contingencies had been met, and it declared that placing the militia under the command of an officer of the United States transferred the militia to the army of the United States and deprived the state of its militia.[11]

Dearborn and Eustis were duly informed that the requisition was not in conformity with the Constitution and that, even if it had been, Connecticut objected to placing its militia "under the immediate command of an officer or officers of the Army of the United States" rather than under the command of its state militia officers. Eustis's response was that the reasons assigned for noncompliance were "not less extraordinary than the act itself." To remove all doubt, he declared that he had been instructed by the president to state that a condition of imminent danger "actually exists" and that the requisition of General Dearborn should "be forthwith carried into effect." Eustis dismissed the problem of officering by simply stating that the militia's company officers "will command or be commanded, according to the rules and articles of war." Dearborn attempted to conciliate Connecticut, announcing on July 17 that the command over the companies could be assigned to one of the state's majors. The Council stubbornly insisted, when they met on August 4 to reconsider, that the militia was being called out to perform ordinary garrison duty and not to repel any invasion. Until the circumstances stipulated by the Constitution were met, the Council advised, the governor should not comply with the requisition.[12]

Griswold informed Eustis on August 13 that Connecticut's position had not changed. The phrase "imminent danger of invasion" was not the condition expressed in the Constitution authorizing the federal government to call upon state militia, and the president's declaration was obviously drawn from the mere fact that war had commenced. If such a consequence of a declaration of war be admitted, Griswold wrote, "it would follow, that every war, of that character, would throw the militia, into the hands of the national government—and strip the states, of the important right, reserved to them." Griswold declared in a proclamation that it was "the prerogative of the state to hold its militia for the maintenance of its lawful privileges, and never to permit them to be withdrawn from its authority, except in cases expressly mentioned in the Constitution." A committee of the legislature argued, among other things, that "it is not a *defensive*, but *offensive* war," that the use of militia for garrison duty converted militiamen into "standing troops of the United States," and that the United States was "a confederated, and not a consolidated Republic." Finally, it denied that the state's militia could be demanded by the president "to assist in carrying on an offensive War."[13]

Many of the same issues were raised in Massachusetts, where tensions ran high as a result of the declaration of war. Elbridge Gerry, an unpopular Republican governor who defended the national administration although he received several threats of assassination, was replaced by Caleb Strong, a Federalist.[14] The transition of government meant that the federal government's call for militias would be received much differently. Dearborn summoned forty-one companies of Massachusetts militiamen, which would entitle a brigadier general to command, but the highest-ranking officer drafted was a lieutenant colonel. In fairness to Dearborn, because the militia was dispersed to so many different locations, no detachment rated more than a lieutenant colonel.

Governor Strong responded by asking the justices of the state supreme court, first, whether the governor had the right to determine whether the exigencies contemplated by the Constitution existed that required him to place the militia in the service of the United States and, second, whether the state militia could be commanded by any officers but those of the state. The justices replied that the governor did indeed have that right. Since the Constitution did not give that power explicitly to Congress or the president, it was reserved to the states. Any other construction, the justices reasoned, would give the national government the right to call the whole of the militia from the states, subjecting them to the will of the president and Congress "and produce a military consolidation of the states without any constitutional remedy." On the second question, the justices asserted that placing militiamen under regular army command "would render nugatory the provision that the militia are to have officers appointed by the states."[15]

On August 5, 1812, Strong informed Eustis of his decision not to comply with the requisition, which he had based not only on the Supreme Court opinion but also on the advice of his Council. There was no apprehension of invasion, he declared, and thus no exigency under the Constitution had been met. He did announce that he had called out three companies, commanded by a major, to meet the appeals of the people of Passamaquoddy on the eastern border for protection against predatory incursions. That he assumed they were in the service of the United States is confirmed by his statement that they would remain until the president directed otherwise.[16]

The Massachusetts House of Representatives claimed that Strong's conduct "met [with] the unqualified approbation, not only of this House, but of the great body of the People." The Senate, however, which was controlled by Republicans, dissented. The senators declared, "The hour of danger is not a fit time for abstract speculation, and to decide principles by views to political policy, would be hardly more rational than satisfactory." They argued further, "If it be denied to the National Executive to decide upon the necessity of a detachment of militia, it will render indispensable the support of a standing army."[17]

In Rhode Island, where four companies of militia were called for, much the same scenario was played out. Governor William Jones asked his Council of War on August 12 whether the state's militia could be drawn by the president except in the cases mentioned in the Constitution and whether, in the Council's opinion, those exigencies had been met. The Council replied that although the president decided in the first instance, the governor "has the right ultimately to decide" whether to surrender the command of the state militia to the president. Jones then informed the federal government on August 22 that he would release the militia of his state only "when, *in my opinion*, any of the exigencies provided for by the Constitution . . . exists." On September 24, the Council of War reaffirmed its advice "that it is not expedient under the existing circumstances . . . to order the detached militia of this State into the service of the United States."[18]

Public opinion, already heated by the dispute between federal and state authorities, was further agitated by an inflamatory pamphlet written by John Lowell late in 1812. He stated that he expected soon to see Massachusetts and Connecticut declared in a state of rebellion, to see habeas corpus suspended, "and by commissions to Gen. [William] King and the [Maine] volunteers whom he has raised, to coerce the refractory states." Lowell also predicted "a law placing the militia under the orders and lashes of the officers of the standing army, and our papers will soon give us another affecting detail of the ceremonies with which the deserters from the militia *are shot*." Beyond the overheated rhetoric, Lowell also argued that Madison's interpretation of the use of the militia would lead to "one vast military consolidation." Lowell actually encouraged the militiaman drafted into service contrary to the Constitution "to kill his assailant, or to collect his friends to rescue him."[19]

Lowell also denounced the use of volunteers, "a mongrel breed of soldier citizen and citizen soldier," as an "insidious way of *destroying the militia*." If Congress could raise 50,000, they could raise 500,000 volunteers. The purpose, Lowell argued, was to defeat the intent of the Constitution and transfer the whole militia to the control of the president. One way to frustrate this plan was for state militia officers to insist that volunteers do their state militia duty.[20]

Neither New Hampshire nor Vermont presented any immediate problems (the problems came later) to the Madison administration. Republican governor William Plumer of New Hampshire, in fact, declared to his legislature on November 18, 1812, "To admit that [the President] has power to call upon the Governors of the several states, to order a portion of the militia into service, but that those Governors can with propriety *refuse* to carry those orders into effect, would establish a principle of insubordination incompatible with all military principles." He noted that he had complied with Dearborn's requests and that five companies were then in the service of the United States. Both houses of the New Hampshire legislature endorsed Plumer's sentiments. Governor Jonas Galusha of Vermont, a Republican, also cooperated with Dearborn. In a message to his legislature on October 9, he complimented his militiamen for their prompt response in marching to the frontier.[21]

The other New England governors were denounced around the country. In a letter published in the *Richmond Enquirer* in spring 1813 and widely reprinted, an anonymous author questioned whether the United States was dependent upon "indirect and irresponsible agents" to execute its call or whether it could have agents "directly responsible" to carry out this power. The New England governors' position, the author insisted, was the same as the requisition under the old Confederation government, a weakness that paved the way for the writing of the Constitution. "We should pause, then, before we adopt a construction which would thus visit the imbecility of the parent upon the child." The spirit of the Constitution, the author said, was that "the national *force* ought to be called out to execute the national *will*." He added, ". . . there is nothing better calculated to bring this republican government into contempt, to produce mistrust among our citizens and render us the scorn of Europe, than a successful attempt to paralyze its powers." Joseph Gales, in the *Daily National Intelligencer,* declared such arguments "conclusive" and insisted that "9/10's of the intelligent federalists in the nation will agree with us, that the non-combatant governors have shown an entire ignorance or contempt of their constitutional duties."[22]

Only in Maryland was there any sympathy or support for the New England position on militia. There the Federalist-dominated House of Delegates approved resolutions on December 22, 1812, declaring that the call for militiamen under the federal law of April 10, 1812, did not meet the exigencies stated in the Constitution. Nor was it contemplated in the Constitution that the general government, entrusted with control of the militia in certain emergencies, would, "by perverted interpretations . . . use that power in the absence of emergencies." Furthermore, use of militiamen to garrison forts was "an unwarrantable stretch of power, which must ultimately lead to a consolidation of these United States into a military government." A separate resolution passed two days later by a two-to-one margin approved the conduct of the governors of Massachusetts, Connecticut, and Rhode Island and stated that their action was "constitutional, and merits our decided approbation." The Republican-controlled Senate, however, passed a resolution on January 2, 1813, supporting the declaration of war and the power of the president to call out the militia.[23]

In Virginia, Governor James Barbour declared to his legislature that the Constitution "placed the whole physical force of the nation under the control of the national authority" and that the occasion on which the militiamen would be employed, and the manner, was to be determined by the federal government. He also argued that it was perfectly correct "that a federal officer of superior grade, should take the command" of the militia. Governor Arthur Middleton of South Carolina also asserted in his annual message that each state had a duty to support the constituted authority even if it doubted or disapproved of the policy of war. Opposition would paralyze the war effort and would tend to produce defeat and disgrace.[24]

President Madison was undoubtedly relieved that no state outside New England refused the services of their militia. In his Fourth Annual Message on November 4, 1812, he asserted that the New England governors' refusal to release their state militia was "founded on a novel and unfortunate exposition of the provisions of the Constitution relating to the militia." If the authority of the United States could be frustrated, he said, "in a state of declared war and . . . under apprehension of invasion . . . , they are not one nation." He warned that the recourse of the government might be "large and permanent military establishments which are forbidden by the principles of our free government, and against the necessity of which the militia were meant to be a constitutional bulwark."[25]

Another problem that arose between the New England states and the federal government related to the distribution of arms under the law of 1808. The states were plagued by equipment shortages. Governor Plumer of New Hampshire suggested to his legislature in June 1812 that it was difficult to know precisely the deficiency of firearms among the state's militiamen because of the practice, widespread among soldiers, of borrowing arms and accoutrements from each other. He recommended that all battalion musters be held on the same day. Similarly, Governor Galusha of Vermont informed his legislature in October 1812 that the state had received 1,000 stand of arms (weapons and accouterments) under the Act of 1808, but it fell "far short of the real deficiency." Most of the arms distributed, he noted, were to the detached militia, "who were destitute." He urged the legislature to buy more arms, ammunition, tents, and camp equipage.[26]

A committee report from the Rhode Island House noted in November that not a single stand of arms had been delivered to that state under the Act of 1808. Why the arms due to the state had been withheld, the report continued, "the Committee are unable to explain," but it appeared to the committee that the southern and western states had received "their full complement." Governor Jones related to the legislature on February 16, 1813, that while a thousand stand of arms had been delivered, he was still trying to get Rhode Island's full share. In June, Jones stated that there was no hope of "being placed in any adequate state of defence, by the United States."[27]

On February 27, 1813, the Massachusetts legislature asked the governor to apply to the national government for that state's proportion of muskets due under the law of 1808. Governor Strong forwarded the resolution to President Madison on March 1. Two weeks later, Secretary of War John Armstrong responded that arms received by the federal government had been "inconsiderable," and "the President has deemed it most conducive to the general interest to supply in the first instance the frontier states and the militia who have come forward in the service of the country." When the state of the arsenals justified it, Massachusetts would receive its proportion of arms under the law.

A Massachusetts Senate committee report in response to Armstrong's letter declared the provisions of the law were "simple, precise, and definite, admitting neither of a perversion of purpose nor latitude of construction—of the favouritism of partiality, or an indulgence of caprice." The committee estimated Massachusetts's fair share of arms at about one-tenth of the $1 million that had thus far accrued to the fund. Citing a War Department report in December 1812 that showed eleven states, the District of Columbia, and the Territory of Illinois receiving arms, the committee declared it was "wholly unable to comprehend, or perceive, even on the alleged principles of distribution, how the withholding from the State of Massachusetts . . . can be justified or palliated." The committee recommended the drastic action of withholding from the direct taxes paid by the state to the federal government the proportion of funds that was due Massachusetts from the federal government to enable the state "to adopt those measures of defence which the general government neglect to provide for it." The legislature, however, adopted a resolution merely calling upon its senators and congressmen to work to obtain Massachusetts's fair share of the arms. If the federal government failed to provide arms, the governor was authorized to purchase weapons needed for defense. The state treasurer was authorized to borrow $100,000 to meet Massachusetts's defense needs.[28] The national government's failure to provide arms and other aid for defense was one of the grievances that later led to the calling of the antiwar protest meeting, the Hartford Convention.

In the remaining thirteen states and five territories outside New England, the militiamen were even less well equipped and less well organized. The shortage of arms and camp equipage was a common lament even in the better organized states. In New York, Governor Daniel D. Tompkins complained to Maj. Gen. Henry Dearborn on June 28, 1812, that the U.S. quartermaster general "has not a tent, camp kettle or knapsack in the arsenal . . . [and] as to cannon, muskets, ammunition, I can find no one here who will exercise any authority over them or deliver a single article upon my requisition." Tompkins urged Dearborn to furnish the militiamen with weapons and other desperately needed supplies.[29]

In Pennsylvania, where the militia was supposedly well organized, numerous problems arose when the militia was called out in 1812. Governor Simon Snyder informed his legislature on December 3, that the calling into service of 4,000 Pennsylvania militiamen was "effected with as much celerity and completeness as our militia law, fund, and system would permit." He noted that the state law did not provide for paymasters or for defraying the expenses of marching detachments to the rendezvous. The law provided for the position of quartermaster general but not a salary. Also, some regiments and companies had neglected to choose officers, and there was no mode for calling classes into service. He also urged providing indigent militiamen with blankets and suitable clothing.[30]

Maryland Governor Levin Winder asked his General Assembly in December 1813 to improve the state's militia system. "In its present state," he complained, "it is almost a dead letter." He was particularly upset that "those who understand the defects of the system, contrive to avoid the service, [while] others will engage in it with cheerfulness and consent to bear an undue proportion of its burthen and sufferings." Delaware, in effect, did not have a militia system when the war began. A February 2, 1811, law abolished all fines for missing militia drills and thereby created a largely moribund system.[31]

Elsewhere, despite impressive and detailed militia laws, the situation was worse. In North Carolina, for example, Governor William Hawkins, in order to comply with the call in 1812 for its 7,000-man force to be held in readiness, was virtually compelled to organize his militia anew. The state militia system remained in a dreadful state of organization, even as Hawkins delivered his annual message to the legislature in November. Most militiamen were unarmed, but fortunately Hawkins arranged to receive 2,000 stand of arms as part of its quota under the Act of 1808. Even so, there was a shortage of powder, ball, and cartridge boxes. The supply organization of quartermasters, commissaries, and contractors was in shambles and lacked many staff officers at the lower grades. "It may, with utmost confidence, be said," Hawkins asserted, "that our present system cannot be productive of anything bordering upon even a tolerable discipline."[32]

Eight companies of North Carolina militiamen were called out by Maj. Gen. Thomas Pinckney on July 4, 1812, four to protect Fort Johnston, near Wilmington, and four to defend Fort Hampton, near Beaufort. This experience not only showed how destitute the militiamen were of all the articles of war, even blankets, but also revealed how totally unprepared the supply departments were to provide these items. Fortunately, Pinckney was able to release most militiamen by September as new recruits were signed up.[33]

In Georgia, Governor David B. Mitchell admitted on the eve of the war the weakness of his militia, and he issued a general order in January 1812 calling upon the adjutant general to ensure that militia trainings were carried out and the militiamen aroused "from apathy and indifference." "It is a lamentable truth," he wrote to Gen. John Floyd, "that Georgia has never made any provision for the service of her militia, unless indeed a few thousand stand of muskets, one half of which are hardly fit for service, be considered as such." Mitchell declared that he had no qualms about who should command Georgia militiamen called into the field; "They will be under the immediate command of their own officers, but their duty and operations will be directed by those of the United States."[34]

In his annual message in November 1812, Mitchell called upon his legislature to revise the militia laws thoroughly, as well as to purchase arms and ammunition. He also cited the shortage of artillery, especially for coastal defense. When George Jones, the mayor of Savannah, called upon Mitchell in March 1813 for coastal fortifications to protect his city, the governor could only cite the "painful and serious truth that the State has not the command of a single piece of artillery, neither has she any ammunition except a small quantity of powder." Mitchell hoped the city could procure "a half dozen good six pounders" from among the prize vessels that might be brought to the city.[35]

Although Mitchell promised to cooperate with federal officers, he did reserve his right to dispose of the state militia as he saw fit. In August 1812, General Pinckney called upon Georgia to send a regiment to St. Mary's and four companies to Savannah. Mitchell did not call out the companies for Savannah. A year later Mitchell wrote that he considered this action "one of the most fortunate circumstances that has ever occured [sic] to me in the whole course of my public life. . . . It is now evident," he continued, "that the troops if sent down would have been entirely useless and by this time probably one half of them dead or dying and the balance deserted and gone home." Moreover, the expense of maintaining them would have consumed the state's resources and left nothing to encounter the hostile Indians, who were then waging war upon the frontier.[36]

In the Mississippi Territory, Governor David Holmes warned Secretary Eustis on the eve of the war that his militia was desperately short of arms. He hoped the government would lend a thousand stand of arms. When the war began and Brig. Gen. James Wilkinson issued a call for Mississippi militia, Holmes responded that while he could furnish any number of men Wilkinson wanted, it was to be regretted "that the militia are almost entirely destitute of arms and ammunition. This may render our situation truly deplorable," he added, "unless we can be furnished, without delay, by the United States." Many militiamen were not just unarmed; Holmes informed Eustis that about 200 of the 500 men called out were also without blankets, many without shoes. In addition to expenses for subsistence, camp equipage, and medical and hospital stores, Holmes declared he would also obtain blankets and shoes; the troops had consented that the amount for the latter two items be deducted from their pay. To obtain these supplies, Holmes advised Eustis, "I shall draw upon the war department." Wilkinson provided 300 stand of arms, but according to Holmes most were "entirely unfit for use."[37]

In Louisiana, the situation of the militia was much the same. A slave insurrection near New Orleans in January 1811 pointed to the need for a better militia organization. Slaves estimated variously at 180 to 500 in number revolted at Colonel André's plantation about thirty-six miles above New Orleans. At least two whites, including the major's son, were killed. The first reports stated that Colonel André organized armed citizens, killed several of the insurgents, and captured eighteen to twenty of them. Eventually, a varied force of regulars under Gen. Wade Hampton, volunteer militia, crews of merchant vessels, and even a company of "free men of color," commanded by a Major Dubourg, were organized and completed the task of subduing the insurrection. The leader, one of Colonel André's slaves by the name of Gilbert, and about a dozen other insurgents were put to death. Governor William C.C. Claiborne lamented the lax and disorganized state of the militia and informed Col. John Ballinger after the insurrection had been put down that he hoped the incident would "induce the Legislature to give us a more energetic militia system." He also wrote to Colonel André, "We are now all convinced of the necessity of a well-organized militia, and I really will not permit the ensuing Legislature to adjourn until they shall have passed a strong militia law."[38]

In his message to the legislature on January 29, 1811, Claiborne declared that the "lax and disorganized state of the militia" was due to the defective militia law. Among other things, he recommended circumscribing exemptions from militia duty, prescribing specific times for musters and greater frequency, and increasing the fines for nonattendance at musters, "so much so as to make the wealthiest of our citizens unwilling to incur them." He also urged vesting the officers with more power to "punish the disobedient and disorderly with fines and if necessary with imprisonment." The law, passed by the territorial legislature on April 29, did indeed answer many of Claiborne's requests. More frequent musters were required (there were, for example, company musters on the last day of every month except May), and the increased fines for nonattendance ranged from twenty dollars for officers to seven dollars for privates. Claiborne forwarded the act to Secretary Eustis and called the legislation "sufficiently rigorous," but it was clear that he was not entirely happy with the law. He argued that "the contrariety of language spoken by the citizens of Louisiana, & the dispersed situation of the settlements are great obstacles to rendering the militia an efficient force."[39]

Claiborne said essentially the same thing on July 30, 1812, to the first legislature of the newly created state of Louisiana, declaring that the militia "does not exhibit that arrangement, order & discipline which can alone render it respectable." Claiborne, however, vetoed the militia bill passed by the legislature because of "contradictory" provisions, which he insisted "would tend to throw the whole militia into a state of confusion & chaos." The legislature adjourned without acting upon the bill returned to them. Louisiana entered the War of 1812 under an obsolete militia law of April 1811.[40]

Thus, despite the fact that the basic militia law of 1792 had been on the books for two decades, there was still no uniform organization of state militia. The problems created by this situation meant that the federal government, perhaps contrary to its expectations, found that state militias, particularly when they were called out with some urgency, were typically unavailable or were so poorly organized, ill equipped, and undisciplined as to be practically useless. Moreover, several New England states withheld their militias on constitutional grounds, and others were reluctant to call out their militiamen without assurances from the federal government that the militiamen would be paid. Consequently, the federal government increasingly sought to rely on regulars and volunteers, but it was not always possible to do so.

Chapter 5

The Militia and the War in the West

While Congress debated the merits of militiamen versus regulars on the eve of the declaration of war, a spirited discussion on the same issue occurred in the Indiana Territory after the Battle of Tippecanoe in November 1811 between Col. John P. Boyd, commander of the Fourth Regiment, U.S. Infantry, and Governor William Henry Harrison, commander of the forces at Tippecanoe. Boyd was addressed by a group of citizens in Vincennes who referred to the "brave Regulars" and called the militiamen "spirited but untutored." Harrison's supporters viewed this as an attempt to take away some of the credit due to Harrison. Boyd, perhaps unintentionally, exacerbated the issue when he referred to the "dastardly" conduct of the militiamen engaged in the Battle of Tippecanoe in a widely reprinted letter to Secretary of War William Eustis on December 11, 1811. Harrison was prompted to respond to the "severe animadversions" in a public statement noting that, of the ten volunteer militia units in the battle, only two "abandoned their posts." One of the units later rallied and took up "a post of greater danger." In effect, Harrison admitted some failings of the militia, but he preferred to emphasize the fact that parts of the militia stayed at their posts and performed their duties creditably.[1]

The public view of the militia during the War of 1812 was colored by perceptions like those described above. Supporters of the militia cited the positive aspects of militia conduct during military engagements and were prone to overlook incidents that evidenced poor conduct and a lack of discipline. Conversely, opponents found fault with virtually every aspect of militia performance and tended to overlook creditable conduct. In evaluating the performance of the militia during the War of 1812, it is difficult to assess the numerous reports of incompetence. There are far more negative reports than positive ones. No doubt, the reason was partly self-serving officers who transferred blame to militia-men that more properly belonged to them. Officers who viewed the militia favorably, however, like Harrison, also cited improper conduct by militiamen. It is perhaps natural that comments about misconduct found their way into print far more often than reports that the militia-men had performed their duties. Obviously, ill behavior gains more at-tention than good, and the following account reflects the evidence that is available. Common sense suggests, however, that militia performance could not have been as bad as the reports indicate. Harrison's point that we should not overlook the individuals who went about their business and did their job should be kept in mind.

In no part of the country was there greater enthusiasm for war than in the West. Western leaders, aware that their militiamen would bear the brunt of fighting in this region, were confident that they would fight well. Fortunately, the British had few regulars to wage war in the West. Western militias often faced an Indian foe as untrained and ill equipped as they were. Unfortunately, events did not bear out expecta-tions, nor did Westerners maintain their initial enthusiasm for war.

After the Battle of Tippecanoe, citizens of the West predictably urged that the militiamen be called out to protect the frontier from Indian violence. Resolutions to Governor Ninian Edwards of the Illi-nois Territory, for example, lamented the failure of the national gov-ernment to offer aid and support against the Indians on the most vul-nerable parts of their frontier. Edwards, in fact, informed Secretary of War Eustis that he united with other governors in the West in appre-hending "a formidable combination of Indians and a bloody war." Eustis responded by informing Edwards that under a law of January 2, 1812, two companies of rangers would be raised in Ohio, one in Indiana, one in Illinois, and one in Kentucky, "competent to protect the frontiers." These rangers were to cooperate with a detachment of regular troops that was establishing a post at Peoria village. The command was given to Col. William Russell (U.S. Army).[2] It should be noted, however, that there was very little coordination between the regulars and the volun-teer rangers, and very little protection was afforded by either.

Even before the war was declared, the Army of the Northwest was formed with approximately 1,500 Ohio volunteer militiamen called out by Governor Return J. Meigs, to which the Fourth Regiment of U.S. Infantry was added. The force was assembled by Governor Meigs at Dayton and was turned over to the command of Gen. William Hull, governor of the Michigan Territory, who was designated by President Madison to command. Unfortunately, Hull, a Revolutionary War vet-eran, was past his prime, and his relationship with the militia was tenu-

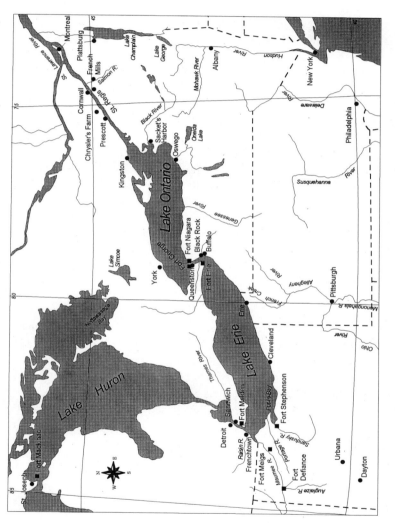

The Northern Front. Courtesy of the Laboratory for Remote Sensing and Geographic Information Systems, Department of Geography, The University of Memphis.

ous from the very beginning. At the staging base in Urbana, Ohio, the militiamen refused to bend to discipline. Lt. Jonah Bacon of the Fourth Regiment noted that the Ohio militiamen "were . . . without either" subordination or discipline. One evening at Urbana he heard a noise and, when he ran out to determine the cause, he was informed that "it was only some of the Ohio militia riding one of their officers on a rail." Capt. Charles Fuller, also of the Fourth Regiment, testified later at Hull's court-martial that orders to the militia to stop promiscuous firing of weapons in camp "did not entirely suppress it." Fuller was vague about a reported mutiny of some militiamen. He observed that he had heard of sentences being passed on "two or three ring-leaders." More likely, he was referring to punishment dispensed by courts-martial for sporadic insubordination. Fuller was explicit, however, that some volunteers refused to march from Urbana and that a "Captain Cook's company was sent back" by General Hull. Fuller claimed that he only heard of posters on trees encouraging men not to march. The lack of discipline in the Ohio militia was such that General Hull placed the Fourth Regiment of regulars at the rear of the column marching to Detroit to suppress further mutinies and desertions. Lt. Col. James Miller quoted Hull as saying, "By God, Sir, your regiment is a powerful argument. Without it I could not march these volunteers to Detroit."[3]

Such evidence raises questions at least about the validity of assertions by such individuals as Col. Lewis Cass, who commanded one regiment of Ohio militia, when he wrote to Secretary Eustis in September 1812 that "had the courage and conduct of the general been equal to the spirit and zeal of the troops, the event would have been as brilliant and successful as it now is disasterous [*sic*] and dishonourable."[4]

When Hull crossed the Detroit River to assault the British post of Malden, the Michigan militia (approximately 200 men) did not cross. Hull did not explain why, but presumably, based on their later conduct, it was because they were considered unreliable. Also, a large number of Ohio militiamen refused to cross into a foreign country for constitutional reasons. The exact number declining to cross is unclear. At his trial, Hull stated, "This number was about one hundred and eighty." Cass claimed that "about 100" Ohio militiamen did not cross, but he also added that 30 to 40 of them "made off and returned home in safety." Lieutenant Bacon stated that on one occasion 30 to 40 refused to cross, and on another about 100. Still another source, Maj. John Whistler, believed that there were 68 Ohio militiamen in the fort who refused to cross, but he added, "I do not know how many were in the town."[5]

Hull's conduct was no doubt influenced by his perceptions of the low quality of the militiamen who did cross. It was clear that he had no confidence in the militiamen he commanded. As he said at his trial, "What proportion of the militia, which I had with me at Sandwich, would have been effective to lead against the enemy, the Court may judge from general experience." He claimed to have only 1,300 effectives, and only Lieutenant Colonel Miller's 300 regulars "had seen any service." He added that the militiamen although "very ardent and patriotic in their expressions had had no experience, and neither men nor officers had ever been tried." He then asserted, "It is not extraordinary, that I should have felt some want of confidence in these raw troops." Hull confessed that his experience during the Revolutionary War "had fixed in my mind a mistrust of the services of the undisciplined militia. . . . Indeed the organization of the militia corps I had with me was particularly calculated to create distrust with respect to them." Another reason for distrust of militiamen was that "all their officers held their commissions in virtue of an election . . . of the men whom they were the nominal commanders." Elected officers, he noted, would be unwilling to incur the displeasure of their men and would instead court their troops' favor, which was "totally incompatible with military discipline." He also argued that he was not bound, as some of his junior officers seemed to think, by a majority vote. Many of the officers, he added, "have not yet learned even military language," and most of them, "when they joined my army, knew no more of the duties of a soldier than was to be learned from militia musters and parades about their own homes."[6]

Hull denied that the affair at the Aux Canard Bridge on July 16 was anything but a "skirmish"; in fact, it "could hardly be a test either of courage or discipline." In truth, little was achieved in this skirmish except to give American troops under Colonel Cass their first baptism of fire. After momentary confusion following the first clash, the American troops reformed and, Cass reported, "moved on with great spirit and alacrity" to drive the British off. Two prisoners were captured.[7]

On the other hand, Hull believed that the conduct of the militiamen under Maj. Thomas Van Horne in another engagement was more representative of its fighting capabilities. Van Horne was sent by Hull on August 4 to connect with a supply column that had reached the River Raisin and wanted an escort. Van Horne's force was composed of some 150 riflemen and "a number of militia-men who had refused to cross into Canada." When Van Horne's force was attacked on August 5 by about 40 British and 70 Indians, the militia, Van Horne recalled, "retreated in disorder by squads." Of those reported missing, 70 later showed up at the fort. Among the 17 dead from Van Horne's encounter in the Battle of Brownstown were 5 officers, most killed "attempting to rally their men." Hull denied that Van Horne's force had been inadequate. Had the militiamen not "fled in the first moments of an attack, with the utmost disorder and precipitation," he asserted, " . . . the detachment was sufficient."[8]

Hull also argued that the troops were loyal to their state leaders and not to him. If he had had Gen. Duncan McArthur arrested, he said, "I have no doubt his men, who had elected him, would have turned their arms against me, with as much alacrity as they professed to use them against the enemy." It may well be that it was a combination of both loyalty to their state leaders and a lack of confidence in their commander. Hull lost all the confidence of the troops when he gave up a promised attack on Malden and retreated to Detroit. Hull was alarmed by the news at the end of July of the fall of the American fort on the island of Mackinac. He believed he would soon be overwhelmed by hordes of Indians. Rather than retreat to Detroit, as he did on August 7 and 8, he admitted later that had he followed "the dictates of his conscience" he would have retreated to the Miami. That he did not do so was perhaps because Colonel Cass had declared that "the Ohio militia would desert him to a man." The disloyalty of the militiamen went beyond words. At the critical moment of the siege of Detroit by British Gen. Isaac Brock, at least two companies of the Michigan militia deserted to the enemy. Moreover, Hull claimed he received information "that a larger body were about to join him [Brock]." Lieutenant Colonel Miller confirmed Hull's view. He recalled hearing Col. Elijah Brush, commander of the First Regiment of Michigan militia, exclaim, "By God, he believed his men would have run away to a man."[9]

While Hull's surrender of Detroit may have been militarily inexcusable, it is nevertheless not difficult to understand the frame of mind that led him to do so. At his trial he was adamant that he had had no choice. Regarding Cass's reference to the tears of the troops when he surrendered, Hull stated cynically that it was obviously not the Michigan militia, "because a part of them deserted, and the rest were disposed to go over to the enemy rather than fight him." Perhaps, he continued, it was the Ohio volunteers, "who mutinied in the camp at Urbana, and would not march till they were compelled to do so by the regular troops." Or perhaps it was those who refused to cross into Canada and at Brownstown under Major Van Horne "ran away at the first fire, and left their officers to be massacred." In conclusion, Hull stated, "With one third of the residue of my force absent, and with nothing to rely upon out of the fort, but untried and undisciplined militia, officered by men, most of whom were in hostility to me, and had even conspired against me, what was I to expect from a contest?"[10]

Hull's surrender of Detroit to the British on August 16 aroused mingled sentiments of apprehension and anger in the western country. One of the consequences of this event was the emergence of William Henry Harrison to lead the effort to retake Detroit from the enemy. Harrison, the governor of the Indiana Territory, had previously been designated by the War Department to defend the western frontier from Indian depredations. He was authorized to call upon Kentucky to augment his troops from the Indiana and Illinois territories. When news of Hull's surrender was received in Kentucky, Harrison was there, arranging for Kentucky militiamen to join an expedition against Indians in the Illinois Territory. Leaders in Kentucky, acting on popular sentiment, recommended to Governor Charles Scott that Harrison be appointed a major general of the Kentucky militia to lead the force to recapture Detroit. The legal obstacles that Harrison was not a citizen of the state, that only one major general was authorized, and that the position was already filled were overcome by making Harrison a brevet major general.[11]

Kentucky's action, as noted earlier, set up a problem of command of the Northwestern Army, but the Madison administration, which had designated Brig. Gen. James Winchester of Tennessee to command the Kentucky and Ohio forces against Detroit, bowed to western pressures and placed Harrison in command of the Northwestern Army.

While Harrison was raising his force to recapture Detroit, he sent out two expeditions against hostile Indians. One under Col. Allen Trimble with about 500 Ohio militiamen got as far as Fort Wayne when half the troops refused to proceed farther, presumably for many of the same reasons that General Hopkins's men cited, namely, lack of supplies and lack of confidence in the leadership. Trimble's only accomplishment was to destroy two small Indian villages. A second force commanded by Lt. Col. John B. Campbell was a combined force of regulars and militiamen. The latter group included a Pennsylvania rifle company and a company of one-year volunteers known as the Pittsburgh Blues. This expedition advanced into the Indiana Territory about eighty miles west-northwest of Greenville, Ohio, and captured one Indian village, killing 8 and taking 42 prisoners. Three other villages evacuated by the Indians were burned. In the early morning of December 18, 1812, while encamped near the Mississinewa River, which flowed into the Wabash, an Indian force of approximately 300 launched a surprise attack. After an hour of desperate fighting, the Indians were driven back with an estimated loss of 100 killed and wounded. Campbell's loss was 8 killed and 45 wounded, 4 of whom died later. In his report on the Battle of Mississinewa, Campbell singled out the Pittsburgh Blues for praise: "They fought with the coolness and intrepidity of veterans."[12]

Meanwhile, General Winchester's troops on the left wing of the

Army of the Northwest, suffering greatly from exposure, disease, and a lack of supplies, finally managed in early January 1813 to move to the rapids of the Maumee, which flows into the west end of Lake Erie. General Harrison intended to use the post as a rendezvous point for some 4,000 men as well as a collection point for supplies and a staging base for an assault upon Detroit and the British post of Fort Malden. Harrison was beginning to express doubts to his government about continuing the operations. Expenses were mounting alarmingly, and he hinted broadly that the campaign should be abandoned until spring. James Monroe, temporarily heading the War Department after the resignation of Eustis, declined for political reasons to assume that responsibility, no doubt because he feared that his and the Madison administration's reputation would suffer in the West if the campaign were called off. Harrison vacillated and worried that the terms of most of his militiamen ran out in February.[13]

While collecting his troops and forwarding supplies to the rapids, Harrison instructed Winchester to make no advances. Winchester, however, failed to obey his orders. He was induced to do so by pleas for protection from Indians by inhabitants of Frenchtown (now Monroe, Michigan), on the Raisin River about thirty-five miles from the rapids. No doubt, the report of a considerable quantity of corn and flour at Frenchtown destined for Fort Malden entered into Winchester's calculations. Accordingly, on January 17, 1813, approximately 650 Kentucky militiamen under Lt. Cols. William Lewis and John Allen were sent to Frenchtown. As they arrived the afternoon of the next day, they encountered and drove off a force of about 50 Canadian militiamen and 200 Indians. American casualties in this skirmish amounted to 12 killed and 55 wounded. The militia performed admirably in this engagement. Pvt. Elias Darnall recalled, "In this action the Kentuckians displayed great bravery, after being much fatigued with marching on the ice. Cowardice was entirely discountenanced. Each was anxious to excel his fellow-soldiers in avenging his injured country."[14]

Winchester rushed additional troops to Frenchtown, including 250 regulars under Col. Samuel Wells, and personally joined his troops, which now numbered about 1,000 men. Unfortunately, Gen. Henry Procter, the British commander at Fort Malden, dispatched an even larger force to Frenchtown. Winchester failed to take proper defensive precautions and left his troops in an exposed position. When Procter attacked on January 22, the regulars took the brunt of the first assault. When militiamen were sent to their support, both were outflanked by Indians and Canadian militia. The American regulars and militiamen fled in panic, but they were pursued and cut off, and most were killed.

The remaining American militiamen, although in a defensible position, were surrounded and short of ammunition. Also, General Winchester and Colonel Lewis had been captured. Maj. George Madison, the American militia leader, was persuaded to surrender upon Procter's assurances of protection from the Indians and proper treatment as prisoners of war. Unfortunately, Procter left behind some 80 wounded Kentuckians, many of whom were killed and scalped by drunken Indians. Other prisoners were killed or carried off on the march to Malden. Altogether, as many as 400 American troops were lost at the disaster on the River Raisin at Frenchtown, giving the Westerners a new battle cry, "Remember the Raisin!"[15]

The disaster at Frenchtown was not a consequence of a failure of the militia. In this instance, they fought bravely until they were overwhelmed by a superior force. The blame must be attached to Winchester, who foolishly extended his forces deep into enemy territory and then failed to take proper defensive precautions, thereby allowing his entire force to fall to the enemy.

After the disaster at Frenchtown, Harrison moved his remaining forces of approximately 3,000 to the rapids. He briefly considered an offensive operation against Malden, but because of uncertain weather and the approaching expiration of the terms of service of a large number of his Kentucky and Ohio militia, he abandoned what had been an extremely expensive and unproductive winter campaign. The troops spent their remaining time productively, building a defensive fortification near the foot of the rapids on the Maumee River, eventually named Fort Meigs. Designed by Capt. Eleazer Wood, a graduate of West Point, the nine-acre fort was located on an elevation about 150 yards from the river. Harrison proposed to use the fort as a staging base for his assault on Canada in the spring.[16]

The government's attitude changed when John Armstrong, Jr., of New York replaced James Monroe as secretary of war in February 1813. Armstrong took a particularly intolerant stance toward the excessive use of militiamen in the West. His attitude was revealed in a private letter to the publisher of the *Philadelphia Aurora*, William Duane. Alluding to the waste in the West, he expressed astonishment that Kentucky governor Isaac Shelby had wanted 15,000 men for the 1813 campaign "and that they must be mounted like Asiatics, and to do what? To take a work defended on three sides by pickets! To fight an enemy, not more than two thousand, of all colors and Kinds."[17]

Faced with a shortage of funds and appalled at the waste of money he perceived in the West, Armstrong reordered the priorities and switched the emphasis to the Niagara and St. Lawrence frontiers. He

William Henry Harrison, by Rembrandt Peale. Courtesy of the National Portrait Gallery, Smithsonian Institution.

informed Harrison that vessels were being built to win control of Lake Erie and that Harrison and his troops would be transported across the lake to Malden. In the meantime, Harrison was to hold his position. If there was a "want of force," he should "retire to the frontier settlements" and place the wilderness between himself and the enemy. Harrison was also instructed to avoid additional calls for militias and to encourage the recruiting of troops for the three regular regiments to be assigned to his command.[18]

Harrison was dismayed. "I must confess," he wrote Armstrong on March 27, "that the Idea never occurred to me that the Government would be unwilling to keep in the field at least the semblance of an army of Militia until the regular troops could be raised." He doubted regular regiments could be raised in the West, citing a "disinclination to the service which appears to prevail in the western country." He suggested "a large auxiliary corps of Militia," and he informed Armstrong that prior to receiving Armstrong's letter he had called for 1,500 Kentucky militiamen to protect the stores at Fort Meigs.[19]

In a private letter, Harrison explained his concerns to Armstrong. He too had little use for militiamen and much preferred to use regulars. "Militia can only be employed with effect, to accomplish a single distinct object, which will require little time and not much delay, on the way." He admitted that thousands had been rushed into the field with little thought that they would require subsistence, ammunition, and artillery. These items were now abundant, and he asserted that a large force was necessary to impress the Indians. "It is decidedly my opinion," he wrote, "that the employment of a large force would not only be the most certain, but in the end most economical." He again expressed doubts that a large regular force could be raised in the western country, and he urged instead that a large volunteer force be called out "to serve forty or fifty days after their arrival at the Rapids" and move towards Malden. Harrison argued that "the Indians who may not have joined the British standard will suspend their operations against our frontiers until they see the result." While command of Lake Erie would greatly facilitate operations, what if naval superiority was not gained? "What will be our situation unless we are prepared to take the other course?" He urged Armstrong to release the balance of the 3,000 men organized in Kentucky for the protection of the western posts, and he warned ominously, "if any disaster happens to any of the posts for the want of troops to protect them, the popularity of the administration in the western country will receive a shock [from] which it will never recover."[20]

Indeed, fearing threats to Fort Meigs, Harrison issued a call on April 9 to Governor Shelby for 1,500 additional troops on the grounds, as he informed Shelby, "our force should be treble theirs; at present it is inferior." Harrison assured Armstrong that once the circumstances were understood, he was certain that it would "meet your approbation." In Kentucky, despite its early enthusiasm, judging from Governor Isaac Shelby's letters to General Harrison and messages to his legislature, a major concern was getting the militia to perform its duty. By early 1813 it was difficult to raise militiamen to replace those who had initially volunteered. Perhaps the setbacks suffered by Kentuckians, particularly at the River Raisin, affected the enthusiasm for military service. In fact, the state had to resort to the draft to fill their complement of troops. Shelby wrote to Harrison after inspecting a regiment to be commanded by Gen. Green Clay that the "great part of them appeared to be men under size and in other respects hardly Kentuckians." Moreover, the "better kind of people" hired substitutes.[21]

Armstrong discounted the possibility of an attack on Fort Meigs, characterizing the clamor for troops as "artificial alarms." He wrote smugly to Samuel Huntington of Ohio that there would soon be a regular force in the West "competent to the whole service of offence or defence," leaving the militiamen "to their civil pursuits."[22]

Armstrong probably never appreciated that but for Harrison's prompt action the West might have suffered yet another disaster. In fact, the British commander, Gen. Henry Procter, with about 2,400 men, including about 1,200 Indians led by the renowned Tecumseh, attacked Fort Meigs on April 30. Fortunately, Harrison was prepared and had on hand about 1,200 effectives, mostly militia, in the fort, and General Clay was on the way to the fort with about 1,400 reinforcements. Heavy rain hampered the British seige, but Harrison and his men endured a severe bombardment with light casualties (sixteen killed).[23]

Clay's Kentucky militia arrived at the fort on May 5, while it was under siege by the British. Harrison had managed to contact Clay and arranged a concerted plan of attack. A force of about 800 under the command of Lt. Col. William Dudley would land on the north bank of the Maumee, opposite the fort; spike the guns that were bombarding the fort; and then retreat across the river to the safety of the fort. A second force under Clay would land on the south bank and join with a sortie from the fort to disable the British guns on that side of the river and then withdraw into the fort. Unfortunately, the attack did not go as planned. While Dudley's force captured and spiked the British guns, his undisciplined militia, despite orders to withdraw, pursued the enemy into the woods only to be met by a counterattack. Three-quarters of Dudley's regiment were either killed or captured. Among those killed was Dudley himself, who was attempting to recall his men. On the south side, Clay's force landed too close to the fort and came under British fire. A sortie from the fort commanded by Col. John Miller, however, that was composed of about 350 regulars, volunteers, and militiamen successfully spiked the British guns and retreated safely to the fort with Clay's men and forty-one prisoners.[24]

After the battle on May 5, on May 9, Procter abandoned his siege of Fort Meigs and withdrew. Tecumseh reportedly said after the withdrawal, "It is hard to fight people who live like groundhogs." Harrison remarked in general orders on May 9, referring to Dudley's men, "It rarely occurs that a general has to complain of the excessive ardor of his men, yet such appears always to be the case whenever the Kentucky militia are engaged. It is indeed the source of all their misfortunes. They appear to think that valor can alone accomplish any thing." While lamenting the loss of Dudley's men, Harrison's official letter to Armstrong on May 13 also cited positive conduct by other militia. It was not surprising that the Pittsburgh Blues and the Petersburg (Virginia) volunteers behaved well, he wrote, but that Capt. Uriel Sebree's company of Kentucky militia, which fought under Colonel Miller on May 5, "should maintain its ground against four times its numbers," he said, ". . . is astonishing."[25]

Neither Harrison nor Clay was blamed for the loss of Dudley's men. Rather, the blame was generally leveled at the militiamen themselves. The influential editor Hezekiah Niles published approvingly a letter from a correspondent in the West: "The want of discipline and subordination in the militia, is indeed truly lamentable," the author wrote, "It is most clear that it is owing to this cause we have now to lament the loss of so many brave countrymen." Niles also published an extract from a letter by William Creighton, Jr., a future Ohio congressman, saying that Dudley's men, "in spite of the repeated calls which were made from the fort to bring them back to their boats, [they] suffered themselves to be amused and drawn into the woods by some feint skirmishing, while the British troops and an immense body of Indians were brought up."[26]

In the meantime, as Harrison predicted, recruiting of the regular regiments lagged. Armstrong blamed Harrison, who had ordered Brigadier General McArthur early in April to Fort Meigs to assist in its defense. McArthur and Brig. Gen. Lewis Cass were assigned to recruit the Twenty-sixth and Twenty-seventh Regiments in Ohio, and Col. Thomas D. Owings the Twenty-eighth Regiment in Kentucky. By July 1813, Owings and Cass had each raised about 700 recruits each, and

McArthur fewer than 500. Harrison argued that considering the situation the rebuke was unmerited.[27]

Ironically, Armstrong perhaps inadvertently contributed to the lack of success in recruiting regulars. On February 26, 1813, he authorized Cong. Richard M. Johnson of Kentucky to raise a regiment of mounted volunteers. Colonel Owings noted that his recruiting was hurt by Johnson's proposition to give his recruits a dollar a day for four months. Moreover, he added, Kentuckians were partial to cavalry service. He claimed he could have filled a regiment of cavalry in four weeks.[28]

Johnson's mounted riflemen were destined to play an important role in the 1813 campaign in the West. Armstrong intended to assign Johnson's force to defend the frontier from Indian attacks, but Johnson had other ideas. He informed Armstrong on April 13, 1813, that his troops would be able to take the field by May 10 and that they had volunteered only for invading purposes. Armstrong, however, decided that Johnson's troops would probably not be needed, and he wrote Johnson on May 5 to inform him of the fact. Johnson, however, had called out his volunteers in response to the attack on Fort Meigs. Citing this crisis, as well as public sentiment and the advice of Governor Shelby, Johnson informed Armstrong on May 12 of his action, declaring, "We fondly hope to meet your approbation & sanction."[29]

Harrison met with Johnson in Cincinnati, where Johnson's force was gathered. By this time the crisis was over. Harrison agreed with Johnson that it was probably not wise to disband the mounted volunteers, as they "could never again be brought into the field." Harrison and Johnson decided that the regiment would sweep the frontier, and in early June they moved about 180 miles in six days toward the mouth of the St. Joseph River on Lake Michigan, encountering few Indians. Then they moved to assist Gen. Green Clay at Fort Meigs, threatened by another British force. The threat failed to materialize, and Harrison ordered Johnson's regiment to march to Lower Sandusky, where he anticipated an attack. Johnson remained hopeful; as he informed Harrison, "To be ready to move with you to Detroit and Canada against the enemies of our country, is the first wish of our hearts."[30]

Secretary Armstrong, however, ordered Johnson's regiment to proceed to Kaskaskia, Illinois, to assist in the defense of the Illinois and Missouri Territories. Johnson argued to Harrison that this movement would consume most of the time remaining of their service and that they should stay where they could be of some use to Harrison. Harrison, nevertheless, instructed Johnson to proceed as ordered. Armstrong, however, changed his mind and proposed using Johnson's men in the invasion of Canada. They would, he suggested, "be useful in making demonstrations by land while you go by water." Johnson's regiment had only just arrived at Urbana, Ohio, when it was called back.[31]

By early July, Armstrong recognized that a sufficient number of regulars was not going to be raised for offensive operations against Canada. He authorized the use of Johnson's force and instructed Harrison to make up the deficiency of regular troops with militia. Harrison quickly appealed to Governor Shelby to send "as many good men as you can conveniently collect," up to 2,000 men. He also invited the Kentucky governor to accompany the men personally to "be the guiding Head and I the hand." Harrison also called upon Governor Meigs for two regiments of militiamen and invited him to take the field with his militia.[32]

In late July, General Procter returned to Fort Meigs and again laid siege. Harrison informed Armstrong that the fort was "in every respect in a better situation for defence than when besieged before." He suspected that the attack was a diversion and that Procter's real object was likely the fort at Lower Sandusky, which Harrison admitted was "untenable," but he added that "there is nothing in it of any value but two hundred barrels of Flour and I have made arrangements for withdrawing the garrison and leaving the Fort."[33]

Maj. George Croghan of the Seventeenth Infantry, however, a nephew of George Rogers Clark who was only twenty-one years old, in command of a little over 200 men in Fort Stephenson at Lower Sandusky, was determined to hold onto the fort. Harrison took exception to Croghan's insubordination, but after explanations were offered he relented and allowed him to stay in command. Croghan was still ordered to retreat if possible when the British approached. He did not retreat, however, and refused demands for surrender when the British appeared before the fort on August 1. The following day a British assault of about 500 regulars and 700 to 800 Indians was repulsed with heavy casualties, inflicted particularly by Croghan's one artillery piece, a six-pounder called "Old Bess." The gun was ably managed by Sergeant Weaver of the Virginia volunteers and six members of the Pittsburgh Blues who were accidentally in the fort at the time of the attack. The British then withdrew. Croghan suffered only one killed and seven wounded, while Procter reported twenty-six killed, twenty-nine taken prisoner, and forty-one wounded. Croghan was voted the thanks of the nation by Congress, was awarded numerous swords and medals, and was brevetted a lieutenant-colonel for his heroic defense of Fort Stephenson.[34]

On August 11, Harrison informed Armstrong 4,000 militiamen would be needed for the campaign. He announced that Commodore Oliver Hazard Perry was ready to sail in pursuit of the enemy. Lacking seamen, Perry took volunteers from a Pennsylvania militia regiment. The remainder of the regiment, Harrison noted, would join his army "provided they get two months pay beforehand." Perry needed more volunteers for his little navy, and Harrison gave him 100 of his best men. Efforts were made to get every qualified seaman. Meanwhile, Harrison prepared to cross the lake as soon as Perry delivered a victory. He informed Armstrong that he would have approximately 2,000 regulars and 3,000 militiamen ready to embark between the tenth and fifteenth of September once Governor Shelby and the Kentucky volunteers arrived.[35]

On September 10, Perry finally engaged the British fleet near Put-in-Bay and destroyed it after a desperate struggle. He then penned his famous letter to Harrison, "We have met the enemy and they are ours," which permitted Harrison to plan his assault on Canada. Perry carried Harrison's force to Fort Malden, which surrendered on the twenty-third without opposition; nearby Amherstburg was taken four days later. Harrison wrote Armstrong that Procter had retreated to Sandwich and that he would pursue him, but there was "no probability of overtaking him as he has upwards of 1,000 horses and we have not one in the army." Harrison's force amounted to about 5,000 men, approximately 60 percent of whom were Kentucky militiamen with no constitutional scruples about going into Canada, unlike the approximately 500 Pennsylvania militiamen who "with the exception of about 100 refused to cross the line."[36]

Harrison fretted that already his militiamen had "become restless and desirous of returning home." They were willing to stay as long as there was "a prospect of overtaking the enemy but no human influence will keep them any longer." Fortunately, Colonel Johnson, going around by land, arrived in Detroit with about a thousand of his mounted regiment on September 30. They began the chase of Procter and caught him approximately fifty miles east of Detroit. On October 5, Johnson's troops played a crucial role in breaking through the British lines with a cavalry charge, then wheeling about and catching the British and the Indians in crossfire. The remaining Kentucky militiamen played only a minor role in the battle. Harrison won a great victory at the Battle of the Thames. In his report to Armstrong, Harrison gave credit to Johnson's force: "Veterans could not have manifested more firmness."[37]

Although the British suffered only twelve casualties, another 600 were taken prisoner at the Thames. The Indians lost at least three dozen killed, and others were undoubtedly carried away. Most important, Tecumseh was killed in the battle, reportedly by Colonel Johnson himself. With the death of Tecumseh and the loss of his marvelous leadership qualities, the Indian confederacy collapsed. The war was effectively over in the West. Moreover, the American militiamen had redeemed their reputation. An article published in the *Daily National Intelligencer* noted that only about 140 regulars were among Harrison's force during the battle. The militia, "uninfected by constitutional scruples," gave a veteran enemy a "lesson on backwoods tactics." This was another "specimen of the enterprise and spirit of the yeomanry of the country, when properly organized and brought into action," which was quite different from the Boston militiamen, "who show their valor and prowess only in empty bravadoes and ridiculous menaces against the constituted authorities of the country!"[38]

Harrison's continuing troubles with Armstrong resulted eventually in his resignation. After his troops were directed to Sackets Harbor for defensive purposes on November 3, 1813, Harrison, with nothing further to do, asked for permission to return to his district. At a public dinner held in his honor at Philadelphia in December 1813, he was called upon to make a toast, and he responded by obliquely attacking Secretary of War Armstrong and those calling for reliance upon regulars to prosecute the war. He prefaced his toast by stating, "Believing, as I do, that a sentiment is gaining ground unfriendly to republicanism and injurious to the nation, and knowing from my own experience, that the sentiment is not well founded," he gave his toast: "The militia of the United States—they possess the Roman spirit, and when our government shall think proper to give them that organization and discipline of which they *are* susceptible, they will perform deeds that will emulate those of the legions led by Marcellus, and Scipio."[39] Relations between Harrison and Armstrong, never good, deteriorated even more in the months that followed.

When Armstrong bypassed the chain of command and sent orders directly to Brig. Gen. Benjamin Howard to remain in charge of frontier defense rather than assuming command at Detroit as Harrison had ordered, Harrison wrote indignantly to Armstrong, "I think, Sir, I have a right to complain of that order, both as to its matter and manner." He hinted broadly that he might retire if he did not receive more consideration.[40]

Sending orders directly to an officer, bypassing his superior, was not an uncommon practice in the War Department. The justification was that delays would occur by sending such orders through military channels. The commanding officer was usually sent a copy of the order as a courtesy. Armstrong's response to Harrison was not conciliatory. "As a general principle," he wrote, "it cannot be doubted but that the Government has a right to dispose of the Officers of the Army as they may think best for the public interest." Shortly afterward Armstrong ordered Maj. Andrew H. Holmes to lead an expedition against Mackinac. At the same time, however, he sent a courtesy copy of his letter to Harrison. Col. George Croghan, Holmes's superior, refused to allow Holmes to leave without orders from Harrison. Croghan wrote Harrison, "Were I a general commanding a district, I would be very far from suffering the secretary of war, or any other authority, to interfere with my internal police."[41]

Eventually, the matter was resolved, with President Madison's intervention, by enlarging the scope of the expedition and by Armstrong's placing Croghan in command. This incident was apparently the last straw for Harrison, who submitted his resignation to Armstrong on May 11, effective May 31, 1814. Harrison may have hoped that the president would encourage him to stay in the army and would perhaps rein in Armstrong, but Armstrong did not give Madison time to reflect. When Madison returned to Washington from his home in Virginia, he learned that Armstrong had not only accepted Harrison's resignation but had also filled the vacant major general slot with Andrew Jackson. Madison was furious, but he accepted Armstrong's action. This incident, however, triggered an investigation by Madison into Armstrong's conduct that would lead to a reprimand several months later.[42]

Croghan's combined force of approximately 700 regulars and Ohio militiamen left Detroit on July 3 on his expedition against Mackinac Island. Bad weather and other factors delayed his assault until August 4, but the well-entrenched British repulsed his attack with heavy casualties. Croghan gave up the assault and returned to Detroit. In his account of the battle, Croghan was generous in his praise of the Ohio militia, who were "wanting in no part of their duty. Col. [William] Cotgreave, his officers and soldiers, deserve the warmest approbation."[43]

Brigadier General McArthur replaced Harrison as commander of the Eighth Military District and was instructed to assist Maj. Gen. Jacob Brown on the Niagara peninsula. By the time he raised a force of 1,000 men in late July 1814 and was ready to move from Cleveland to Buffalo, the Battles of Chippewa and Lundy's Lane had already taken place. McArthur was concerned that his movement would be too late, and he worried that the British might move against Detroit during his absence. He therefore called out 1,000 militiamen from Kentucky and 500 from Ohio to march to Detroit immediately. McArthur joined Brown on August 8, but such was his concern that Brown released McArthur and some of his force to return to Detroit. McArthur's fears proved to be groundless.[44]

McArthur's call for militiamen upset Governor Shelby. He wrote

Armstrong that it was "a matter of surprise" that Kentuckians should be called to march through the populous state of Ohio to garrison a post on their frontier. Shelby stated that he would comply with the callout, but he declared that the troops should be given one or two months' pay in advance. It was clear that the burden of the war was testing Kentucky's resolve.[45]

The war wound down in the West without any more major engagements. One of the last expeditions, carried out in November 1814 by General McArthur, was a sweep toward Burlington on the Grand River. McArthur's account of the campaign, which had no significant results, noted the usual problems and the mixed results in using militia. Only twenty Michigan militiamen agreed to accompany his movement, he wrote, but six deserted, and the remainder were sent back. On the other hand, his volunteer rangers performed well.[46]

The military successes in the West during the War of 1812 were attributable to the militia. Overall, however, the record was undistinguished. Victories at the Thames and the successful defense of Fort Meigs and Fort Stephenson were offset by defeats at Brownstown, Detroit, and the River Raisin. Innumerable problems were caused by the use of militia, and greater success would undoubtedly have been possible with a well-equipped, disciplined regular force. Nevertheless, the Indians were defeated and, with the success of Commodore Perry, the British were expelled from the West.

Chapter 6

The Militia and the
War on the Northern Front

The northern front, the St. Lawrence and the Niagara peninsula, was the most active and critical front during the War of 1812. Here the British contested Americans more severely and over a longer period than in any other region. Here also, more than in any other area of the country, the mettle of the militia was tested. Sadly, the performance of the militia reflected in microcosm its general lack of effectiveness throughout the war, weak discipline, poor leadership, and lack of supplies. Occasionally, when the circumstances were right, the men performed adequately when they were properly motivated and properly led.

The Niagara region was bounded on the north by Lake Ontario and on the south by Lake Erie. The peninsula that separated the two protagonists was bisected by the north-flowing Niagara River (and its famous falls). To the west was Upper Canada, to the east New York. At the southern or Lake Erie end of the river was Fort Erie in Canada. Not far away on the American side lay Buffalo and Black Rock, the only sizable towns in the region. Down the river, below Grand Island, Fort Schlosser in New York and Fort Chippewa in Canada guarded each other. Below the falls, the small American village of Lewiston faced nearby Queenston on the Canadian side. Facing each other across the river on the Ontario shore were the British Fort George and the American Fort Niagara. The Niagara frontier was unprepared, even for defense, on the eve of the declaration of war in 1812. Citizens of Black Rock, alarmed by the military activity on the Canadian side, warned New York congressman and militia quartermaster general Peter B. Porter on April 15, 1812, about the lack of arms and ammunition. A volunteer militia force had been organized to stand sentry at Lewiston, Slosser, and Black Rock, but, they added, "there is not five muskets that is fit to use in this place & they are not to be had in this quarter."[1]

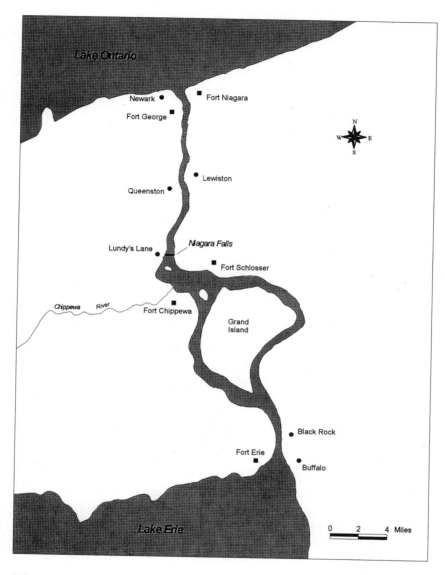

The Niagara Front. Courtesy of the Laboratory for Remote Sensing and Geographic Information Systems, Department of Geography, The University of Memphis.

New York's militia quota under the act of April 10, was 13,500, and Governor Daniel D. Tompkins was well aware that his militia companies called out were destitute of arms, camp equipment, blankets, and other items. He suggested, hopefully, to Porter that as U.S. volunteers were entitled to two months' pay and an allowance of sixteen dollars for clothing under the Act of February 6, 1812, "Perhaps the whole [militia] will now sign as *Volunteers* considering the advantages of that act." A week after the war began, Tompkins, warned that Fort Niagara was endangered, hastily authorized the movement of two cannons, with balls, powder, and other supplies, to the Niagara frontier, and he appointed Brig. Gen. William Wadsworth to command the militia at Black Rock. Wadsworth, however, confessed that he lacked military experience and was "ignorant of even the minor duties of the duty you have assigned me," and accordingly he asked for a "military secretary." Tompkins complied with Wadsworth's request, but he also assigned Brig. Gen. Amos Hall to overall command until Maj. Gen. Stephen Van Rensselaer could assume the post in mid-July.[2]

Maj. Gen. Henry Dearborn, the regular army officer commanding the northern front, mobilized the militia to protect Fort Niagara. Militiamen flocked to the frontier in such numbers that they quickly exceeded the quartermaster's ability to meet their supply needs. General Hall informed Governor Tompkins on July 4 that his force at Black Rock amounted to 2,800, including 300 regulars. Some 1,000 militia, however, could "remain but a short time in service. They have left their farms, their crops, their all, and will be ruined if they cannot soon return to their homes." They could not be accommodated anyway, due to shortages of tents and camp equipage. Hall added, "The disorders incident to camps thus formed of citizens will prove more fatal in one season that [*sic*] two campaigns of hard fighting."[3]

After taking command, General Van Rensselaer wasted little time before he projected offensive operations. A planned attack on a ten-gun British schooner at Prescott (opposite Ogdensburg) on the St. Lawrence was aborted, however, when only sixty-six men volunteered for the service.[4] It seems that Van Rensselaer had failed to check first with his militiamen as to who would volunteer to cross into Canada. Nor does he seem to have learned from this experience, for he repeated the mistake later, with infinitely greater consequences.

Van Rensselaer complained constantly to General Dearborn about the condition of his troops. Some were without shoes; they lacked all types of supplies, including ammunition. Many were sick, and morale was low. Hull's troops, taken prisoner at Detroit, were marched through Queenston, on the opposite side of the Niagara River, "in full view of my camp," Van Rensselaer wrote. "The effects produced by this event are such as you will readily imagine." The effect obviously produced on Van Rensselaer was one of foreboding, for he wrote, "While we are thus growing daily weaker, our enemy is growing stronger," and he warned Dearborn that he could act only on the defensive. Dearborn gave contradictory advice in response. He encouraged Van Rensselaer to retaliate, to avenge the misfortunes of Detroit at "the earliest opportunity," and to "be prepared to make good a secure retreat, as the last resort."[5]

Van Rensselaer was senior officer of the New York militia, and as a Federalist (he was the party's candidate for governor in 1813), it was hoped that he would bring other Federalists to support the war. He had no previous military experience, but he was assisted by his kinsman Col. Solomon Van Rensselaer, who had fought under General Anthony Wayne in the Indian Wars of the 1790s. Solomon complained that General Van Rensselaer's usefulness was being undermined by Quartermaster General Porter, John C. Spencer, and others "to answer party purposes . . . He cannot enforce that subordination which is so necessary to the safety and the glory of the troops he commands."[6]

Governor Tompkins indeed received complaints that the militiamen lacked confidence in Van Rensselaer.[7] The general admitted later that criticism about his lack of action prompted him to plan an attack across the Niagara River at Queenston Heights. The assault was supposed to begin on October 11, but it had to be aborted when a boat with all the oars mysteriously disappeared down the river. The invasion began on October 13 when a small force of about 200 regulars and militia, led by Col. Solomon Van Rensselaer, began the attack against withering fire from the British. After Colonel Van Rensselaer was wounded, Capt. John E. Wool of the regulars rallied the troops to scale the heights. Initial attempts by the British to counterattack, which led to the death of their commander, Gen. Isaac Brock, were rebuffed. General Van Rensselaer called for reinforcements, but the New York militia, on the American shore, observing the dead and wounded being carried across the river, refused to cross, despite everything Van Rensselaer could do to stir them.

In his report to General Dearborn the next day, Van Rensselaer asserted, "I can only add that the victory was really won; but lost for the want of a small reinforcement. *One third part of the idle men might have saved all.*" Historians have generally followed Van Rensselaer's lead in laying the blame for the loss at Queenston Heights on the militia. It should be noted, however, that about 500 militiamen did volunteer to cross. Among the approximately 950 American prisoners, there were

378 militia. Those who crossed apparently behaved well, at least until attacked by Indians, whose war whoops precipitated a rapid flight by many to the bank of the river where, one observer noted, many "regulars and militia" hovered. When General Van Rensselaer, who had crossed to the Canadian side, returned to gather reinforcements, he had to share his boat back to the American shore with soldiers fleeing the battle. The effect of this retreat on the militiamen can easily be imagined. They had flocked to the shore when the battle began, under no discipline or any particular command by militia officers. When they were belatedly asked to volunteer by General Van Rensselaer, the battle was going badly; not surprisingly they refused.[8]

Unfortunately, Brig. Gen. Alexander Smyth's 1,500 regulars were not used for the attack. Smyth was given command of the regular forces on the Niagara frontier on September 13, 1812, and it became clear that he did not want to serve under a militia officer. He arrived in Buffalo and reported by letter to General Van Rensselaer on September 29. Smyth declined a personal interview, stating that in his opinion the best place for an offensive was between Fort Erie and Chippewa, so he was encamping near Buffalo to prepare for such operations. Van Rensselaer responded to this display of arrogance by declaring that he had studied the situation carefully and was determined to adhere to his plan for a crossing at Queenston Heights.[9]

Smyth's letter suggested that unless compelled to do so, he intended to operate separately rather than place his force under a militia officer. Van Rensselaer, in fact, entertained the idea that the two forces might operate separately, with the regulars attacking Fort George, near Lake Ontario, while his militia force took Queenston. Despite Van Rensselaer's efforts to effect a meeting, Smyth stalled. Van Rensselaer thus failed to have a council of war, but he determined to attack anyway. He explained to Secretary of War Eustis, "Such was the pressure upon me from all quarters that I became satisfied that my refusal to act might involve me in suspicion and the service in disgrace."[10]

On October 10, Van Rensselaer ordered Smyth to strike his tents and march to Lewiston (twenty-seven miles from Buffalo). The intended assault was aborted on the eleventh, however, and Van Rensselaer, for reasons that are unclear, countermanded his order and instructed Smyth to return to his camp. The next day, October 12, Van Rensselaer again placed Smyth's force on alert for another march. Smyth's troops eventually made it to Lewiston after the battle was over. Smyth's assessment was that had he been ordered down in time to assist in the assault, "all would have been well." He faulted Van Rensselaer for attacking prematurely, for crossing at the most difficult part of the river, and for failing to ascertain beforehand whether the militia would cross over. Still, Smyth's account does not excuse Smyth's reluctance to cooperate beforehand.[11]

Governor Tompkins informed the New York legislature after the Battle of Queenston that "reverses are to be expected in the first outsets of inexperienced troops." He also called attention to the inequities of the militia draft. Those over forty-five years old, he noted, presumably the wealthiest part of the community, were exempt from militia duty and were subjected to no contribution or duty in time of war. Moreover, because the penalty for disobeying calls for service was "pecuniary only," the eligible wealthy, by paying "a trifling amount," escaped the dangers and burdens of service. The indigent alone were required to make the sacrifices of defending their fellow citizens and for a compensation that was "a mere pittance." Tompkins urged that "the hardships and perils of defending the country shall be more equitably diffused."[12] It is unlikely that Tompkins was pandering to the public for political gain. What he said was true, but changing the militia system during a war was questionable.

In the aftermath of the Battle of Queenston, Van Rensselaer asked to be relieved of his duties. Smyth assumed the command, but he inherited the same undisciplined and discontented militia, and his regulars were little better than raw militiamen. Capt. William King reported that the Twelfth and Fourteenth regular regiments lacked arms and equipment, as well as clothing, tents, and medical supplies. The Fourteenth's arms were in "infamously bad order," and the troops were "ignorant of their duty." He added, "They are mere militia, and, if possible, even worse; and if taken into action in their present state, will prove more dangerous to themselves than to their enemy."[13]

Smyth wrote Secretary Eustis on October 20, 1812, asking for more regular troops. "Place no confidence in detached militia," he wrote, "they have disgraced the nation." In fact, Col. Thomas Parker advised Smyth to call off the campaign, citing the lack of discipline in the regulars and the little confidence that could be placed in the militia. Parker asserted that the militia at Buffalo included only one company "that would not corrupt any regular troops that they might be associated with." Even that company would not be willing to be subjected to regular discipline. The militiamen and volunteers, he wrote, should be formed into a distinct brigade and "put under strict drill. If they will not bear this, they had better be at home."[14]

While Smyth awaited the arrival of about 2,000 Pennsylvania militia, a mutiny broke out in Brig. Gen. Daniel Miller's brigade in Buffalo on November 1. At least 100 militiamen stacked their arms and left camp, while another 100 stacked their arms and stood by them. No effort was made to return those who left, but those who remained were placated by General Miller with a promise of better quarters. Lt. Col. J.W. Livingston, aide to Governor Tompkins and acting deputy adjutant general, inspected General Miller's brigade on November 4, after which he declared that the brigade was "little better than an undisciplined rabble." The want of order, he believed, was due to "the ignorance of the officers and the great familiarity which exists between them and their men." Nor was it likely to change, he noted, "while such materials are employed for officers."[15]

At least four militiamen were shot for desertion and one for mutiny. One officer, Capt. John Phillips, was court-martialed but was found not guilty for not using his "utmost endeavors to stop a mutiny." General Smyth approved the decision; yet he also declared that "an officer present at a mutiny, who never draws his sword and uses only words, cannot be said to use his utmost endeavors to suppress it." General Miller and several of his officers were dismissed and the remaining members of his brigade consolidated with other units.[16]

On November 9, Smyth informed General Dearborn that two militia regiments, one at Utica and another at Manlius (near Syracuse), as well as a volunteer company at Buffalo, had mutinied because they had received no pay. Also, another volunteer militia company threatened not to cross into Canada unless it received pay and a clothing allowance. To add to his laments, Smyth noted a great amount of sickness in his camp.[17]

Meanwhile, 2,000 Pennsylvania militiamen called out by Governor Simon Snyder on August 25 to rendezvous at Meadville on September 25 moved tardily toward Buffalo. Governor Snyder pointedly noted in his call that the patriotism of the volunteers was "too sincere and ardent to permit them to make any objections to crossing the boundary line of the United States; otherwise they will render no service to their country." Smyth asked General Dearborn on November 9 whether the Pennsylvania militiamen could be forced to cross the line. "I am told they will refuse." When the Pennsylvania militiamen finally arrived in Buffalo on November 18, Smyth quickly queried their commander, Brig. Gen. Adamson Tannehill, on this point. Tannehill replied that 413 of the approximately 2,000 troops had volunteered.[18]

On November 10, Smyth issued a bombastic proclamation calling for volunteers, declaring that his troops would soon "plant the American standard in Canada." Nevertheless, Smyth twice embarked his troops, and twice disembarked them, without making a crossing. It did not appear that the British would have offered much opposition to a landing. In fact, while the troops were on board ships after the first embarkation, three American sailors crossed over to the opposite shore and spent two hours burning houses and stores, shooting "fowls, ducks, and pigs," and returned unmolested with loot taken from the houses.[19]

Smyth's defense was that he had been ordered by General Dearborn to make the assault with 3,000 men and that on the first occasion he had only 1,465 men and on the second only 1,500. Although as many as 7,000 troops were in and around Buffalo, many were physically in no condition to cross over, others were in such a state of discipline that they would have been totally unreliable, and some, such as the Pennsylvania militia, simply refused to cross into Canada. Smyth gave a hint of his feeling in a statement to a committee of citizens on December 3. "The affair at Queenston," he wrote, "is a caution against relying on crowds who go to the bank of the Niagara to look on a battle as on a theatrical exhibition, who if they are disappointed of the sight break their muskets, or if they are without rations for a day, desert."[20]

Smyth supposedly said after the second debarkation that he "could not depend on the militia and had not regular troops sufficient." The outraged militiamen reportedly offered $1,500 for his person (presumably alive), and they "fired off all of their ammunition and disembodied themselves." Smyth was "universally denounced as a coward and a traitor; he was shot at several times, and was hooted through the streets of Buffalo. He was shifting his tent in every direction in order to avoid the indignation of the soldiers." Reportedly, "every tavern keeper in and near Buffalo, declined the infamy of his company."[21]

Among those harshly critical of Smyth was Brig. Gen. Peter B. Porter, who embarked with volunteer militiamen and was bitterly disappointed when they were disembarked. He openly denounced Smyth as a coward and a traitor. In a letter to the editor of the *Buffalo Gazette* on December 8, he ascribed the "late disgrace . . . to the cowardice of General Smyth," and he promised to submit "a *true* account" of those events. Smyth, who had not responded to taunts heretofore, now challenged Porter to a duel, and the two met on the fourteenth on Grand Island. Shots were exchanged without damage, and after "mutual explanations" a reconciliation was effected. The next day, Porter's account of the events appeared in the *Buffalo Gazette*. He stated that he had received assurances from General Smyth, which "as a man of honor I am bound to believe," that he was following instructions from the secretary of war and General Dearborn. Still, Porter estimated a force of between 2,000 and 2,600 in the first embarkation. "The men," he declared, "were in fine spirits and desirous of crossing," so the order to disembark produced "great discontent and murmuring." After the second order to disembark on December 1, Porter wrote, "A scene of confusion ensued which is difficult to describe, about 4000 men, without order or restraint, discharging their muskets in every direction."[22]

Smyth disputed Porter's figures and again asserted that only 1,500 men were willing to cross the river. He added, "It is an error to rely on troops except those who are *bound to obey*." He asserted that only 360 Pennsylvania militiamen were prepared to cross. It was true the remainder went to Black Rock but, he said sarcastically, "I presume to be spectators."[23]

Obviously, Smyth did not assault Canada because he lacked faith in the militia and believed his force inadequate not only quantitatively but also qualitatively. In fact, the militiamen on hand gave literal meaning to the word "mob." A dispute arose between a Mr. Pomeroy, a well-known Federalist who kept a hotel in Buffalo, and certain volunteers, particularly those from Baltimore (some of whom may have participated in the riot there in July) and the so-called Irish Greens from Albany and New York City. On November 25 a mob of some forty or so from these companies stormed the hotel, broke furniture, damaged the hotel, and actually set it afire three or four times. Each time the fire was put out by local citizens for fear it would consume the village. A citizen who tried to intervene was bayonetted but not mortally. An artillery company was brought in to clear the house. The mob resisted with fury; at least two were killed, and others were wounded. Several went to get their weapons, intending to return and engage the artillery company, but they were dissuaded by their officers. The artillery company had to place its encampment under guard to deter any assault. About 300 regular troops were posted to protect the village of Buffalo.[24]

In the aftermath of Smyth's cancellation of the invasion, large numbers of militiamen deserted. Some 600 Pennsylvania militiamen deserted within twenty-four hours, and nearly that many left in the next few days. Discontented since their arrival, the Pennsylvanians, living in tents, had been much exposed to the weather and sickness. General Tannehill lamented that a large number of officers joined their troops in deserting. He hinted to Smyth that his remaining force (267 privates, plus officers, noncommissioned officers, and musicians) should be dismissed before they added to the exodus. He argued that to hold his force any longer, raising expenses without any benefits, "would only be an accumulation of the same evil." General Smyth organized the remaining force into a battalion under one of the majors and dismissed General Tannehill and the other field officers. This battalion, however, was disbanded within two weeks.[25] The Pennsylvania militiamen contributed nothing to the campaign; their presence was in fact a disruptive element.

Much chagrined by his failure to invade Canada and perhaps fearing for his safety, Smyth asked for and was granted permission to retire from the army.[26] He turned over the command to Col. Moses Porter, who presided over a much diminished force as the year drew to a close.

Elsewhere, Maj. Gen Henry Dearborn finally began his belated march toward the Canadian border near Lake Champlain in November 1812. He included in his army of 5,000 approximately 2,000 New York and Vermont militia. Not only was the season late and the weather bad, but the army was short on supplies and tents. When Dearborn learned that only about half of the militiamen would cross the border, he called off his campaign. No additional fighting occurred during the winter of 1812-1813, as both sides waited until spring to renew the conflict.[27]

Thus the first year of war had passed, and the nation was reeling from unanticipated military failures. A war had been declared, but the nation was unprepared to fight. The militia, which was to be the primary force for waging the war, was simply not organized, trained, disciplined, equipped, armed, or ready. The failures of the first year, in fact, revealed that militias were unlikely to be useful at all for conducting any offensive operations—and only marginally useful for defensive purposes.

Editor Joseph Gales reluctantly concluded in the *National Intelligencer* in December 1812 that the war was not going well for the Americans. "Every day's experience," he wrote, "tends to force on our minds a conviction we are unwilling to receive, that the volunteer militia are not precisely the species of force on which to rely for carrying on war, however competent they may be to repel invasion." The doctrine that they could not be ordered beyond the limits of the United States contributed to "the disastrous events of Queenston and the disgraceful scenes recently exhibited at Black Rock."[28]

The wet spring of 1813 delayed the planting and made farmers reluctant to respond to calls to volunteer. A friend informed Peter B. Porter on May 10, 1813, "Nothing short of a cannonading will start them." After planting was done, he said, "all say they will then turn out for ten or twelve days."[29]

In the meantime, John Armstrong, Jr., of New York replaced Eustis as secretary of war in February 1813. Armstrong had useful insights into how to prosecute the war, but he lacked the resolve to persevere with his plans and allowed others to modify his proposals. His weakness was shown shortly after he took office. He recommended offensive operations, proposing first that General Dearborn attack Kingston, the British naval station at the head of the St. Lawrence, then move against

York (present-day Toronto) and the ships being built there, and then proceed against Forts George and Erie, at each end of the Niagara peninsula.[30] Dearborn, however, supported by Comm. Isaac Chauncey, commander of the U.S. fleet on Lake Ontario, persuaded Armstrong to alter the plan by attacking York first, then Forts George and Erie, before moving against Kingston.

While the Americans were occupied in the successful attacks upon York and Fort George, the British assaulted Sackets Harbor, the American naval headquarters at the eastern end of Lake Ontario, on May 29, which was lightly defended by about 400 regulars and approximately 500 militiamen led by militia general Jacob Brown. The militiamen fired prematurely, broke ranks, and fled. Lt. Col. John Mills of the Albany volunteers was killed trying to stop the flight of his troops. In his battle report, Brown was critical of the militia, which he described as "raw troops unaccustomed to subordination." Fortunately, with support from the regulars and some militia, Brown drove off the British. He was rewarded with a commission of brigadier general in the regular army.[31]

While approximately 2,000 Americans occupied Fort George, the British operated nearby, successfully harassing the troops inside and still menacing Americans along the Niagara peninsula. Thus free to carry out offensive operations, a British force of about 300 regulars and forty militia, commanded by Lt. Col. Cecil Bisshopp, landed on the morning of July 11 below Black Rock. Raw American militiamen acting as pickets fled without giving an alarm. Maj. Parmenio Adams, commanding about 200 militiamen at Black Rock, although surprised and called upon to surrender, was able to retreat in good order. The British set fire to the military barracks and blockhouse and ate breakfast at the home of General Porter, who fled before their arrival. The British also plundered public stores and the houses of some inhabitants.

Porter went to Buffalo, rallied Adams's men, added another militia company and some thirty to forty Indians from the Six Nations, and led them back to Black Rock. He routed the British, who fled in boats. As the British floated down the Niagara River, the American militiamen and Indians followed along the bank and laid down a murderous fire. At one point the British hoisted the flag of surrender, but it was a ruse to escape, which they accomplished. Among those wounded on the boats was Colonel Bisshopp, who subsequently died. Altogether, the entire British loss (killed, wounded, and prisoners) amounted to nearly 100. American losses were minimal, with four killed and as many wounded. Two Indians were also wounded. This was the first battle in which Indians were used on the American side. Porter praised their gallantry in his letter to General Dearborn, and he added that they "committed no acts of cruelty." It was true they asked permission to scalp the slain, but they "evinced no displeasure" when this was refused. Porter also praised the militiamen, whose conduct "would have reflected credit on veteran troops," but he tempered this praise by saying, "and it is not less creditable to them as soldiers and citizens than that of their companions who basely deserted them, is disgraceful."[32]

The Battle of Black Rock marked the emergence of Peter B. Porter as the quintessential militia leader of the war. A friend and ally of Daniel D. Tompkins, Porter had served in the state legislature and Congress. He actively supported war and was one of the "War Hawks." His brother, Augustus, headed the firm of Porter, Barton, and Company, the main contractor for U.S. forces in the Northwest, headquartered in the town of Black Rock, now a part of Buffalo. Part guerrilla leader and part military chieftain, Porter played an important role on the Niagara frontier for the remainder of the war. He never received a regular commission, which he richly deserved, perhaps because he never secured an independent command that allowed him to gain distinction. Still, he was extremely successful in getting the most out of his troops, and he demonstrated persuasively that militiamen, capably led, were effective fighters.[33]

Porter was concerned that the government was focusing on other places to the neglect of the Niagara frontier. He was provoked to write a bitter letter to Secretary of War Armstrong. Every man of common sense, he asserted, knew that for the past two months "a vigorous and well-directed exertion of three or four days" would have defeated the whole enemy force on the Niagara frontier. Instead, the frontier was exposed, and the American force at Fort George "lies panic-struck, shut up and whipped in by a few hundred miserable savages." Brig. Gen. John Boyd, commander of the American forces at Fort George, even urged Porter to induce 200 Indians to join the Americans at Fort George to "punish the temerity of the scouting parties of the enemy."[34]

Porter instead proposed an offensive, with about 1,200 men, composed equally of regulars, volunteers, and Indians crossing the river, attacking Chippewa, and then moving toward Fort George, while Boyd would send a force in the opposite direction and catch the British in a vise. Porter believed a "united force of 3000 men" could easily capture all the British stations to the head of Lake Ontario and "disperse the whole of their army." Boyd responded that he was barred "from undertaking any enterprise when the hazard is not more than counterbalanced by the probability of success."[35]

Apparently anticipating a negative response, Porter, with about 200 Indians joined to 200 regulars and volunteer militia, crossed the

Niagara River near Fort Erie on August 3 and captured a considerable quantity of livestock and public and private stores. The Indians, Porter related, were "active and expert" in taking prisoners and were generally well behaved. While cattle and horses were being transferred across the river, however, "a few unprincipled rascals from our shore crossed the river and with a few Indians strayed off, unknown to the officers, and plundered several private homes." Porter and "respectable" Indian leaders undertook to restore the ill-gotten plunder, but he informed Gen. Boyd that he could not with propriety ask the Indians to return cattle and horses that were private property. The value of the property was about $1,000, and Porter suggested that perhaps it would "be best for the Government to pay for it than to take it away." Boyd responded that since the expedition "was intended to effect a desirable public object," he approved selling the cattle and horses and dividing the proceeds among the Indians.[36]

For various reasons, lack of control of Lake Ontario, a change in command with Maj. Gen. James Wilkinson taking over, and other circumstances, the proposed attack on Kingston was delayed. When the British fleet appeared offshore near Fort George in early August, Boyd, fearing an attack, urged Porter to bring on his force immediately. They arrived on August 14, but by then the scare had abated. Porter's volunteers and Indians, impatient to engage the enemy, gained Boyd's approval to assault British pickets near Fort George. On the morning of the seventeenth, Maj. Cyrenius Chapin, Porter's second in command, led about 300 volunteers and Indians, with 200 regulars under Maj. William Cummings, against the British pickets. A heavy rain kept the enterprise from being totally successful. The enemy escaped but suffered heavy casualties, and at least fifteen were captured. Americans lost two Indians killed and a few wounded. Despite a taste of battle, Porter's volunteers feared their absence left Buffalo exposed to British depredations. Boyd permitted Porter's force to leave on August 29, but the British fleet reappeared off Fort George the next day. Porter stopped his troops at Lewiston and advised Boyd that he had sent Major Chapin on to Buffalo to raise more troops and that he would await orders.[37] Once again a threatened attack failed to materialize.

In anticipation of a movement of regulars from Fort George, 2,000 militiamen were called out for three months' service on August 25. Those who had served in 1812 were specifically exempted. Governor Tompkins assigned the command to Brig. Gen. George McClure and reminded him that the defense of the frontier might be left to the militia. The usual problems were encountered in gathering the troops; arms were short and only half of the camp equipment arrived. McClure assured

Tompkins on September 10 that he would establish military discipline. That same day, McClure called upon his troops in the bombastic fashion of Smyth, to support their country and yield to discipline, for "without it an army is no better than a mob . . . useless to their country and a plague to themselves."[38]

McClure continued to issue embarrassing, melodramatic proclamations. On October 2, he urged the militiamen to accompany him across the Niagara, and he ridiculed those who cited the injunctions of the Constitution. "The General desires no faint-hearted effeminate poltroons, who cannot bring their courage to the *sticking point* to go with him," he declared. "The path of duty, of honor and glory is before you." McClure also appealed for 1,000 volunteers to join him.[39]

At this same time, General Harrison's defeat of the British at the Battle of the Thames enabled Secretary Armstrong to bring Harrison's regulars to the Niagara frontier for defensive purposes. About 1,300 arrived in Buffalo on October 24 on their way to Fort George. McClure, now at Fort George, persuaded Harrison that offensive operations were appropriate to dislodge a British force at Burlington Heights, about fifty miles to the west. Early in November, McClure informed Governor Tompkins that Harrison had authorized a further requisition of 1,000 militiamen to repair to Fort George by November 12. With a reinforcement of 1,500 volunteers and militia, McClure wrote, "I will undertake to obtain possession of Burlington Heights." He added that his men were "under good discipline and perfect subordination; an equal number of the enemy cannot, I am confident, stand before them." Harrison also wrote Tompkins that it was urgent for the attack to be made before the enemy strengthened its position.[40]

Secretary Armstrong, apparently unaware of the plans at Fort George, issued orders to General Harrison on November 3 to send his troops to reinforce Sackets Harbor. Harrison protested that this would leave Fort George practically defenseless. McClure implored Harrison not to abandon the expedition, but Harrison had no alternative. His troops embarked for Sackets Harbor on November 15, which "knocked in the head" the proposed Burlington expedition.[41]

McClure apparently believed he had to use the volunteers for some purpose or they would return home. On November 21, he informed Governor Tompkins of a projected "movement towards the enemy," but he mentioned only raiding some mills for flour. He also noted with some concern that the term of service of his regular militiamen was growing short. In fact, Armstrong authorized McClure on November 25 to call 1,000 militiamen to replace those whose terms were expiring. Tompkins immediately alerted Maj. Gen. Amos Hall to organize the requisite number of men and march them to the frontier as quickly as possible.[42]

Meanwhile, on November 26, McClure marched about 1,300 men out of Fort George toward Burlington. After about twenty miles, confronted by bad roads, bad weather, and evidence that the enemy was preparing to meet their advance, McClure chose, upon the "advice of every field officer in the brigade," to retire to the safety of the fort. Still, he claimed, 400 barrels of flour had been seized, and the attention of a large British force was diverted from employment elsewhere. With militia terms running out, he urged the volunteers to stay. "The situation of Fort George," he declared, "will be truly precarious if left to be defended by but a small force." On December 6, he informed Tompkins that when the militia left he would have only 200 regulars and 100 Indians. He hoped to induce 200 to 300 militiamen to stay by giving a bounty of two dollars per month for two months.[43]

The situation was worse than McClure anticipated. On December 10 he had present for duty only sixty regulars and about forty volunteers. The militiamen left him "almost to a man." It was no use offering bounties; "A very inconsiderable number were willing to engage for a further term of service on any conditions." Learning the enemy was approaching, a council of the principal officers deemed the fort untenable, and McClure ordered an evacuation. He noted in a letter to Armstrong, almost matter-of-factly, that the village of Newark was then in flames, "in conformity with the views of Your Excellency disclosed to me in a former communication." He added that the conflagration would deprive the enemy of winter quarters in the vicinity of Fort George.[44]

McClure's burning of Newark was a misunderstanding of Armstrong's instruction that the defense of Fort George "may render it proper to destroy the town of Newark." President Madison was forced to explain to the outraged British that the action was the result of "a misapprehension of the officer & not an order from the govt."[45]

McClure understood his action might bring retribution against Americans along the Niagara frontier. He wrote Armstrong that the enemy was "much exasperated, and will make a descent on this frontier if possible." On December 18, he called the militiamen of Niagara county out en masse. But it was too late. After reoccupying Fort George, the British crossed the Niagara on December 19 and surprised and overwhelmed the Americans at Fort Niagara. Sixty-five were killed and 422 taken prisoner. The British suffered only 6 killed and 5 wounded. Lewiston was also burned, as well as a Tuscarora village nearby.[46]

Brig. Gen. Timothy Hopkins, in Buffalo, reported to Governor Tompkins that he had called out his brigade and that he hoped for the aid of the militia from Genesee. His men, however, were unwilling to come under the command of General McClure, whose conduct had "disgusted the greater part of the men under his command and they have no confidence in him." Hopkins advised the governor that "the militia of this country have stood so many drafts and have been so much absent from their homes and business it will be very difficult to keep them out any length of time." The destruction of Newark, he said, had "incensed the people of Canada," and he warned "nothing will save any part of this frontier but a respectable force." Only 400 men answered McClure's call for militia. The men were more concerned about "taking care of their families and property by carrying them into the interior than helping us to fight." McClure added that he had ordered Colonel Chapin confined for treason. "There is not a greater rascal exists than Chapin," he wrote, "and he is supported by a pack of *tories* and enemies of our Government. Such is the men of Buffalo. They don't deserve protection." McClure denounced Chapin as "an unprincipled disorganizer" who "headed a mob for the purpose of doing violence to my feelings and person" and, he noted, "five or six guns were discharged at me by his men."[47]

John C. Spencer, son of the prominent New York jurist and a future congressman and cabinet officer, wrote Governor Tompkins that the "infamous Chapin" and his company refused to consider themselves under McClure's command. Chapin had been placed in confinement but was released "by force by the Buffalo tories." Spencer believed McClure a "good officer" but added, "He is wholly incompetent to the command of this frontier. At all events, you may rest assured that he is universally detested by the inhabitants; that his soldiers have no confidence in him, and that his officers unanimously concur in the opinion of his unfitness to command." Spencer recommended that Tompkins himself raise a force and lead them into Canada or that he appoint a popular man fit for the station, such as Peter B. Porter.[48]

McClure wrote Lt. Col. Erastus Granger from Batavia on Christmas Day that he would not go again to Buffalo unless he was convinced he would be treated differently. He advised Granger that Maj. Gen. Hall was in command of the militia and volunteers in Buffalo. Three days later, McClure informed Granger that he was going to visit his family. "The gross insults which I have received from many in Buffalo will apologise for my absence," he wrote. "When I return again with the regular troops I will be able to do myself justice."[49]

Clearly, McClure blamed the militia. On December 25 he appealed to Secretary Armstrong for more regular troops. "The militia will do to act with regulars, but not without them," he stated. "In spite of all my exertions to insure subordination, my late detachment ultimately proved to be very little better than an infuriated mob." He attributed the fault to officers "seeking popularity, and who, on that account, were afraid of enforcing subordination and introducing strict discipline."[50]

General Hall informed Tompkins that he had gathered 2,000 militiamen by the twenty-sixth in Buffalo, mostly volunteers. They could be kept "but a few days." About 200 men were also gathered at Black Rock where, on the evening of December 29, the British attacked. Colonel Chapin rushed to the scene with about 400 militia, but they were green and undisciplined and fled in great disorder when the first shots were fired. Chapin, trying vainly to stop them, was captured. Hall arrived later with about 1,500 men. At first they laid down a "smart fire," but they soon broke ranks and retreated in disorder, and "neither entreaties nor threats" could stop them. Hall's Indian allies did not give the expected support, and as for the Chautauqua militia, "terror . . . dissipated this corps." Every effort to rally the troops, Hall informed Tompkins, "proved ineffectual and experience proves that with the militia retreat becomes a flight, and, a battle once ended, the army is dissipated."[51]

The British looted and burned both Black Rock and Buffalo the following day. Gen. Lewis Cass, observing the ruins of Buffalo shortly after the attack, called it "a scene of distress and destruction such as I have never before witnessed." He was harshly critical of the militia, who although greatly outnumbering the British, "behaved in the most cowardly manner. They fled without discharging a musket." The *Manlius Times* editor agreed: "To the want of discipline, of subordination and proper concert is to be attributed the fate of Buffalo and Black Rock. Our forces were not only sufficient to have repelled but to have captured the invaders." Even worse, some American militiamen were seen plundering what the enemy did not take.[52]

The assistant deputy quartermaster general, John G. Camp, denied that there was a scarcity of arms and ammunition. He insisted that all who applied got them and that an additional 7,000 rounds of musket cartridges were available for distribution on the day of the battle. Unfortunately, he noted, many militiamen did not use the arms distributed to them. At least 300 stand of arms, he observed, were destroyed in houses where they were left by militiamen who deserted their arms as well as the village of Buffalo. "If one-half of the troops that were on duty the day previous to the action," he exclaimed, "had made use of half the means Government had provided for them the villages of Buffalo and Black Rock would still have been flourishing."[53]

Thus, at the end of another year, disaster had again befallen the

Niagara frontier, and great suffering was visited upon the inhabitants. Again the blame was placed on the militia. The federal government might reasonably have expected the New York militiamen to be capable of defending the frontier, but the glaring failures of leadership and lack of discipline among the drafted militiamen made it painfully obvious that they were not. As James Wadsworth wrote Governor Tompkins, the disaster at Buffalo had "spread fright and consternation among all ranks, broken down the ardor and spirit of the militia, and it will require some time for it to recover." He added, "The frontier will remain defenseless until a regiment of regulars is sent on."[54]

The situation elsewhere in the northern New York–Lake Champlain region in the summer and early fall of 1813 was particularly unsettled because of frequent raids by Canadian militia. Typically, the American militiamen called out in response were from rural areas and always arrived too late to engage the raiders, who had retired back into Canada. In late July 1813, for example, a British raiding party led by Lt. Col. John Murray looted and burned considerable property in and around Plattsburgh, New York, on Lake Champlain. Brig. Gen. Benjamin Mooers, the New York militia commander, with his troops so disorganized, wisely refused to engage the British raiders. The raids and frequent militia callouts were demoralizing not only to the people who suffered from the attacks but also to the militiamen, who resented the disruption of their lives.[55]

The regular American army in this region was commanded in 1813 by Maj. Gen. Wade Hampton, who chose not to be diverted by the raids, leaving the people along Lake Champlain to deal with the problem themselves. His decision was met with only grudging acceptance. When Governor Jonas Galusha ordered the Vermont militia to assist in the defense of Plattsburgh in September 1813, the order was effected only "at the *point of the bayonet*," according to one observer. This action perhaps contributed to the subsequent election of a Federalist governor, Martin Chittenden. In his first message to the legislature on October 23, 1813, Chittenden spoke of the intent of the framers of the Constitution. They had not, he said, contemplated that "the whole body of the militia were, by any kind of magic, at once to be transformed into a regular army for the purpose of foreign conquest." Rather, the militia was designed "for the service and protection of the respective states."[56]

On November 10, Chittenden issued a proclamation summoning his militiamen home, declaring that the militia of Vermont "must be reserved for its own defence and protection *exclusively*—excepting in cases provided for, by the Constitution of the United States—and then under orders derived *only* from the commander in chief." His order, however, backfired. Vermont militia officers refused to comply, declaring the proclamation "a gross insult to the officers and soldiers" and an "unwarrantable stretch of executive authority, issued from the worst of motives, to effect the basest purposes." Brig. Gen. Jacob Davis, sent to Plattsburgh to bring the militia home, was arrested and was released only after he had posted $5,000 security to appear at the next session of the U.S. District Court in New York City.[57]

Chittenden was vigorously denounced in Republican newspapers and resolutions of state legislatures. The *New York Columbian* characterized his proclamation as the "most scandalous and unwarrantable stain on the political history of America that ever disgraced its annals" and urged that he be tried for treason. The only question was whether a civil court or a court-martial was the proper tribunal. Governor William S. Pennington of New Jersey asserted to his legislature in November 1813 that the Constitution gave the command and disposal of the militia to the federal government, "not by implication, and construction, but by clear, unambiguous and express provisions." Otherwise, the caprice of state executives in denying the state militia to the federal government during emergencies could defeat and paralyze the operations of the general government. This doctrine, he said, was "fraught with incalculable mischief, and . . . it carries in its bosom the seeds of national dissolution." The legislature adopted a resolution denouncing "the ravings of an infuriated faction, either as issuing from a legislative body, a maniac governor, or discontented or ambitious demagogues."[58]

Chittenden was criticized in Congress by Solomon Sharp (Ky.), who introduced a resolution declaring that the attorney general of the United States should prosecute Chittenden for violating the statute against enticing soldiers in the service of the United States to desert. James Fisk of Vermont stated that very few persons in Vermont and none of the state's delegation approved of the proclamation, but he believed the House had no right to influence courts of justice and that the resolution was improper. After cursory debate, in which Chittenden's action was characterized as treason, the resolution was tabled.[59]

Hampton was meanwhile trying to raise a force to menace Montreal and, perhaps, if events were auspicious, to assault the city itself. In October 1813, Secretary Armstrong ordered Hampton to move his force down the Chateaugay River to meet an army proceeding down the St. Lawrence led by General Wilkinson. Fifteen hundred militiamen refused to cross the line. This development undoubtedly came as no surprise to Hampton, for he had already informed Armstrong of the possibility that a large percentage of Brig. Gen. Elias Fasset's Vermont militiamen would not cross the line.[60]

Hampton was repulsed by a smaller British detachment before he ever reached the mouth of the Chateaugay, and he was forced to retreat. Learning that Armstrong had given the quartermaster general orders to construct huts below the border on the Chateaugay River, Hampton informed Armstrong that in "fulfillment of the ostensible views of the Government," he considered the campaign "substantially at an *end.*" Armstrong asserted later that this order was merely a contingency plan, but in any event Hampton was not in position to effect a junction with Wilkinson's army when it came down the St. Lawrence. Bitter recriminations followed, as Wilkinson seized this pretext to call off an assault on Montreal that he had not wanted to make anyway.[61] Hampton took his army back to Plattsburgh, placed the men in winter quarters, and hastily left the military district, no doubt to avoid arrest and court-martial at the hands of his bitter enemy Wilkinson.

As the year 1813 drew to a close, the government could point to mixed results on the northern front. Along the Niagara, early successes were marred by devastation and defeat at the end of the year, and the vital waterway, the St. Lawrence, had not even been threatened. Large numbers of militiamen still refused to cross the international boundary, and they continued to display a lack of discipline and retreat before the enemy. The country faced the next campaign still relying on militias to bear a large part of the burden of military action.

Armstrong relieved Wilkinson from his command in March 1814 and announced a court of inquiry. The order came too late to stop an ill-advised attack across the border at La Cole Mill. A British force outnumbered eight to one inflicted 150 American casualties. When Hampton was also allowed to resign on March 16, both commanders on the northern front had to be replaced. Maj. Gen. Jacob Brown was assigned to the Niagara frontier, and Maj. Gen. George Izard was given command along Lake Champlain. Brig. Gen. Alexander Macomb, soon to make a name for himself on this frontier, was the ranking officer under General Izard.[62]

Macomb was temporarily in command when he called upon Governor Chittenden in April 1814 for 500 men at Burlington and 1,000 at Vergennes. Both were within the state of Vermont and not subject to the strictures of Chittenden about the use of militiamen outside the state. When federal officials attempted to organize the militiamen into 100-man companies, however, many militiamen simply refused to be mustered and returned home. Macomb lamented: "The difficulties made by them on being collected for muster was truly ridiculous & I deem it my duty to say that no reliance can be placed on them as a source of defense." Later he wrote, "They did not give us even an opportunity of mustering them and they very soon discharged themselves."[63]

Macomb was also in charge of the defense of Plattsburgh when the British attacked in September 1814. Secretary Armstrong had ordered General Izard and 4,000 troops to join the American forces on the Niagara. Despite Izard's protests that this move would leave Plattsburgh vulnerable to the enemy, Armstrong, who had heard exaggerated claims of enemy forces on the frontier before, insisted on Izard's march. Shortly after Izard left, however, Gen. George Prevost appeared before Plattsburgh in early September with approximately 10,000 troops. Macomb had only about 1,500 regulars to face a force, as Macomb styled them, "the conquerors of France, Spain, Portugal, and Indies, led by the most experienced generals of the British Army." He called upon New York militiamen to turn out en masse.[64]

Macomb also asked Governor Chittenden for militia. He did not give any specific number of troops, but Chittenden replied that attention would be paid to his request and aid would be afforded "as should be found necessary, and in my power constitutionally to grant." When no troops materialized, Macomb urgently renewed his request on September 1. Chittenden replied that he would ask for volunteers, despite the plea of the commander of the Vermont militia, General John Newell, that he and his militiamen would cheerfully obey any call to repair to Plattsburgh. Chittenden informed Newell that he did not consider himself authorized by the constitution or law to order militiamen out of the state. He believed, he said, a request for volunteers "would have more effect than an attempt to assume unauthorized power." Eventually, Gen. Samuel Strong led Vermont volunteers to Plattsburgh in great number, reaching perhaps 2,500 men.[65]

By September 4, General Mooers had gathered about 700 New York militiamen to protect a northern approach to Plattsburgh. They were joined by 250 regulars commanded by Maj. John Wool. On the sixth the British approached the American line. The militiamen skirmished briefly with the British advanced party but broke and fled precipitously, despite their officers' efforts to make them stay and fight. Many militiamen returned to their homes. Wool's regulars contested the enemy approach, but they were compelled to retire. A mitigating circumstance explaining the militia reaction was that New York dragoons, who wore red coats, were on the heights watching the enemy, and the militiamen mistook them for the enemy attacking in their rear. General Mooers was disgusted with the performance of his militia, as attested in his general orders on September 8. "The general regrets that there are some who are lost to patriotism and to honor . . . , fled at the first approach of the enemy, and afterwards basely disbanded themselves and returned home; thereby disgracing themselves, and furnishing to their fellow soldiers an example of all that brave men detest and abhor."[66]

The British captured most of Plattsburgh that first day of fighting, but they paid a price. Three officers were killed and their soldiers suffered about 100 casualties. The Americans had about forty-five casualties.[67] The American forces took refuge on the east and south side of the Saranac River and destroyed the two bridges leading to their side. Here the remaining militiamen helped to drive the British back. Fortunately for the defenders of Plattsburgh, Lt. Thomas Macdonough and his fleet on Lake Champlain destroyed the British fleet on the morning of September 11. Prevost, without assured supply lines, gave up the siege of Plattsburgh and withdrew.

Afterward, General Macomb generously bestowed accolades on his militia. His general orders of September 14 declared that their zeal reflected "the highest lustre on their patriotism and spirit . . . They have exemplified how speedily American citizens can be prepared to meet the enemies of their country." In his report of the battle, Macomb wrote, "The militia behaved with great spirit after the first day. . . . The Militia of New York and the Volunteers of Vermont have been exceedingly serviceable, and have evinced a degree of patriotism and bravery worthy of themselves and the states to which they respectively belong."[68]

General Mooers, however, was not so generous. His general orders of September 13 showed that he had not forgotten the actions of some of his men. In discharging the militia, he expressed the hope that the individuals who had basely deserted "will meet their reward by being despised as cowards, not deserving to be free men." Mooers, however, praised those who had stayed behind; they had shown "to their country and to the enemy what may be expected in case of any future invasion of this frontier."[69]

Even Governor Chittenden, displaying his flexibility, hailed the victories of Macdonough and Macomb, "supported by our patriotic, virtuous and brave volunteers." He seemed to offer an olive branch, declaring that "the conflict has become a common, and not a party concern," and he exhorted everyone in the state to unite for the common defense of the country. The new attitude did not extend, however, to allowing the state's militiamen to be commanded by regular officers. Late in October 1814, the Vermont council reaffirmed unanimously that the state's militia, when detached to the service of the United States, were to be commanded only by an officer appointed by the state, "or by the president in person."[70]

On January 31, 1814, Governor Tompkins recommended to the

New York legislature that two regiments of volunteer infantry and a battalion of mounted riflemen be organized to relieve the detached militia. He also recommended that the volunteers receive additional pay and that they be allowed to choose their own officers. Obviously, the failures of the militia in 1812 and 1813 convinced him that a more permanent and substantial force was needed. Fortunately, the federal government authorized a volunteer militia regiment. Tompkins selected Gen. Peter B. Porter and Col. John Swift, a prowar Federalist, as commanders. Porter and Swift issued a broadside on March 25 calling for six-month volunteers. They noted that the legislature was considering appropriating additional money for volunteers. The rendezvous was set for May 1 at Canandaigua.[71]

Porter was warned that it would be difficult to raise troops unless a bounty was offered. He was also apprised that opponents of the war were openly discouraging enlistments. But enlistments were slow for other reasons. Many complained that the militiamen had not been paid for their last service. Also, Capt. William B. Rochester informed Porter that many complained the state had been already "too much oppressed by repeated drafts of militia. Appeals to patriotism are unavailing," he said, and he lamented the "noxious influence of *peace men.*"[72]

Unfortunately, the legislature failed to approve the bounty for volunteers. One of Porter's officers who had enrolled thirty men conditionally upon the anticipated bounty was forced to discharge them. Other problems arose. May 1 had been set as the date for the rendezvous, but lack of tents and camp equipage forced Porter to halt the march of troops to Canandaigua. On a positive note, Porter declared to Governor Tompkins that about 1,000 recruits had been engaged, and he intended to collect his force by the twentieth, providing that he received the promised camp equipment. Porter added that approximately 500 Indians would join his force, providing they received their pay and annuities or gifts from the federal government.[73]

Tompkins declared that supplies had been sent on and that those who had not been paid when they were discharged last year would be paid. The problem was that many commanders had neglected to have the muster rolls certified by regular officers as required. As for the troops called out under state authority, the legislature had simply failed to appropriate the money, but Tompkins hoped that the next legislature would make up for the omission. Despite Tompkins's efforts, Porter declared that he was "egregiously . . . disappointed" with respect to supplies. As late as July 3, he had "not yet received a rifle, sabre, bayonet, blanket, and but a partial supply of tents." He added wistfully, "Had I foreseen the situation in which I was to be thrown, nothing would have induced me to have undertaken the task I did. But I embarked, and if I have but ten men I will persevere."[74]

With all of the recruiting problems, supply difficulties, and organizational concerns, Porter was not able to rendezvous his volunteers until June 29, nearly two months later than planned. He was able to gather about 1,000 volunteers and 500 Indians. Maj. Gen. Jacob Brown, commanding the regulars on the Niagara frontier, agreed to add a regiment of Pennsylvania volunteer militiamen to Porter's command. Porter informed Tompkins that with this force and the support of General Brown, "I hope to gain some credit for the volunteers."[75]

On July 3, Brown crossed the Niagara with 3,500 men and invested Fort Erie, which quickly surrendered. The next day, Porter's volunteers and Indians, about 1,500 in number, joined Brown's army moving north in search of the British army. Porter's troops were assigned the task of clearing the woods of British militiamen and Indians sniping on Americans encamped near Street's Creek, two miles south of the Chippewa (or Welland) River. About three o'clock on the afternoon of July 5, they advanced single file at a right angle to the Niagara, extending about three-quarters of a mile from the river. Encountering a small British and Indian force, Porter's volunteers engaged and routed them. Pursuing them into the woods, they reached a clearing in front of the Chippewa and there met the main force of the enemy. General Brown's account was not flattering. Porter's force, he reported, gave way "and fled in every direction, notwithstanding his personal gallantry, and great exertions to stay their flight. The retreat of the Volunteers and Indians caused the left flank of Gen. Scott's brigade to be greatly exposed." Perhaps aware that his account was damaging to the volunteers, Brown tempered his criticism but not very successfully. The volunteers, he added, could not be expected to contend with British regulars, so it had not surprised him to see them "retire before this column."[76]

Porter complained to Brown that while his report was complimentary to Porter, it did "great injustice to the troops under my command." Porter asserted that his troops retreated in good order after encountering the main British force, but "the rapidity of the pursuit, became on our part, a flight, & presented that part of our movements which alone could have met your view, and undoubtedly led to the remarks in your report." He asserted that his troops did regroup and participate in a counterattack. Years later Porter wrote, "My error . . . was remaining too long under an unequal fire, or possibly in attempting to rally at all, for I lost by it besides other valuable men the three principal officers of the Pennsylvania Volunteers." He also contended that Gen. Winfield Scott's brigade was supposed to have crossed Street's Creek to

Above, Jacob Jennings Brown, by an unknown artist (after J.W. Jarvis). Courtesy of the the National Portrait Gallery, Smithsonian Institution. *Below*, Peter B. Porter, by C.G. Crehen. Courtesy of the Buffalo and Erie County Historical Society.

support the volunteers, but that force was only crossing the bridge as the flight of the volunteers was taking place. "Had General Scott been at hand to support the volunteers when they first met the British line," he argued, the Battle of Chippewa "would doubtless have presented quite a different aspect." In a draft of this letter, Porter made the point, no doubt seriously, that his volunteers contributed to the American victory, because the British became deranged in their pursuit and were never quite able to reorganize in battle formation.[77]

The Battle of Chippewa showed that American regulars, well drilled, disciplined, and competently led, could defeat a comparable force of British regulars. Scott's brigade in particular performed brilliantly. Porter believed the most essential ingredient was leadership. The common soldier, he claimed, identified with his commanding officer. "If an officer prove recreant in battle, his example will poison & make cowards of the whole corps to which he belongs." He also argued, not very plausibly, "a farmer fresh from the plow, may by a drill of six weeks, *under proper officers*, be rendered as efficient in all the duties of the field as a soldier of ten years standing."[78]

The volunteers still lacked discipline. Shortly after the Battle of Chippewa, Porter sent Lt. Col. Isaac W. Stone with a small force to dislodge enemy troops at St. David's (about three miles from Queenston). After driving the British out, Stone returned to find the village plundered and in flames. He denied any knowledge of the perpetrators, but it was known that American militiamen and Indians were responsible. General Brown dismissed Stone on the grounds that the senior officer was responsible.[79]

On July 25 another clash with the British occurred near Niagara Falls at Lundy's Lane. Porter's volunteers participated, but their numbers had been reduced to about 300. (Four companies had been sent to Buffalo, and two companies were retained by General Brown to guard the camp at Chippewa. The Indians had left.) In the battle, as Porter informed General Brown, his troops were "conspicuously engaged with part of the regular troops in successfully repelling those desperate charges of the enemy's line to regain their artillery." He further asserted, "They fought with the coolness & discipline of regular troops." General Brown, reporting to Secretary Armstrong, complimented Porter's militia volunteers, who "stood undismayed amidst the hottest fire, and repulsed the veterans opposed to them."[80]

Porter's report bared his frustrations to Governor Tompkins. In proportion to those engaged, he wrote, "we lost more than any other corps" and, he believed, more officers as well, for a total of sixty-five. "I mention this not to boast," he stated, "but to show how unequally the policy observed towards volunteers bears upon them." Moreover, victory had been turned into defeat by General Brown's order to retreat. According to Porter, Brig. Gen. Eleazer W. Ripley, who commanded, "ought not to have been dictated to by a wounded man four miles from the scene of action." Porter asked permission to retire from service, because his force did not "warrant a Brigadier's command." He wrote bitterly that he was certain no militia general would "gain any military fame while united to a regular force and commanded by their officers." The militiamen would always be "the tools and drudges of the regular troops."[81]

Tompkins encouraged Porter not to relinquish his command. He had written to Washington on the subject of Porter's rank, presumably to see whether he could be offered a regular commission. Tompkins asserted the federal government would probably agree to the states' raising their own armies and "officering them with officers of the same grade in the army." If he persuaded the state legislature, Porter would be prominent in those plans.[82]

General Brown also urged Tompkins to increase Porter's command, stating that he was "a brave and efficient officer. In the midst of the greatest danger I have found his mind cool and collected, and his judgment to be relied upon. These are rare qualifications, and therefore it is that I desire all the militia force may be continued under his command." Brown had called for 1,000 additional militia. "This State has suffered in reputation this war," Brown wrote, ". . . I find the inhabitants of this frontier more disposed to skulk from the danger which threatens them than to arm in defense of their country and her rights."[83]

After the Battle of Lundy's Lane in early July, the Americans retired to Fort Erie with Maj. Gen. Edmund P. Gaines in command while Brown recuperated from his wounds. On the morning of August 15, about 2,000 British attempted to dislodge the Americans. Porter's New York and Pennsylvania volunteers, about 300 men, closely engaged a British column for two hours. The British were repulsed, and those killed included their commander, Col. Hercules Scott. A tremendous powder magazine explosion set off by an American soldier accounted for most of the 920 British killed, wounded, missing, and captured. Porter termed the battle a "brilliant action" and declared himself "satisfied with the conduct of the whole of my Brigade." Gaines's report to Secretary Armstrong praised Porter for his "military skill and courage in action, which proves him worthy the confidence of his country and the brave volunteers who fought under him."[84]

After the August 15 battle, General Gaines called out 4,000 New York volunteers for one to three months. Porter, chosen to raise and organize this force, hastened to Canandaigua. The response was enthusiastic but tardy. General McClure declared, "Unless some effectual mode of punishing delinquents is speedily adopted, future calls on militiamen will be useless, such is the language of those who have, and are still willing to do their share of duty." Nevertheless, Porter received reports that militiamen were "flocking in by companies" and that the turnout was "more liberal than possibly could be expected." Still, he was "apprehensive there will be a deficiency of arms and other implements . . . I observe they nearly all pass without any."[85]

A problem was created when Brig. Gen. Daniel Davis of Genesee County ordered out his whole brigade without authority. If regularly ordered out he would take the command from General Porter, which Governor Tompkins's aide, Lt. Col. J.B. Yates, said "would occasion very general dissatisfaction." Yates suggested that Porter be given a brevet rank of major general "to obviate any difficulty that may occur." General Davis, however, willingly served under Porter, who in fact had been given the rank of major general on August 22, although the announcement did not arrive until mid-September.[86]

While Porter was gathering this force in Buffalo, his old volunteers at Fort Erie engaged in another clash with the British on September 4. About 100 volunteers led by Lt. Col. Joseph Willcocks and Maj. Abraham Matteson sallied out and assaulted a British breastwork. After a sharp engagement of fifteen to twenty minutes, the Americans withdrew in good order, having inflicted heavy losses on the British. Unfortunately, Colonel Willcocks, a lieutenant, and three others were killed. Major Matteson in his report to General Ripley declared that the volunteers had "behaved in Spirit and manner characteristic of spartan bravery." Matteson added in a cover letter to Porter that General Ripley had "expressed great satisfaction and remarked that it was a brilliant action." Porter announced the engagement to his assembled militiamen in a general order. He concluded with pride, "The New York Volunteers have on this occasion, as well as every other that has occurred during the whole campaign, reflected honour on the State."[87]

His health restored, General Brown was back in command at Fort Erie. He urged Porter on September 8 to hurry his troops across the Niagara, "the more the better." Porter crossed on September 11 with approximately 1,000 men; another 500 came later. Brown hoped to mount an offensive operation against the British commander, besieging his position. He also urged Maj. Gen. George Izard, who was bringing troops from Plattsburgh to the Niagara frontier, to join him in an offensive. There were few British regulars between Kingston and Fort Erie, he wrote, and their militiamen "are worse than ours, they are good for nothing."[88]

Brown wasted no time in launching an offensive. On September 17, in a heavy rain, American forces attacked enemy batteries. In a severe engagement, the batteries were carried, the principal work was blown up, the guns were spiked, and the Americans retreated to the fort. British killed, wounded, and missing numbered around 800; the American total was 511. Four regular officers were slain, and five of Porter's officers were killed, including General Davis. Porter praised his veteran volunteers, who added "a new lustre on their former brilliant achievements." He also lauded his recently recruited militia volunteers. "They were not surpassed by the heroes of Chippewa and Niagara in steadiness and bravery," he declared. Brown also praised the militiamen to Tompkins: "The militia of New York have redeemed their character, they behaved gallantly."[89]

Porter had a narrow escape in the engagement of the seventeenth in which he suffered a slight wound to his hand. During the battle he moved with two or three of his aides from one of his columns through some woods to make contact with the other column. In the woods, however, he encountered sixty to eighty of the enemy, who were apparently confused about which way to go. They knew the Americans were operating to the rear, and they were now confronted by Porter and his staff. Porter coolly approached the soldiers, called upon them to surrender, seized a musket from one of the soldiers, threw it upon the ground, and called upon the others to do the same. Some voluntarily did so, but suddenly one soldier put his bayonet to Porter's breast and demanded his surrender. Porter grabbed the musket, but was wrestled to the ground by several of the soldiers. Fifteen or twenty now aimed their guns at him and called for his surrender. At that moment, however, more Americans arrived on the scene. Porter calmly called again for their surrender. When they refused, the Americans opened fire, killing several and taking the remainder as prisoners. Porter escaped with only a sword cut to his hand, which he declined even to mention in his report.[90]

Porter's courage and coolness amply demonstrated his leadership. If, as Porter argued, troops took the hue of their commander, then this incident illustrates why he was such a successful leader of militiamen and why they performed well for him and not for others. At a public gathering in his honor at Batavia near the end of October as his force was being disbanded, he said modestly, "If I have been more fortunate than the commandants of militia who have preceded me on this frontier, the whole credit is due to the brave officers who now surround me."[91]

The engagement of the seventeenth of September was the last

heavy fighting on the Niagara frontier that year. Unable or unwilling to mount an offensive, General Izard, now commanding on the Niagara, discharged Porter and his volunteers late in October, and the remaining regulars evacuated and blew up Fort Erie on November 5.

The New York legislature in October 1814 approved giving volunteers an additional five dollars a month above the pay and allowances from the national government. Unfortunately, the deputy paymaster for the northern frontier, J.L. Richardson, informed Porter on October 28 that he had no funds. In a general order of November 2 discharging his force, Porter advised those badly needing money that he and three of his officers had obtained a loan, "a small sum of money which will be distributed among this corps &, it is hoped, will enable them to meet their present necessities." The settlement of volunteer pay took a year, but claims for invalids and troops improperly mustered and pay for court-martial boards lingered for decades.[92]

Virtually no additional fighting occurred on the Niagara frontier for the remainder of the war. After all the fighting and suffering, no military objective had been gained, and the situation remained fixed. In retrospect, after the humiliations and defeats suffered in 1812 and 1813, the 1814 campaign did restore the pride of American regulars and somewhat redeemed the reputation of the New York militia. In recognition of their achievements during the War of 1812, Congress voted to strike gold medals for Generals Brown, Jackson, Scott, Ripley, Gaines, Macomb, and Miller of the regulars. Peter B. Porter was the only militia officer recognized.[93] His honor was a fitting and symbolic recognition that the militiamen had, after all, contributed to the war effort.

Chapter 7

The Atlantic Front and the Battle of Bladensburg

The entire Atlantic coast lay open to British incursions during the War of 1812. The American government, lacking money, did virtually nothing to raise fortifications for the protection of the inhabitants. The tiny American navy was spread too thin to offer much resistance or protection. Nor were the state militias much of a deterrent to British raids along the coast. During the war great turmoil was caused by the frequent threats, which necessitated militia callouts to respond to a menace that often failed to materialize, and the militiamen were sent home. When the attack proved real, the militiamen almost always seemed to be disorganized and poorly equipped, and they usually fled when confronted by the enemy.

The British were very active along the Atlantic coast and in the Chesapeake Bay in 1813. Under the command of Admiral Sir George Cockburn, they made several raids upon the largely unprotected communities on the Upper Chesapeake Bay. Havre de Grace, Fredericktown, and Georgetown, Maryland, were looted and burned in early May. The militiamen at these places put up little resistance, save for one lone, heroic militiaman, John O'Neill (or O'Neale), a naturalized Irishman, who stood his ground at Havre de Grace. He was captured by the British while trying to rally militiamen to fight. O'Neill was subsequently released and became a celebrity. He was voted a sword by Philadelphians.[1]

Maryland clearly felt imposed upon. Maryland, the most Federalist state outside New England, adopted the attitude that the national government, having declared war, now had the responsibility not only of providing for the defense of the states but also of compensating states for any expenses incurred by them in providing for their defense. The British navy hovering off the coast raised the anxiety of Marylanders about their vulnerability. Governor Levin Winder wrote on March 20,

1813, to recently appointed Secretary of War John Armstrong to ascertain "in the event of the militia of the state, being called out for its defence, whether the expense will be defrayed by the United States." Winder obviously knew the answer to the question, for he wrote a committee appointed by the town of Easton nine days later, informing them that the laws of Maryland vested full power in the militia commander to call out the troops in the event of invasion. If this exigency occurred, he explained, an application should be made to the president, who was authorized to place the militia in federal service, and the expense would then be borne by the national government. He advised the committee that he would forward their memorial to the secretary of war, and "if he thinks it advisable to station a force at Easton, it may be under the direction of the President of the United States and paid by the general government."[2]

In fact, President Madison authorized 500 troops for the defense of Annapolis on March 24 and 2,000 for Baltimore on April 16. Winder, still not satisfied, wrote Madison on April 26 that the enemy had visited Sharps Island and taken the supplies it needed. He lamented the fact that Maryland had only limited means for its defense and argued that the national government had a responsibility to protect states against invasion and defray all the expenses of a national war. "To us it is a painful reflection," he concluded, "that after every effort we have made, or can make for the security of our fellow citizens and their property, they have little to rely on, but the possible forbearance of the enemy."[3]

Winder informed the Maryland legislature on May 17 that requests for aid from the national government had not been answered. If the federal government failed to provide for the common defense, he asserted, "the law of self preservation . . . would demand that every effort . . . should be made for the safety of the State." He asserted, however, that ultimately "all expenses incurred in affording protection . . . ought to be reimbursed by the United States," and he urged the legislature to create an officer to keep accounts and vouchers of expenses to submit, eventually, to the national government.[4]

A deputation was sent from the Maryland Council to President Madison in the spring of 1813 carrying a resolution of the state, but Madison remained firm that he would pay only militiamen called out by the national government. Winder, faced with the obstinacy of the federal government, cautioned his militia officers about the need for careful expenditure of state funds. He wrote Gen. Thomas M. Forman on June 1, 1813, for example, "it becomes us all to be as sparing of expense as we possibly can be, as well as to expose the militia to as little inconvenience as possible." As the enemy had gone down the bay, he suggested, it would serve no good purpose to keep the militiamen called out in service.[5]

On June 22, the British assaulted Craney Island (at the approach to Norfolk, Virginia) with about 2,500 men. They were driven off, however, by American guns. British casualties may have amounted to 200, while the American force of perhaps 700 men had none. Three days later, about 2,000 British attacked Hampton, Virginia. Although one account stated that the American militia of less than 450 men "put up a spirited defence," they were forced to retreat before overwhelming numbers. Hampton was then subjected to many acts of rape, murder, and pillaging.[6]

With the British navy operating along the Atlantic coast, nervous inhabitants of seacoast towns in North Carolina, calling themselves defenseless, petitioned Governor William Hawkins for assistance. General Pinckney had given Hawkins authority to call out the state militia, "so many . . . as the occasion may require," in the event of actual or threatened attack, but as Hawkins well understood, militiamen without firearms and equipment would do little to deter a British attack. In June 1813, Hawkins wrote his two U.S. senators, James Turner and David Stone, enclosing petitions for assistance from inhabitants in Wilmington and Beaufort. "I deem it unnecessary to mention to you," Hawkins said, "that the State is *destitute* of *munitions of war*."[7]

Around July 1, a British force landed on the North Carolina coast in Carrituck County, near the Virginia border. Maj. Caleb Etheridge summoned two companies of the state militia, but they lacked weapons and Etheridge urged Governor Hawkins to send supplies. Hawkins replied that none were to be had immediately, or else he would have been disposed to purchase them on his own responsibility. He urged Etheridge, "With the aid of the patriotic citizens on your frontier, whose property is most in danger," to procure whatever supplies they needed and rely upon the government to compensate them later. "They are called out upon a requisition of General Pinckney," he added, "and the United States are bound to remunerate them."[8]

On July 12, British forces commanded by Adm. George Cockburn took possession of Portsmouth Island, near Ocracoke Inlet. North Carolina militiamen were hastily collected, and as usual, there were shortages of all kinds of supplies. Hawkins was besieged by requests for arms and ammunition. Typical of these was a letter from Col. Thomas Banks. Banks noted that on July 15 he ordered his troops to assemble at Elizabeth City. By noon the next day, he reported, he had gathered over 500 men, "but melancholy to say we had not more than 150 shot guns which could be depended upon & no ammunition." Fortunately, a schooner,

Globe, was in port and was willing to lend arms and cannon. According to Banks, reliable sources indicated that the British had returned to sea, and he had discharged his troops. He asked that the governor "direct in what manner the men are to be paid, for if this should be neglected, we may not be able to command men at any future time upon any sudden emergency." Another letter from Joseph H. Bryan, a quartermaster at Edenton, indicated that he had taken the initiative of going to Norfolk, Virginia, and buying 1,000 pounds of lead and powder, plus flints and cartridge paper on credit. He enclosed a bill amounting to less than $1,000, stating he hoped he had done the right thing.[9]

The excitement created by the British incursion generated many offers of support, which were often of the good news–bad news category. Maj. General Duncan Cameron, for example, wrote to Hawkins on July 23, that a battalion muster had just been held at Hillsborough, and "a very respectable company of volunteers was raised to be placed at the discretion of the Governor." He added that they would be armed with rifles, but he noted "the number of those I fear will be few; and indeed I am apprehensive that they will be very deficient in arms—of ammunition they will have not to carry from home; and if called into service must be furnished elsewhere."[10]

Many of the militiamen gathered at Wilmington were quartered in the houses of private citizens, in part because of a lack of camp equipment, while other militiamen were loaned camp kettles by inhabitants. It was obvious, however, that many of the militiamen found conditions not to their liking. Capt. Abner Pasteur, the commander at Fort Hampton, related to Hawkins that when one company arrived during the day on August 11, twenty deserted in the evening.[11]

The British were also active along the northern Atlantic coast, particularly the Maine coast in the fall of 1814. Eastport was seized in July, and in September, Castine was captured. Capt. Charles Morris, commander of the U.S.S. *Adams*, a twenty-eight-gun corvette, took refuge up the Penobscot at Hampden, where he hoped to fend off a British land force of 350. Learning of the approach of the enemy, Morris prepared his defenses and called upon the local militia to assist. Lieutenant Lewis of the U.S. Artillery arrived from Castine with twenty-eight men, and about 370 militiamen showed up. As Morris noted, however, "Many of the militia were without arms and most of them were without ammunition." Morris distributed muskets and ammunition from his ship to the militia. On October 3, three more companies of militiamen arrived. When the British made their first assault, however, the militiamen broke and fled in great confusion. Morris was forced to spike his guns, burn his ship, and retreat.[12]

When the British attacked near New London, Connecticut, in August, however, the local militiamen did not turn and flee. Instead they behaved bravely and repulsed the British attack. The British sustained fifteen killed and sixty-two wounded. No Americans were killed, and only five or six were wounded.[13]

The focus of the war shifted in the late summer and fall of 1814 to the Chesapeake Bay and Gulf coastal region. Again, the mettle of the militia would be tested, and the results were mixed. Washington's citizens were also alarmed by the British activity along the Atlantic coast and in the Chesapeake. The previous year, in mid-July 1813, some 300 volunteers responded to an alarm and were accompanied down the Potomac by both Secretary of War Armstrong and Secretary of State James Monroe. Many demanded fortifications for the defense of Washington. According to Maj. Gen. John P. Van Ness, commander of the District of Columbia militia, Armstrong "appeared rather indifferent, and expressed an opinion that the enemy would not come, or even seriously attempt to come to this District." In truth, Armstrong, under severe fiscal constraints, doubted that the District, given its remoteness, could be made safe physically by fortifications. The numerous points needing protection, he argued, would have "exhausted the Treasury." Rather, he said, "bayonets are known to form the most efficient barriers."[14]

Armstrong was undoubtedly correct, but his attitude, to say the least, disconcerted the residents of the District. Under pressure, he agreed to a proposition by District bankers to lend the government $200,000 to be used for the protection of the District. The money, however, was to be paid into the Treasury on August 24, 1814—the very day the British captured Washington. "The events of that day," Armstrong declared, "put an end to the business, and at the same time furnished evidence of the fallibility of the plan, had it even been executed, by showing that no works on the Potomac will, of themselves, be sufficient defence for the Seat of Government."[15]

President Madison was more sensitive to the concerns of the people of the District. No doubt he was also alarmed by the increased activity of the enemy in the Chesapeake in the early summer of 1814. Consequently, he met with his cabinet on July 1, and he created a new Tenth Military District on the Potomac. The next day, without consulting Armstrong, Madison named Brig. Gen. William Winder to command the District. Winder's chief qualification was that he was a nephew of Levin Winder, governor of Maryland. Obviously, Maryland's cooperation was critical to the defense of the District. About 1,000 regulars were assigned to the District, and 10,000 militiamen were to be held in

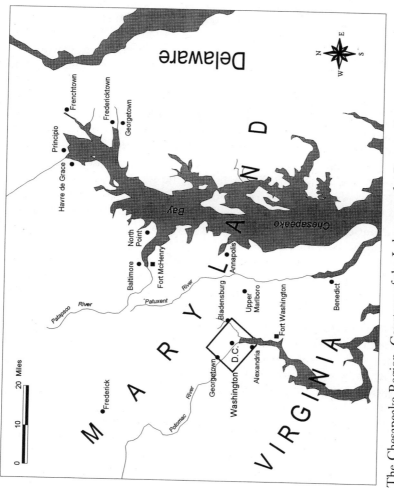

The Chesapeake Region. Courtesy of the Laboratory for Remote Sensing and Geographic Information Systems, Department of Geography, The University of Memphis.

readiness by neighboring states and the District of Columbia for a call from General Winder.[16]

Winder immediately suggested to Armstrong that a force of 4,000 militiamen be assembled "for one, two or three months." Armstrong, ever mindful of expense and convinced that militiamen who were not fighting would drain the Treasury, disagreed. He argued that militiamen could be used most advantageously "upon the spur of the occasion, and to bring them to fight as soon as called out." Winder insisted, quite correctly, that if the enemy did come to the District, it would be nearly impossible to collect a force upon the spur of the moment and bring them to bear upon the enemy. They would be little better than "a disorderly crowd, without arms, ammunition, or organization, before the enemy would already have given his blow." Armstrong remained adamant. He instructed Winder on July 12 to call out militiamen only "in case of actual or menaced invasion of the District," to avoid unnecessary calls, and "to proportion the call to the exigency." Winder did not appear to be mollified. On July 16, he wrote Armstrong that although the governor and Council of Maryland had taken steps to comply with the government's requisition for militia, "I fear, from my recent experience, it will be in vain to look for any efficient aid upon a sudden call upon the militia."[17]

In fact, the president shared Armstrong's view on the use of the militia. In June the British arrived about forty miles below Washington at the mouth of the Patuxent River. The Georgetown and Washington city militiamen were mobilized and marched down the river, and the British withdrew. Madison wrote Governor James Barbour of Virginia that with the objects of the enemy uncertain an immediate callout of the state's militia would waste resources, would exhaust the government's means, and would hazard everything. Once the enemy's object was clear, the resources and militia could be used effectively.[18]

On July 17 the British again reappeared on the Patuxent River. Three companies of the district militia were dispatched by General Winder toward the Patuxent. When they arrived at Woodyard, about ten miles from Washington, they learned that the British had retired down the river. Despite his earlier protests about needing to have militiamen readily available, Winder dismissed the militiamen rather than retain them to prepare defenses or for training. In fact, he declared, in terms that Armstrong no doubt approved, "The facility with which they can turn out and proceed to any point, renders them nearly as effective as if they were actually kept in the field; and the importance of them individually attending to their private affairs, decides me, even in doubt of the enemy's probable movement, to give this order."[19]

During the first month, Winder was constantly on the move and paid little attention to organizing his command. Not until July 23 did he designate Bladensburg, four miles north of Washington, as the rendezvous for the Maryland militia. He did not inspect the regulars of the Thirty-sixth and Thirty-eighth Regiments under his command until July 27, and he did not establish his headquarters in Washington until August 1.[20]

Winder inspected the militia of Washington on August 2, and he reported to Major General Van Ness, their commander, that the firearms of the uniformed companies were in order and ready for service. The remainder of the corps, while not to the standard of regulars, were "still effective and in better order than the army of militia usually are, or indeed, can reasonably be expected." The volunteer rifle companies' firearms, however, were "altogether unfit for service."[21]

The matter of arms, or rifles, for the volunteer company became an issue later on in the charges brought against Secretary Armstrong by the Washington community. According to J.I. Stull, captain of the Georgetown Rifles, a force of approximately 120 men, he appealed to Armstrong to release some of the rifles in the Washington arsenal. Armstrong refused, insisting that the rifles were intended for the northern army and could not be spared. Consequently, when the rifle companies were called out after the British landed, they were forced to take muskets, and they were further delayed in procuring ammunition and flints. As for the rifles that Armstrong refused to release, Stull noted, "It was understood and believed that those very arms . . . were destroyed by the British on the 25th August."[22]

Winder confronted many problems raising the Maryland militiamen for his command. On July 27 he informed Armstrong that the governor of Maryland "has been, in vain, endeavoring to assemble the neighboring militia at Annapolis; he had called on Frederick county, and some militia were coming in from thence." He added, however, "All this force is . . . called out by the authority of the State laws, and is not under my command. But they do and will cooperate toward the general defence." Problems persisted in raising the Maryland militia. On August 13, Winder wrote Armstrong from Baltimore that because the 2,000 militiamen called out in April counted as part of the July 4 quota, and because the Eastern Shore militia were needed for local defense, the Maryland militiamen to be assembled at Bladensburg, "instead of being three thousand, will not exceed as many hundred." Winder stated that he would have the governor summon all drafts from the western shore, but because they would amount to no more than 1,500, "I apprehend that, after all shall be assembled . . . , they will not exceed one thousand men." In the aftermath of the Washington debacle, Winder attributed the inefficiency in collecting the militiamen to "the incredulity of the people on the danger of invasion" and "the perplexed, broken, and harassed state of the militia" in various Maryland counties.[23]

Winder also intended to incorporate Pennsylvania militiamen into his command. On July 23 he proposed to Armstrong that as the Pennsylvania militiamen assigned to his district were in remote locations and could not be gathered quickly in an emergency, "might it not be expedient to draw from the remotest points, leaving that portion of the militia nearest the probable scene of action, to be called out on the spur of the occasion?" As late as August 13, Winder was still counting on a regiment of militia from Pennsylvania.[24] Because its militia was being reorganized, however, Pennsylvania was unable to comply with Winder's request.

On August 13, Winder issued general orders declaring that he had learned "with great pain" that a large number of Maryland's drafted militiamen had refused or neglected to go to Bladensburg as ordered. He suggested that many were "under the mistaken impression that there is no legal power to compel their compliance." He announced to all who neglected to attend that he would institute a court-martial with the power to impose a fine of eighty dollars upon each delinquent or one month of imprisonment for each five-dollar fine imposed. Unfortunately, Winder gave the militiamen until August 27 to rendezvous before steps would be taken to enforce the law. By that time the British had already burned Washington.[25]

As it developed, only 250 militiamen were at Bladensburg on August 18, the day the British landed at Benedict on the Patuxent with a force of about 4,500 regulars. This event, seemingly so unexpected, aroused a frenzy of activity. The militiamen of the district were called out en masse, and dispatches were sent to Maryland and Virginia for additional militiamen. Winder predicted to Armstrong, "The result of all these operations will be certainly slow, and extremely doubtful as to the extent of force produced."[26]

Confusion abounded. Secretary Armstrong even roused himself from his lethargy regarding affairs of the district. Heretofore he had largely ignored Winder. Perhaps he was overly sensitive because Madison had dictated affairs in the Tenth District and had selected Winder as commander of the district without consulting Armstrong. Perhaps it was also because Madison, after concluding his months-long investigation into Armstrong's conduct of his office, delivered a reprimand on August 13. The secretary was chastised for exceeding his authority and failing to consult Madison before exercising the powers of his office.

Now, after being exceedingly reticent about giving unsolicited advice, Armstrong urged Winder to obstruct the march of the enemy and to "drive off all horses and cattle, and remove all supplies of forage, and etc., on their route." He later recommended placing a force at the rear of the British to threaten their communications or, alternatively, withdrawing to the Capitol and placing artillery to induce them to engage in a siege operation, for which they were unprepared.[27]

No doubt Winder received plenty of advice during this confusing period. Madison wrote on August 21 to Monroe, who had gone off to scout the British movement, that "extensive & pressing calls have been made for militia, and we hope they will be prompt." Madison's opinion, which he no doubt shared with Winder, was that "as our troops will in general be raw, tho' numerous, the true course will be to pelt the Enemy from the start with light troops, taking advantage of grounds & positions for artillery, and throwing in all sorts of obstructions in the routes." Winder, totally perplexed by the movement of the British, was indecisive and unable to devise any plan to oppose their march. He envisaged numerous possible objectives. On August 22, the British camped at Upper Marlboro. From there, Winder later explained, "he could take the road to Bladensburg, to the Eastern Branch bridge, or Fort Washington, indifferently, or it might be to cover his march upon Annapolis."[28]

By August 23, Maj. Gen. Robert Ross, the British commander, had marched his troops, virtually unscathed, to within nine miles of the Eastern Branch bridge leading into Washington. Winder withdrew to the bridge with about 2,500 men. From this point, he explained later to a congressional investigative committee, he could harass the enemy if it moved toward Fort Washington or could follow if the enemy reversed its march and moved toward Annapolis, or he could rush to Bladensburg, five miles to the north, where he had a force about the same size, if it moved in there. A group of 700 Virginians led by Lt. Col. George Minor arrived that evening in Washington. They had no arms or ammunition, however, and Minor alleged that they spent the morning of the twenty-fourth collecting these items from the government arsenal, each flint painstakingly counted by a young armorer at the arsenal. As a consequence, just as they were ready to march to Bladensburg, they were met by the troops retreating from the battle.[29]

As soon as Winder received positive information that the enemy was on a march toward Bladensburg on the morning of the twenty-fourth, he hastened to that place with his troops. The American force, including Winder's, amounted to perhaps 7,000 men, while the British numbered no more than 4,500. Still, there was a vast difference in the quality of the two forces. In fact, Armstrong was quoted as saying injudiciously prior to the engagement that "as the battle would be between Militia and regular troops, the former would be beaten." In the aftermath of the battle, Winder candidly stated much the same to a correspondent of the *Baltimore Patriot*. He regretted that his force had not put up a stronger resistance, he said, but he believed that the British force outnumbered his. Moreover, "our force was principally militia, and that of the enemy all regulars and picked men."[30]

There was also a vast difference in the leadership of the two forces. In his statement to the congressional investigating committee, Winder complained of having to work with "raw, undisciplined, inexperienced, and unknown officers and men." The situation at Bladensburg when Winder arrived was that no one was really in charge. Brig. Gen. Tobias E. Stansbury, commander of the Maryland militia, was nominally in charge, and he made the initial deployment of the troops facing the British. Without Stansbury's knowledge and without authority, however, Secretary Monroe redeployed the troops in such a way that the second line could not support the first. Armstrong characterized Monroe later as a "busy and blundering tactician." Monroe no doubt thought he was helping, which is hardly a defense. Perhaps unaware of his blunder in positioning the troops, he proudly wrote his son-in-law shortly after the event that he had "formed the line, and made the disposition of our troops."[31] His action vividly demonstrates the lack of command at this critical time.

Winder arrived just before the British offensive began, and he had little time to inspect the line of battle. He hardly inspired his men with the will to fight. Instead, he instructed the troops that when—not if—they retreated, they should do so by the Georgetown road. The battle began on August 24 between 12:30 and 1:00 P.M. when British light infantry moved across a small bridge over the Eastern Branch of the Potomac. American artillery and riflemen contested their movement, but the British soon flanked them and forced them to retreat. General Stansbury's force, about 400 yards to the rear, rather than closing in, recoiled from British rocket fire. When Stansbury's right wing, exposed by Monroe's positioning, gave way, "a general flight of the two regiments" threatened to precipitate a rout. One group held firm, but Winder ordered them to retreat and reform in the rear. The first line, however, soon broke into disorder and confusion. The road from Bladensburg forked in three directions. In their panic the troops, forgetting Winder's instructions, streamed in all three directions: some toward Washington; some toward Tenleytown; and some toward Georgetown.[32]

The second line, although positioned too far to the rear to assist the first line, was prepared to stand firm, but Winder ordered the line to retreat and fall back a mile and a half and reform. When it did so, the troops were joined by Colonel Minor's Virginians, and they began to form a new line. Winder came up and soon gave orders to retire back to Capitol Hill. When this maneuver was performed, Winder consulted with Monroe and Armstrong on Capitol Hill to advocate a further retreat back to Georgetown. Given the diminished size of Winder's force and the general confusion, the commanders agreed that the recommendation to withdraw was probably wise. The order to retreat farther ended all discipline, and the defending force simply melted away. The city was left defenseless before the advancing enemy.[33]

The only serious resistance that the British met came from Comm. Joshua Barney's sailors. Barney's flotilla, which had been drawn up the Patuxent River for safety, had been the original objective of the British. But when he blew up his ships rather than allow them to fall into enemy hands, the British altered their objective to assault Washington. Barney and his sailors joined Winder and followed him to Bladensburg. Their guns delivered a devastating punishment to the British before they were eventually flanked and Barney was captured. In fact, the British, largely because of Barney's sailors, suffered greater casualties than the Americans, approximately 250 to 70.[34]

In the aftermath, Hezekiah Niles in his *Weekly Register* called the battle "this lamentable and disgraceful affair." The militia, he noted, "generally fled without firing a gun, and threw off every incumbrance of their speed!"[35] The fleetness of foot of American militiamen was memorialized in a satirical piece called "The Bladensburg Races."

While the militia system failed miserably in this instance, the blame must ultimately rest on the almost total incompetence of General Winder. Throughout the course of the battle he thought only of retreat. Every time the lines were reformed for battle, he called for further retreat. In fairness, he had little to do with the initial formation of the troops for battle, and he did not have the opportunity, as did General Andrew Jackson at New Orleans, of drawing his forces behind a barricade. Nonetheless, it is still difficult not to conclude that if the Americans had had a general who was willing to fight that day, they could have repulsed the British, who were, after all, taking a considerable risk by extending themselves deeply into enemy country. General Ross was well aware of the potential danger of his situation, and he did not tarry long in Washington after burning the public buildings of the city. He withdrew on August 25 after about thirty hours in the city.

The British next turned their attention toward Baltimore. Sir Peter Parker, captain of the British ship *Menelaus*, was already operating on the upper Chesapeake. On August 30, he learned of an American militia force of about 160 encamped near Chestertown, Maryland. The next day, Parker led a force of about 100 men in pursuit of the Americans, commanded by Lt. Col. Philip Reed. The American militia retreated some five miles inland, when Reed stopped his men and formed a defensive line. Parker charged the American line, forcing a retreat, but the militia reformed and drove the British off. Parker was killed trying to rally his men. In addition, ten of the British were killed, while the Americans suffered only three wounded.[36]

After the Chestertown affair, the British lost another leader when they attempted to repeat their success at Washington by capturing Baltimore. Maj. Gen. Samuel Smith of the Maryland militia outranked General Winder, and he raised a force of approximately 15,000 men to defend the city. When the British landed east of Baltimore at North Point with about 4,500 men, Smith sent Brig. Gen. John Stricker with 3,200 men to contest their approach. Stricker deployed and waited on the British, but his advance troops, about 150 riflemen, broke even before the British made contact early in the afternoon of September 12. Also, 700 men under Lieutenant Colonel Amey, posted to protect Stricker's left flank, as Stricker wrote later, "forgetful of the honour of the brigade, and regardless of its own reputation, delivered one random fire and retreated precipitately, and in such confusion, as to render every effort of mine to rally them ineffective." The flight caused confusion among the militia, and Stricker was forced to withdraw toward Baltimore.[37]

One consequence of this engagement, however, was the death of General Ross, shot while reconnoitering the enemy, reportedly by a boy from behind a tree. Col. Arthur Brooke assumed command and pushed the Americans back toward Baltimore. He was prepared to assault the city, when Admiral Alexander Cochrane informed him that because of obstructions in the city harbor (and of course the obstinacy of the defenders of Fort McHenry), he was calling off the attack on Baltimore.[38] The British then retired and the city was saved. Given the size of the defending force, it is unlikely that the British would have succeeded in any event.

After the British withdrew from Baltimore and the Chesapeake Bay area, they shifted their focus to the southern theater along the Gulf of Mexico. Fortunately for the reputation of the militia, the militiamen in the South performed better than their counterparts along the Atlantic seaboard. The Battle of Bladensburg represented probably the worst example of militia performance in the war. It illustrated in microcosm all of the things wrong with the militia in the War of 1812. The govern-

John Bull and the Baltimoreans, by William Charles (1814), Library of Congress, Political Prints, LC-USZ62-7431.

ment was forced to rely on state militia, which could not easily be gathered. When the militiamen were collected, there was a lack of organization, caused by mixing militias from different states, so that it was
difficult to establish lines of command. As usual, most militiamen appeared without weapons, accouterments, or supplies. Had the militiamen not been called out so hastily, many of these problems might
have been worked out; the troops might have borne a resemblance to
a real military force and not a group of strangers unprepared to act as
soldiers.

Chapter 8

Federal-State Relations

The very nature of the militia system, as discussed earlier, depended upon cooperation between the state and federal governments. Given state wariness about federal intrusion in the constitutional division of responsibility over the militia, it is perhaps not surprising that federal-state relations during the first declared war under the Constitution should have been strained. Clearly, however, there was a political element in the objections of the New England governors to the federal use of their militia. In the other regions there was willing cooperation, but state leaders confronted with innumerable problems in meeting federal requisitions of militia, like their counterparts in New England, began to address their situation in ways not contemplated by the Constitution, for example, by forming state armies and suggesting, at least, that taxes might be withheld from the federal government to meet the needs of the states.

As late as 1814, militia organization and the powers of regular officers over the militia created a controversy in Pennsylvania that resulted in a widely noticed court-martial. In late August, after the British burned Washington, Governor Simon Snyder, fearing an attack up the Delaware River, called out volunteer militiamen to defend Philadelphia. Among those volunteering was a detachment organized under Lt. Col. Louis Bache. Eventually, the Pennsylvania militia force was merged with regulars and was placed under U.S. Brig. Gen. Joseph Bloomfield, who commanded the Fourth Military District. Bache's force was ordered to join other troops assembling at Marcus Hook, on the Delaware about fifteen miles below Philadelphia. At the camp, however, because many militia companies were undermanned, Col. William Duane, adjutant general of the Fourth Military District, was forced to merge companies to comply with War Department orders that the companies in federal service must have 100 men. He combined units and, when a surplus of officers resulted, allowed the companies and the officers to work out their command arrangements. When they could not, lots were drawn, and some officers had to go home.[1]

Bache and his detachment of 351 men arrived in the camp in early October 1814, announcing that they were an auxiliary force, subject to orders from Governor Snyder, and that they would not be reorganized and would not serve under any but their own officers. Duane consulted with the new commander of the Fourth Military District, Maj. Gen. Edmund P. Gaines, who ordered Duane to comply with his orders to arrange the troops in compliance with War Department regulations. Duane paraded Bache's force on October 14, divided them into regulation-size companies, and instructed Bache to assign the due proportion of officers to each platoon, which meant that many officers would be sent home. Bache refused, stating that the "detachment under his command would be commanded by none but their own officers; that the men under his command would never submit to any consolidation of the companies."[2]

Bache was arrested, and five subordinate officers were successively ordered to comply; when they refused, all were arrested and ordered to leave the camp. Late that same afternoon, however, having received orders from Major General Worrell of the Pennsylvania militia, Bache returned to the camp. According to Duane a "tumultuous and disorderly" mob of about 500 men gathered that was "very rude and menacing." Although they were dispersed, "discipline and subordination in the camp were at an end."[3] Duane left the camp and informed General Gaines, who ordered the court-martial, which began at Chester on October 20 and moved to Philadelphia four days later.

Bache's defense was that "my detachment was secured against any change, having volunteered under the general orders of the governor, of the 27th August." Bache asserted that General Bloomfield had agreed with the governor that Bache's force was not to be reorganized. Colonel N.B. Boileau, aide-de-camp to Governor Snyder, confirmed that the governor stated to General Bloomfield that Bache's force was not to be reorganized and, furthermore, that the men were entitled to be commanded by their own officers because they believed they had been received into the service of the United States "under that understanding."[4]

Although General Bloomfield was not called to testify, he did write two letters to Duane, dated October 26 and 29, 1814, denying that he had made such an agreement. Duane's position was that once Bache's forces arrived in the camp, they were under the command of a U.S. officer; the camp commander was a Pennsylvania militia officer in U.S. service; the food and forage in camp was paid for by the United States;

and the camp was formed by the United States. When Gaines took command, he stated his position to Duane that the troops were called out "to fight the enemy, with which the governor had no right to interfere; two commanders in a camp was a *military monster*."[5]

In his closing remarks, Bache argued that the attempt to reorganize was "unjust, inexpedient, and wholly ruinous to the service." Many young men were allowed to volunteer only because their parents knew and trusted their officers. Reorganization would "produce general disgust and dissatisfaction among the men . . . no men will volunteer when it shall be known that neither the word of the governor, nor the solemn agreement of the U. States officers can afford either security or protection."[6]

In his summation, Duane observed that the case had roused passions, "tainted by the breath of faction, and held up to the public in the most distorted and extravagant forms." He declared that "the scandalous and humiliating paradoxes which excited so much odium in 1809, have been renewed." He was referring to the Supreme Court case of *United States v. Peters* and General Bright's defense that he was obeying orders from the governor and state law. Now, Duane said, the same doctrine was asserted, that the regulations of the government, the army, and military institutions were "to be overwhelmed by the same authority." But, he said, the state could not sanction resistance to the authority of the United States or permit subversion of subordination and discipline. "An army," he added, "must be governed like the human body— by one head and mind—one spirit and one will."[7]

Bache was found guilty of all charges (but not in every specific). The court was lenient, perhaps because it was sensitive to the political situation, or possibly because it was influenced by Duane's statement that he believed Bache did not understand the seriousness of his actions. The court ruled it was sensible of the "purity of the motives that actuated [Bache], resting as they did upon an honest misconception of his duties." Bache was dismissed from the service of the United States which, as he was a militia officer, was essentially no punishment.[8]

The Bache case was only one of many vexing problems of state-federal relations. Another difficulty was finance, namely, who was to pay the drafted militia. With only limited means, the national government understandably tried to curtail excessive state use of militiamen by refusing to pay for them unless they were called for by the federal government and inspected by a regular army officer. In fact, numerous claims for payment for militia drafts were denied when established rules were not followed. There were occasions, however, where states had to respond promptly to invasion by the enemy before the federal government authorized them. Governor James Barbour of Virginia expressed his anger and amazement when Secretary of War John Armstrong refused to pay for militiamen summoned by the governor to protect Norfolk early in 1813. Instead of "generous and unsuspecting confidence" in furthering the wishes of the government, Barbour declared, states would adopt "the close suspicion of the miser, who before he acts demands solid and unquestionable pledges." To appease Virginia, the administration paid that state's militia expenses. This step, however, angered Maryland, which had also been refused compensation for unauthorized militia drafts. A committee report of the Executive Council of Maryland accused the Madison administration of partiality in assuming Virginia's militia expenses while denying Maryland's. The Council adopted a resolution denouncing the administration's action as "partial, unjust, and contrary to the spirit of our constitution."[9]

Even when the states conformed to all of the federal requirements, such as getting the militia mustered and inspected by a regular officer, the national government was unable, or unwilling, to pay the militia because of a lack of funds. The shortage of money was due to the difficulty that Secretary of the Treasury Albert Gallatin had in borrowing capital from the financial markets, particularly in New England. Consequently, Secretary Armstrong opted to divert most War Department funds to the northern front. As a result, money to pay militia, build fortifications, and reimburse states was simply not available. The bureaucracy was also overwhelmed by bills forwarded for payment, often accompanied by improper or inadequate paperwork, and it refused to pay without adequate documentation.[10]

While the federal government adopted a parsimonious stance, many states went to extraordinary lengths to get the federal government to pay for militia calls. Governor Peter B. Early, for example, expressed this view candidly in a May 1814 letter to Maj. Gen. John McIntosh of the Georgia militia: "In every expenditure to which the crisis may give rise, we ought constantly so to manage that the United States may be made to bear it *immediately* if we can, ultimately if we *must*."[11] Such parsimony would have been commendable if the national government had had money to pay these claims. In fact, the lack of funds meant that virtually no claims were paid, even those that were admittedly valid.

In his December 1813 message to the Maryland legislature, Governor Levin Winder complained, "If the expenses of a war waged by the national authorities are to be borne by the States, it is not difficult to foresee that the state treasury will be soon exhausted and the annihilation of the state governments must follow." Winder indicated that the state's expenses had exceeded $175,000, with a considerable sum yet due. Despite his concern about expenses, Winder recommended that the legislature pay militia volunteers who had come from adjoining states in the spring of 1813 to assist in Maryland's defense.[12]

The question of federal compensation to Maryland militiamen was raised again in the fall of 1814 when they were called out for the defense of Washington and Baltimore. Although he was assured that Maryland would be reimbursed for expenses, William B. Martin, president of the Executive Council, reported to the legislature on December 10 that the national government had failed to respond despite repeated requests. He noted that the state had obtained loans amounting to $436,000, which was believed to be inadequate to meet militia claims already allowed.[13] Thus Maryland was forced to accept a substantial portion of its militia costs and undoubtedly believed it was being discriminated against. In fact, Maryland was simply one state of many that had to bear the burden of their own defense.

Governor Daniel Rodney of Delaware complained to his legislature on January 18, 1814, that an application should be made to Congress for reimbursement of expenses. It was unreasonable for a state to be burdened exclusively for the defense of the state, he argued. According to Secretary Armstrong, replying to a resolution of the U.S. House dated January 15, 1814, the problem was that states were not submitting proper claims for expenses. Virginia was the only state that had done so. Its claims had been adjudicated in the accountant's office, and disallowed expenditures had been returned to Virginia. Armstrong followed with another letter to House Speaker Langdon Cheves recommending more paymaster generals and deputies and setting up a special office to receive war claims.[14]

The fact remains that the states were not promptly remunerated for expenses, and by late 1814 the government had no money for reimbursement. This situation did not reduce the number of complaints. Governor William Miller of North Carolina, for example, informed his legislature in December 1814 that none of the troops or individuals who had furnished them supplies in 1813 had received payment. He asserted bluntly that "patriotism alone cannot be relied upon as a sufficient incentive to endure the hardships and privations of war. Men must be paid or they cannot be expected to fight." Unfortunately, the North Carolina militia called out in July and August 1813 did not comply with the War Department rules that it be inspected and placed on the rolls by a regular army officer. A resolution was adopted appointing a board of auditors to examine and pass on claims, and the legislature authorized $25,000 to settle the accounts. Not until 1916 was North Carolina reimbursed by the federal government for all of the expenditures incurred during the War of 1812.[15]

Similarly, Governor Isaac Shelby of Kentucky admonished Armstrong in August 1814 for the government's failure to pay the state's militia for past service. Shelby complained particularly about the treatment of the men who had marched with him into Canada in 1813. Because the government was withholding their pay, it had become his duty "to be more cautious in future, in complying with demands on this State for troops; and to come to an explicit understanding with the War Department on this subject." Noting that the failure to pay his troops was "damping the ardour of our Citizens," he added that those who served under Colonel Johnson "have long since been paid off in full. . . . The striking contrast presented by the different treatments of these two corps has been observed & remarked upon by every class of our Citizens." In fact, Armstrong's objection was that Shelby's militiamen cost about $300,000 more than a regular force, because they had enough officers for twelve regiments but had fewer bayonets than four regiments of regulars.[16]

Nor were the states willing to bear more than their fair share of expenses. Governor Early himself denied payment to some Georgia militiamen called out on state duty. In regard to paying militiamen ordered to serve at St. Mary's, Early stated to General Floyd late in June 1814, "where the term of service was short like this, I have declined making payment, giving for reason that to do so in all cases would exceed the means at my command, and that the service should be considered as a contribution due from every man to his Country, the more so especially as it was for the immediate purpose of defending his own fire side."[17]

Governor Early stated that he had secured an interest-free loan from a Savannah bank to assist the city in providing for its defense. Less than a month later, he reminded the legislature that the embarrassments of the general government meant that no funds had been deposited with the quartermaster department and, unless the legislature provided funds, the militia force called out to defend Savannah would not be able to march there. He urged the legislators to authorize a loan of $20,000 for that purpose.[18] Georgia was thus also forced to rely on its own resources to carry on the war and to provide for its defense because the bankrupt national government could not.

In February 1815, Governor David Holmes informed Acting Secretary of War James Monroe that he had drawn bills on the federal government of over $3,000. In March, Holmes complained that since the beginning of the war, the Mississippi Territory had kept in the field a considerable part of its effective force. Only two companies had received any remuneration and it had come in pursuance of orders from General Andrew Jackson. In June, Holmes reiterated his plea. "Almost every man in this Territory liable to perform military duty has served a tour of six months during the late war, either in person or by substitute. Very few have received any compensation." The problem, as in so many other cases, was that the Mississippi militia had not been properly inspected by a regular army officer. In January 1816, a committee of the U.S. House of Representatives recommended payment to Mississippi Territory militia, asserting that muster rolls were sufficient evidence, especially when they were operating so far from any regular corps.[19]

In New England, the tensions between federal and state officials raised in 1812 persisted in 1813. During the summer of 1813 the Massachusetts legislature investigated the actions of William King of Maine, who apparently raised a volunteer force without state authority. The legislative committee sought to determine whether King held any military commission under the United States or had accepted arms from the federal government. King responded that he held no commission and had distributed no arms. He admitted, however, that when the state withheld militia from the federal government, he aided the War Department in organizing volunteer corps for the defense of the Maine District. Two regiments were organized, and others had to be turned down. Arms had been distributed to these volunteers. Emphasizing that he had received no compensation for his services, King added that he had exercised his duties as a citizen of the United States as well as a citizen of the state.[20]

The British blockade along the New England coast in the spring of 1814 raised anxiety levels, and state officials, insofar as their principles permitted, attempted to cooperate with the federal government for their defense. In Massachusetts, an arrangement was worked out with the district commander, Brig. Gen. Thomas H. Cushing, who promised to keep the militiamen and regulars separate and to place no regular officer between himself and the militia. Cushing was soon replaced by Gen. Henry Dearborn, however, who promptly violated the agreement when he called out 1,300 militiamen in July. Not only did he consolidate some companies, thereby depriving some militia officers of their command, but he also placed a regular officer over the militia.[21]

In the meantime, Cushing was transferred to Connecticut, where he expected to exercise the same type of control over the militia that he had in Massachusetts. There, however, the situation had developed differently. When two militia regiments were called out in 1813 to protect New London, Connecticut, officials placed the militia under a major general who outranked the regular army officer. Although the militia force was nominally in federal service and was paid and supplied by the federal government, Connecticut effectively retained control over its militia. State officials tried the same tactic in September 1814, however, when a brigade of militia was called out to protect New London, and Cushing obstinately refused to cooperate. Governor John Cotton Smith, supported by his council, assigned a major general over the state's militia. When the state militia refused to follow his orders, Cushing declared that the militiamen had been withdrawn from federal service and cut off the flow of supplies to them. Connecticut was thus forced to assume the financial burden for these militiamen.[22]

In Massachusetts a slightly different set of circumstances led to the same result. Militiamen called out in September to defend Portland, in the Maine district, objected to serving under a regular officer and demanded their own militia officer. Eventually, all the militiamen were placed under a state commander, and thus, in the view of the federal government, they too had been withdrawn from federal service, so that Massachusetts had to assume the financial liability for them.[23]

The result was the same in Rhode Island, but the circumstances were different. When Governor William Jones called out the state militia in the summer of 1814 to protect Newport, the troops were put into federal service to gain financial support. Federal agents had no funds to supply the militia, however, and the state had to bear the costs anyway. Rhode Island's eventual expenses amounted only to $50,000, far less than the $850,000 for Massachusetts and $150,000 for Connecticut. Nevertheless, all three states expected the federal government to make restitution for their sacrifices.[24]

On September 7, 1814, Governor Caleb Strong of Massachusetts wrote the secretary of war and asked explicitly "whether the expenses thus necessarily incurred for our protection will be ultimately reimbursed to this State by the General Government." Acting Secretary Monroe responded on September 17, explaining the views of the government: "The measures which may be adopted by a State Government for the defence of a State must be considered as its own measures, and not those of the United States. The expenses attending them are chargeable to the State, and not to the United States." Monroe's added gratuitous remarks did not soften the blow. He pointed out that any other policy would have "pernicious consequences." Allowing states to undertake their own defense and to call out their militia at will and at federal expense would undermine national authority, he concluded, and would introduce a policy "the tendency of which I forbear to comment."[25]

One consequence of this correspondence was that a Massachusetts legislative committee, headed by Harrison Gray Otis, determined that Massachusetts, faced with increased national taxes, deprived of its commerce, harassed by the enemy, and required to provide for its own defense, must either submit or control its own resources. The committee complained about the men and measures that had brought on this situation and called for a conference of New England states with similar grievances. From this report grew the Hartford Convention to revise the Constitution.[26]

The above report was not gained without vigorous dissent in both houses of the Massachusetts legislature. A Senate minority report signed by thirteen members denounced the Hartford Convention as unwise and illegal. It also argued "that a separate army comports too well with a separate sovereignty, and that these men *may* at some future period be employed to settle domestic quarrels or enforce local interests." The minority attack in the House of Representatives was considered so strong that the majority declared it disrespectful and refused to enter the protest in the journal. In truth, the stance of the House minority was relatively moderate. It even agreed that the "sudden detachments of militia for short periods of service, has left no doubt of the preference for a permanent corps." But the minority also asserted that these troops must be raised under the provisions of the Constitution, with control given to the national government. They warned prophetically, "If this command be denied, neither the letter of the National compact, nor its spirit, by just construction, will sanction a claim to remuneration, and the expence of Troops, otherwise employed must fall exclusively upon the State." The minority also argued that, even with a state army, Massachusetts was obligated to defend the Union; that refusal to comply with legal requisitions not only violated national duty but would tend to the dissolution of the Union. It warned that any compact entered into by the Hartford Convention without the consent of Congress would be unconstitutional and could result in "civil dissentions and convulsions." Worse, the country could become "vanquished and tributary colonies to a haughty and implacable foreign foe."[27]

Because of the constitutional ramifications of the Hartford Convention, more attention has been paid to the challenge to federal authority than to the actual statement of grievances drafted by the delegates. In fact, at the heart of the report was the issue of federal control over state militia. After the preliminary statement, the first major grievance cited was "the claims and pretensions advanced, and the authority exercised over the militia, by the executive and legislative departments of the National Government." If these claims were conceded, it would "render nugatory the rightful authority of the States," and transferring control over the militias to the national government would "enable it at pleasure to destroy their liberties, and erect a military despotism on the ruins." If the declaration of the president be the "unerring test of the existence of these cases, this important power would depend, not upon the truths of the fact, but upon executive infallibility." Therefore, state authorities had as much duty "to watch over the rights *reserved*, as of the United States to exercise the powers which are *delegated*." The convention report also criticized the stationing of regular army officers in districts to command militia units called out. If these drafts or conscriptions be allowed, it was argued, "the whole militia may be converted into a standing army disposable at the will of the President of the United States." Part of the report laid out the proposition that states provide for their own protection and reserve a portion of their national taxes for defense.[28]

Perhaps the most damning indictment of the militia system, and an indication of its failure during the war, was the establishment of state armies. Had the war continued another year, it seems certain that a significant majority of the states would have forsaken reliance upon the militia and established permanent (standing) state armies. By 1815, at least ten of the eighteen states had adopted, or were in the process of adopting, laws establishing state armies. In three other states their governors recommended consideration of such a force.

In New England, Connecticut authorized in October 1812 two regiments of infantry, four companies of artillery, and four troops of horse to serve for the duration of the war. Governor John Cotton Smith, in a message to the legislature in the spring of 1813, made the assumption that must have been made in other states. "The sums it may be necessary to appropriate to this object," he declared, "we have a right to expect will be ultimately refunded by the general government; it being an essential purpose of the confederacy, that expences incurred in a common cause should be defrayed from a common treasury." Hezekiah Niles declared that Connecticut had availed itself of one of the negative clauses of the Constitution that barred states from keeping troops in time of peace and "construed this into an express admission that any state *in time of war* may keep on foot troops."[29]

In October 1814 the Connecticut legislature authorized the governor to raise a body of 1,000 for three years of service. Vermont in 1812 authorized a force of volunteers (number unspecified) to be subject to the orders of the governor for the duration of the war. Rhode Island's legislature directed the governor in June 1814 to raise a state corps and appoint officers "as soon as the President of the United States consents to receive them into service." Massachusetts approved a corps of 10,000 men in October 1814.[30]

In the Middle Atlantic region, Governor Daniel D. Tompkins, while saluting the achievements of the New York militia, reminded his legislature in late September 1814 of his earlier declaration that the burden of militia duty fell most heavily upon the poorer class. He again asked for reform of the militia system, arguing that the population and resources of New York enabled it to raise 10,000 state troops and 10,000 minutemen uniformed, equipped, and disciplined for local defense "as a substitute for ordinary militia." A few days later, he sent a message to the legislature detailing the various drafts of militia for the Niagara frontier, Sackets Harbor, New York City, and Lake Champlain. Because most militiamen appeared without firearms or equipment, the state spent $5,000 for arms and supplies. Observant persons, he argued, saw that "the expence, public inconvenience, waste and destruction of military stores, and interruption of agricultural pursuits, arising from calls on the ordinary militia . . . are totally disproportioned to their efficiency in service, and that therefore a resort to some other measure to repel invasion and to meet emergencies, is indispensable." He asked for the creation of an advanced corps of 20,000, so that the ordinary militia would be used only as a last resort.[31]

The legislature responded on October 24 by creating a 12,000-man state army and a reserve, making a permanent force of 20,000 men. The troops were, however, to be paid, clothed, and subsisted by the United States, and they were to be raised by "equal classification" (presumably, not allowing for exemptions).[32] The war ended before it could be tested whether the United States government would bear the cost of a New York army or, for that matter, whether the concept of "equal classification" would produce such an army.

Federalists attacked the New York law as conscription. One pamphlet, signed "By an Exempt," denounced it as "the abominable law of *conscription* disguised under the mild and deceptive name of *classification*." Although "ostensibly to relieve the poor . . . ," the author argued, "The real design is to supply the national government with twelve thousand recruits," subject to the orders of the president. The author concluded, the "noble body of militia, which, if well regulated, is a firm bulwark of civil liberty and national independence, shall be transformed into a dreadful engine of military despotism."[33]

As early as December 1812 a resolution was introduced in the Pennsylvania legislature to create two regiments (2,000 men) "to serve during the war in substitution of a portion of the quota of militia which may be demanded by the general government." Nothing was done, however, as Pennsylvania governor Simon Snyder observed to Maj. Gen. David Mead in February 1814. "It is a matter of regret," Snyder wrote, "that no mode of guarding against a sudden invasion of our lake frontier has been adopted less expensive to the State than the one pursued . . . ," and he added, "if calls *en masse* are continued, our ordinary resources will be altogether unequal." Snyder suggested a plan to keep a small force at possible invasion points and a system to alert militia held "in readiness to march in a moment's warning." His suggestion was made, he continued, "to prevent a dissipation of public treasure in the pursuit of measures which appear to me of doubtful utility." Snyder recommended in his December 1814 annual message that his legislature create "a few regiments, to serve during the war, for the defence of the state." A bill dated February 24, 1815, which originated in the Senate, passed to a second reading before peace was confirmed. It called for every twentieth man to volunteer for twelve months of duty and would indeed have created a state army.[34]

In New Jersey, Governor William S. Pennington contended in his message of January 1814: "It is next to impossible that the great body of militia should acquire much proficiency in tactics and discipline," and he urged his legislature to create a select corps such as a rifle corps. Experience showed, he said, that "they form the best corps of irregular troops." In October 1814 Pennington recommended to his legislature a "military corps of more durability than is compatible with the nature of militia service," but the war ended before the legislature could act.[35]

In January 1815, Maryland approved a state force of five regiments of infantry and five companies of artillery for a period of five years or the duration of the war. Use of this force was limited to the region bound by the Susquehanna River in Pennsylvania and the Blue Ridge Mountains and the James River in Virginia. The law stipulated that if the federal government did not accept the whole force, the governor was to scale its size accordingly.[36]

In the South Atlantic states, Virginia created a force in February 1813 of one regiment of infantry, one troop of cavalry, one company of riflemen, and two companies of artillery "to serve during the present war." The force was contingent, however, upon the national government's reimbursing Virginia for "all reasonable expenses incurred in consequence thereof." Perhaps fearing the precedent set by their own state, Madison and Monroe moved swiftly to negate the act. Monroe wrote Governor James Barbour on March 21, 1813, that he had not "examined the constitutional propriety of the measure," but he supposed every object contemplated by the law "might be secured by means of, and under the authority of, this government." Secretary Armstrong informed Barbour the next day that a draft of militia by the governor was approved by the president. Barbour responded on March 24 that the Council of State agreed with him that the law should not be executed, on the basis of their "ardent disposition to cherish concord between the two governments." Eventually, Barbour convened the legislature into extraordinary session. He advised the lawmakers that the general government had taken up their defense, had sanctioned the call of militia, and had authorized another regular regiment "to be officered by our citizens exclusively." Under these circumstances and the fact that carrying the state's law into effect would involve expenses of a half million dollars, as well as establishing "a precedent liable to be perverted to the worst of purposes," Barbour asked the legislature to repeal the law, which was done on May 26, 1813.[37]

Yet in October 1814, Governor Barbour asked his legislature "to consider whether a substitution of a permanent military force . . . would not be preferable to calling out and continuing in service large masses of militia; a system as burthensome to our citizens, as expensive to the commonwealth." He argued that by proper representations to the general government, arrangements could be made satisfactory to both governments. The legislature adopted a resolution asking the governor to query the national government whether the United States would pay for a state army as a substitute for militia.[38]

In early 1815, the Virginia legislature, characterizing the drafts of militia for short terms of service as "wasteful, expensive and improvident . . . , productive of an unnecessary and deplorable waste of lives, without any equivalent of public advantage," again created a force of up to 10,000 men. As before, the plan was contingent upon the federal government's agreement to pay, equip, clothe, and subsist these troops.[39]

North Carolina Governor William Hawkins recommended in late 1814 that his legislature organize a state corps to serve for two years, along with encampments for officers of fifteen days each in the spring and fall, but the war ended before the legislature took any action. South Carolina authorized in December 1814 a state army of two brigades (four regiments) for the duration of the war. It was stipulated that they be kept within the state for defense "unless in the case of an actual invasion of a contiguous state." The force was not to be organized until May 1, 1815, however, which was after the war was over.[40]

In the West, Governor Return J. Meigs, citing the disorganization of the Ohio militia, urged the legislature in his annual message of December 1812 to form companies of mounted volunteers to be held in constant readiness. "When occasion for this species of service . . . has occurred," he said, "so much time has unavoidably been consumed in associating—collecting and organizing—that the object has been lost, the movements not sufficiently simultaneous—too tardy for the emergency." Although the legislature did not act to establish a standing force, the idea resurfaced early in 1815. Thomas Worthington, Ohio's new governor, recommended that the legislature establish an elite corps to muster and train frequently at state expense and be the first to go when calls were made for troops. The plan was under consideration when the war ended.[41]

Kentucky, in effect, created two state armies. In 1813 the legislature authorized a force of up to 3,000 men for six months to be used as Governor Isaac Shelby chose. Near the end of the war, in January 1815, Shelby again cited the urgent need for a state army: "We have too deep an interest at stake to rest our sole reliance upon the General Government," and he recommended a 10,000-man force. Peace came, however, before the Kentucky legislature acted upon the recommendation. Undoubtedly, they would have granted the popular governor's request.[42]

How the state armies would have related to the United States army, and what impact such standing armies would have had upon the concept of republicanism, are just two issues that would have aggravated state-federal relations had the war continued another year. Certainly the question of how the state armies would be paid would have arisen between the states and the national government. Many of the state laws, as noted, were contingent upon the federal government's footing the bill. To say the least, such an eventuality was unlikely.

It is quite possible that the states would have adopted the idea broached in the Hartford Convention and suggested as well by Ohio and Virginia near the end of the war, namely, withholding direct taxes owed by the state to the federal government to cover the state's costs in paying their militias and providing for their defense. The case of Massachusetts and Connecticut is easily understood because of their long-standing differences with the administration. Connecticut governor John Cotton Smith affirmed his support for the recommendation of the Hartford Convention that states assuming the burden of defense should retain a portion of the taxes collected within the state to meet state defense needs. "The plainest principles of justice and self-preservation demand," he said, "that whilst the burden of defence is laid upon the state so much of its resources as may be adequate to that end, should in any event be retained."[43]

Ohio's proposal was apparently more innocent. The state legislature adopted a resolution late in 1814 proposing essentially that the state pay its direct taxes instead to its citizens who had unpaid claims against the federal government. In forwarding the proposal to Treasury Secretary Alexander James Dallas early in January 1815, Governor Worthington declared that because the national government had failed to meet its obligations, "feelings of dissatisfaction are created towards the government, which cannot too soon be removed." Dallas, at least, saw the dangers of such a move. His emphatic refusal brought an apologetic reply from Worthington, who declared that the motives of his legislature were "patriotic." He added that they had no desire, as Dallas had phrased it, "to procure a partial accommodation, for the citizens of Ohio, at the expense of an injury to the fiscal affairs of the General Government."[44]

Dallas did, however, sanction another use of direct taxes. Governor David Williams of South Carolina wrote Dallas on December 22, 1814, that having been informed by Maj. Gen. Thomas Pinckney that he had no funds to subsist his troops, he had recommended to his legislature that their direct taxes be applied to this need. Accordingly, $260,000 had been appropriated and placed in the Bank of South Carolina for that purpose. The $260,000 figure was only an estimate of direct taxes owed; the state promised to make up any additional sum. In fact, South Carolina's share came to nearly $304,000.[45] South Carolina's innovative use of its direct taxes was satisfactory, but it is very likely that had the war continued and the national government remained bankrupt and unable to meet its obligations to pay states for their war costs, many other states would have withheld their funds from the national government to meet their own desperate needs.

State-federal relations during the War of 1812 were thus often turbulent. Partisan politics in Congress precluded a cooperative effort, and Federalist governors used their most powerful weapon in opposition to the war, that of withholding their militias from the federal government. The states' rights arguments used by the Federalists were a convenient shield to rationalize their antiwar opposition. Joseph Gales, in December 1814, editorialized in the pages of the *Daily National Intelligencer* against the Federalist opposition. "The doctrines which they advance in relation to the militia," he wrote, "are calculated entirely to destroy its efficacy." The Federalist contention that the militia was "exclusively a *state force*, and disposable by the National Government, only in cases of *actual* invasion, *actual* insurrection, &c. and then only through the agency of state authorities," Gales asserted, stripped the nation of its "natural defensive force" and would leave the nation at the mercy of the enemy or upon the "liberality of state governments." Such a situation was never contemplated by the Constitution, he declared.[46]

Governor Strong of Massachusetts argued, no doubt with perfect sincerity, that states were the guardians of their sovereignty and the rights of individual citizens. As he informed his legislature in January 1815, it was their duty "to guard the Constitution itself, as well against silent and slow attacks, as more open and daring violations."[47]

The constitutional question was not addressed in Congress until after the war was over. Speaking for the administration, Secretary of War Monroe forwarded the relevant documents to the Senate. In an accompanying letter, he asserted that the right of the government to call out the militia for the purposes specified in the Constitution was "unconditional." "It was obviously the intention of the framers of the Constitution," he argued, "that these powers, vested in the general government, should be independent of the states' authorities, and adequate to the ends proposed." As precedents he cited occasions under President George Washington when the permission of state governors had not been asked for militia drafts. He contended that when militia entered federal service "all State authority over them ceases"; such a national force, paid by the nation, would serve under the command of regular officers. The assertion by the Massachusetts judges that only the president could command the militia in the field, Monroe declared, "pushes the doctrine of State rights further than I have ever known it to be carried in any other instance."[48]

William Branch Giles of Virginia reported for the Senate Committee on Military Affairs on February 28, 1815. He observed that a return of peace had relieved the committee of providing a legislative remedy, but he asserted that in a future war the same question might be raised again and that the problem might deprive the United States of the "most efficient legitimate means of prosecuting . . . war." The pretensions of the state authorities were "not warranted by the Constitution, nor deducible from any fair and just interpretation of its principles and objects." That position, he concluded, would render the national government unable to provide for the common defense and would "change the fundamental character of the Constitution itself, and thus eventually . . . produce its destruction." Not until a decade later, after Massachusetts recanted its position, did the national government consider Massachusetts's militia claim (and it was not paid until 1862). In 1827 the Supreme Court delivered a conclusive decision in *Martin v. Mott* that the authority to call out the militia belonged exclusively to the president.[49]

Chapter 9

War in the South and the Battle of New Orleans

W hile militiamen and their officers frequently confronted professional British soldiers in the North, militiamen in the South were called upon to fight a different kind of war against Indians. The Indians were a traditional enemy, and the militias should have been better prepared to fight them. Nevertheless, the results were mixed. Southern militias encountered many of the same problems plaguing their counterparts in the North and some that were new. When Gen. James Wilkinson called upon Louisiana governor William C.C. Claiborne for assistance after war was declared in June 1812, for example, Claiborne, apparently considering the territorial law of April 1811 invalid, expressed his regret that the lack of a militia law prevented him from cooperating with the regular army for the defense of the state. Although the legislature finally passed a law in February 1813, a lack of weapons and supplies still hampered the organization of the Louisiana militia to meet the needs for war.[1]

Claiborne wrote in May 1813 to James Brown and Eligius Fromentin, the two Louisiana senators, asking their help in securing a loan of arms from the national government. General Wilkinson, he noted, was able to furnish only 600 of the 4,000 muskets that the state needed. "I am making every exertion to organize the militia & to place it on the best possible footing," he wrote, "but the want of arms, and the impossibility of obtaining them, by private purchases, discourage officers & men & check all military ardour." On June 10, learning that the Third Regiment of the United States Army had been ordered out of the state, Claiborne again wrote his senators to represent to the government that the regular force could not be diminished without endangering the safety of the state. "The militia are not & cannot for some time be made efficient," he wrote, "the want of arms & munitions of war, are sources of great embarrassment."[2]

Lack of arms was not the only predicament. When General Flournoy called upon Claiborne in early June to hold 1,500 militiamen in readiness, Claiborne pleaded for time, noting that the militia was "in a state of great derangement" due to the necessity of electing captains and subalterns under the new militia law. Thus, a year after the declaration of war, Louisiana's militia still had not been organized.[3]

In late June 1813, Secretary of War John Armstrong, perhaps in response to the lobbying of the Louisiana senators, promised to send 2,000 stand of arms to Louisiana via Pittsburgh down the Ohio and Mississippi Rivers. For some reason, the number of arms was reduced to 1,500, but the shipment was very tardy. In September, Claiborne informed Flournoy that he was trying to arrange shipment from Pittsburgh, but he feared that they would not arrive for another two or three months. At the same time, Claiborne encouraged Senator Fromentin to see if several hundred sabers could also be shipped to Louisiana. "The Creoles of this country are very partial to cavalry service," he explained, "and in some parts of our State, particularly the Western District, they are the kind of troops that could act with greatest advantage."[4]

Thus the usual problems, lack of arms and supplies, not to mention the lack of organization, discipline, and leadership, plagued southern states and contributed to many of the failures of militia. The war in the South began in July 1813 when militiamen from the Mississippi Territory, having learned that Creek warriors had visited Spanish officials in Pensacola to obtain arms, ambushed the Indians at Burnt Corn Creek in Alabama. The attack was initially successful, but the Indians regrouped and scattered the militia. One account stated, "nothing saved our men from a general slaughter but the inability of the Indians to overtake them." In retaliation, the Upper Creeks, or "Red Sticks," as the war party was called, who were living in Alabama, attacked Fort Mims (about forty miles north of Mobile) on August 30. The fort was caught by surprise, and over 250 people, including women and children, were slaughtered.[5] Reports of the massacre rippled through the South and led to cries for revenge.

Governor David Holmes in the Mississippi Territory was quite willing to cooperate, but the lack of supplies was a constant problem. When the Creek War broke out in 1813, he agreed to summon his troops if he could procure supplies from the regulars. He advised Brig. Gen. Thomas Flournoy on August 12 that "to delay the troops until ammunition, camp equipage, &c. could be sent from Orleans would be

The Southern Theater. Courtesy of the Laboratory for Remote Sensing and Geographic Information Systems, Department of Geography, The University of Memphis.

to abandon the object of calling them out." He promised to try to procure what supplies he could and send them on. When General Flournoy informed Holmes that he did not have the authority to call out the troops, however, and the Mississippi troops could not be entered into the service of the United States, Holmes backed off. "The Territory has not the funds requisite to furnish camp equipage, forage, and ammunition without which troops cannot be marched to a distant part of the country. . . . I shall not embody the troops," he continued, "until I receive further information upon the subject."[6]

Holmes wrote Mississippi territorial judge Harry Toulmin that the failure to embody the force to march to Fort Stoddart was "a source of much mortification, and real distress." He said he assumed that Flournoy possessed the same powers as Wilkinson to call upon the militia. The news of the massacre at Fort Mims on the Alabama River in late August, however, changed the situation as far as Holmes was concerned. He ordered all of the cavalry of the territory into service (four troops, or about 200 men). Supplies were purchased upon the credit of the War Department, and Holmes wrote General Flournoy, "I am confident the President will consider them as in the service of the United States." Holmes explained to Armstrong why he called out the troops, and he confidently assumed that the government would pay for them and that suppliers would accept government IOUs. He announced he had drawn upon the War Department for $2,000, but he promised "no more money will be expended than is absolutely requisite." Flournoy refused to take responsibility for these militia. Holmes traveled to Fort Stoddart to smooth things over, but Flournoy had departed for New Orleans before he arrived. Nevertheless, the cavalry remained in service.[7]

In fact, even prior to the incident at Burnt Corn, the War Department had authorized a draft of militia. On July 13, 1813, Secretary Armstrong had instructed Tennessee and Georgia each to call out 1,500 men. Governor Willie Blount of Tennessee, however, interpreted the letter as only an alert to his militia. After Burnt Corn and Fort Mims, Governor David Mitchell of Georgia, learning of Blount's lack of action, informed the War Department that he was summoning 2,500 men. Blount and his legislature belatedly authorized not 1,500 but 3,500 for service against the Creeks. President Madison approved this additional force, despite Armstrong's protests about excessive costs. To avoid having a militia general, Maj. Gen. Andrew Jackson, outrank Brig. Gen. Thomas Flournoy, the commander of the Seventh Military District, Maj. Gen. Thomas Pinckney's Sixth Military District was extended, and he was placed in command of the Creek operation.[8]

In addition to the above-mentioned force, Brig. Gen. Ferdinand Claiborne's Mississippi Volunteers had been called out earlier. While there was certainly a sufficient force authorized to engage the Creeks, there were serious problems of supply because the contractors were unable on such short notice to gather adequate quantities of food and other necessities to meet the demands of the militia force being collected. Moreover, there were organizational problems and a lack of co-ordination and cooperation among the various forces designated to engage the Creeks. Two armies from Tennessee, one from East Tennessee under Gen. John Cocke, and the other from West Tennessee under Gen. Andrew Jackson, were to converge in northern Alabama under Jackson and drive the Creeks southward. Another force of Georgia militia under Brig. Gen. John Floyd was to proceed westward into Alabama and meet the Tennessee force at the junction of the Coosa and Tallapoosa Rivers. Meanwhile, a fourth army, composed of the Third Regiment of the U.S. Army and Mississippi Territory militia, commanded by Gen. Claiborne, was to advance up the Alabama River and join with the other armies.[9]

Claiborne was the first to act. In early October he advanced towards the Alabama River from Fort Stephens on the Tombigbee. General Flournoy, however, refused to accept Maj. Thomas Hinds's Mississippi Dragoons, despite Claiborne's protests. Flournoy contended that Hinds's force was called out under Governor Holmes's authority and instructed Claiborne to "have nothing to do with them." Flournoy obviously resented being superseded by General Pinckney, and these hurt feelings impinged on the campaign. He advised Claiborne to take a defensive posture until he was joined by Jackson and the Tennesseans. "You had better never fight a battle, than run the risk of defeat," he cautioned, because it would "not only prove the destruction of the frontier inhabitants, but will in all likelihood lead to the destruction of the whole country." Flournoy informed Claiborne in early November that he was returning to New Orleans and that he no longer considered the Third Regiment of regulars under Col. Gilbert Russell under his command, thereby freeing them to join Claiborne. "It concerns me that I am not to be among the conquerors of the Creek Indians," Flournoy wrote. "But this seems to be determined otherwise by a power beyond my control."[10]

Despite Flournoy's cautionary advice, Claiborne, with about 1,200 men, moved into the Indian country and captured the Creek village of Holy Ground, near the juncture of the Alabama and Cahaba Rivers. A large quantity of supplies, which the Indians badly needed, was captured and another village nearby destroyed. Claiborne wrote Secretary

Armstrong that he would have marched on and destroyed other towns but for the condition of his troops, "who were destitute of shoes or cloathing [*sic*], not having been paid for several months past; and the want of provision which from the difficulty in procuring transportation, could not be obtained." He did erect Fort Claiborne, about eighty-five miles above the old Fort Mims on the Alabama River, but in January 1814 Claiborne had to dismiss his militiamen whose terms had expired. Only the Third Regiment of regulars remained to engage the Creeks in south Alabama.[11]

After his campaign against the Creek Indians in the fall of 1813, General Claiborne wrote Armstrong on January 24, 1814, explaining why his militiamen refused to enlist in the regular army. His Mississippi Volunteers were returning to their homes "with eight months pay due to them and almost *literally naked.* They have served for two or three months of an inclement winter, without *shoes or blankets* and almost without shirts." He added that they were "still attached to their country, and properly impressed with the justice and necessity of the war," but "as they believe that some of these sufferings and privations were not unavoidable, they have for some months past almost uniformly declined prolonging their terms of service by enlisting in the regular army."[12]

With the terms of the militia called out in September due to expire in April, Holmes informed Flournoy in March 1814 that he was summoning replacement militiamen without federal authorization because he deemed it essential to keep up a force on the frontier until the war was ended. Six companies were drafted, and Holmes again drew upon the War Department for $1,900 to equip and furnish this militia force.[13]

Meanwhile, in Georgia, Governor Mitchell wrote anxiously that his militia was "destitute of all supplies. This state is not possessed of any camp equipage and of but very little ammunition." Having said so, he wrote that he would "confidently rely upon a refund by the United States of the money I advance for the detachment."[14]

When the Georgia militia rendezvoused in late August at Fort Hawkins in western Georgia, a "small difficulty" presented itself. War Department rules stated not only that the militiamen had to be inspected by a federal officer but that they also had to be organized into companies of 100 privates and 5 officers. Georgia's militia, however, was organized into companies of 75 rank and file and 3 officers. The regular army officer at Fort Hawkins, Capt. Philip Cook, refused to inspect the companies if they were not properly organized. Mitchell informed Armstrong that "a reorganization of them at this time will be productive of serious inconvenience." He also asserted to Cook that the War Department regulation was "contrary to law" and a matter for the governor and secretary of war to settle. He urged Cook to accept the force as organized, lest he endanger "the enterprize for which they have been called into the field." When Cook refused to budge, Mitchell wrote Brig. Gen. John Floyd that Cook's refusal was "of no importance; direct the Adjutant General to prepare the troops, and the Brigade Major to inspect them, who will make a regular return which will be certified by yourself, one copy to me & the other to the Secretary of War." He added, "I will endeavour to make that answer in place of one made by a United States officer."[15]

Although the Georgia militia rendezvoused at Fort Hawkins on August 25, Mitchell advised Armstrong on September 14 that no contractor had yet shown up and no funds had been received from the quartermaster department. Mitchell had been obliged to advance state money, but he warned that he could not do so much longer. He also cautioned that if the troops were allowed to suffer it would cause "a state of discontent which may eventually prove very injurious to the intended service."[16]

By mid-September, General Floyd's force amounted to nearly 2,400 men, but he was plagued by supply problems and sickness that delayed his movement into Creek country. Reorganizing his volunteer and militia units delayed him further. In November he reached the Chattahoochee River and constructed Fort Mitchell. In late November he advanced toward Autosse, an Indian town on the Tallapoosa River. His army was detected by the Indians, who were more sizable in number than Floyd had anticipated. The ensuing battle was hard fought on both sides, but in the end Floyd's artillery and a bayonet charge broke the Indian line, and he won an important victory, killing over 200 Creeks. A shortage of supplies obliged him to retire to Fort Mitchell rather than pursue the demoralized Indians.[17]

Plagued by supply problems and the approaching expiration of his militia terms in February, Floyd advanced about forty miles west of the Chattahoochee and built Fort Hull. From there he again entered into Creek country, but he was surprised on January 27, 1814 by an ambush. Floyd and his men were able to fight off the Indians, but he suffered twenty-six killed and about 150 wounded. The Creeks had forty-nine killed in the attack.[18]

Floyd retired to Fort Hull, and his militiamen, with their enlistments running out, threatened to leave the camp with or without their officers. Floyd withdrew to Georgia, and South Carolina militiamen were called out to assist the Georgians. Floyd left a situation not unlike that left by General Claiborne. While there had been some success against the Indians, no knockout blow had been delivered.

Peter Early, who succeeded Mitchell in the Georgia governorship, informed Secretary Armstrong in November 1813 that the quartermaster department had no funds and that the state legislature had authorized $20,000, which he had gotten by loan for 120 days. He indicated that a portion of this fund would be applied to an additional militia force he had called out following an Indian raid on November 6 on the frontier. Early made it clear that the legislature expected the national government to pay, "the case being one both of actual invasion and such imminent danger of repetition as would not admit of delay, it constitutes I apprehend, a strong claim." On January 12, 1814, not having received a response to his previous letter, Early again wrote Armstrong. He was anxious to know whether the government was going to pay, for the loan came due on March 24. Early also communicated with Congressman George M. Troup to learn whether the government intended to pay the Georgia troops in service. Their term expired February 25, they had not received one cent from the government, and they were suffering great privations.[19]

Early's fears were realized. The troops at Fort Mitchell became mutinous, and General Floyd warned that he might have to relinquish the fort before South Carolina militiamen arrived to relieve them. Early advised General Pinckney in early February that if the troops abandoned General Floyd, "I earnestly hope that all such may be returned as deserters & made to suffer all the privations and punishment due to such conduct."[20]

Whether it was a lack of pay, miserable conditions, or other factors, Governor Early lamented to General Pinckney in fall 1814 that he was "grieved" to learn that the detachment of militiamen "now garrisoning the forts westwardly are in a miserable state of insubordination and entirely without discipline." He asserted that an application had been made for the arrest of the major commanding. In fact, Early urged Pinckney to place Maj. Philip Cook, a regular officer, in command, but Pinckney declined.[21]

General Jackson's Tennessee militia faced the same supply problems that Floyd confronted. Despite his shortages, Jackson aggressively advanced into Creek country. He sent Gen. John Coffee to raid the Black Warrior River towns in October 1813. With his main army, Jackson moved to the area of Ten Islands on the Coosa River in late October and built Fort Strother. On November 3, Jackson ordered Coffee to destroy the Indian town of Tallushatchee, about eight miles away. Coffee estimated he had killed approximately 200 Indians while sustaining five fatalities. In his report to Jackson, Coffee praised his men's "deliberation and firmness": indeed, "all appeared cool and determined."

On November 7, Jackson marched with about 2,000 men toward Talladega, a friendly Creek village under attack by Red Sticks. Approximately 1,100 Creeks were besieging the town. On November 8, Jackson's men encircled the attackers. His plan was to entice the enemy toward his main force and then counterattack. Instead of attacking, however, the militiamen retreated before the approaching Indians. Jackson rushed in his cavalry to break the Indian charge. The militia, Jackson noted, "speedily rallied," but he was clearly displeased. "Had I not been compelled by the *faux pas* of the militia in the onset of the battle, to dismount my reserve, I believe not a man of them would have escaped." Most of the Creeks made their escape, but not before about 300 were killed.[22] As with General Floyd, Jackson's supply shortage forced him to withdraw rather than pursue a defeated group of Indians to deliver a knockout blow.

Gen. John Cocke, a political rival of Jackson, failed to join with Jackson's force as had been planned by the state governors early in the campaign. Instead, Cocke destroyed some towns of the Upper Creeks between November 11 and November 17, culminating in the destruction of Hillabee Towns the next day. Had Cocke cooperated and joined his force with Jackson's, the Creek resistance might have been broken before the end of the year. Jackson was furious, and he eventually brought charges against Cocke, who was acquitted by the court-martial.[23]

Jackson continued to be plagued by lack of supplies and by the expiration of militia terms. At one point his force at Fort Strother dwindled to 130 men. Reports of the chronic lack of supplies and food, in fact, made one group of 200 militiamen marching to join Jackson desert and return home instead. When he was able to gather approximately 800 fresh troops in January 1814, Jackson wasted no time in moving again into Indian country. On January 15 he led about 1,000 men, including friendly Indians, across the Coosa River. By January 18 he reached Talladega, where additional friendly Indians (between 200 and 300) joined. Two days later Jackson approached the enemy encamped at Emuckfau. "The insubordination of the new troops, and the want of skill in most of their officers became more & more apparent," Jackson later informed General Pinckney. The Red Sticks, perhaps realizing that Jackson was overextended and vulnerable, attacked on January 22, but they were repelled. Jackson decided to abandon his campaign and began to withdraw toward Fort Strother. After crossing Enitachopco Creek on the twenty-fourth, he was again assaulted by the Red Sticks. The First Regiment of West Tennessee Volunteer mounted gunmen was assigned the task of rear guard. Earlier, they had performed well, but now they unfortunately broke and ran. Jackson's account of the battle asserted that "This shameful retreat was disastrous in the extreme." Fortunately, the regulars and artillery held firm and after a desperate fight drove off the enemy. Jackson contended that but for "the unfortunate retreat of the rear guard in the affair of the 24th inst., I think I could safely have said that no army of militia ever acted with more cool and deliberate bravery." Upon reflection, he added that the failures on the twenty-fourth "ought rather to be ascribed to the want of conduct in many of their officers than to any cowardice in the men." The commander of the West Tennessee Volunteers, Col. Nicholas Tate Perkins, and Lt. Col. John Stump, second in command, were court-martialed for cowardice, disobedience, and abandoning their posts. Perkins was acquitted, but Stump was cashiered.[24]

Returning to Fort Strother, Jackson began to assemble a capable army. When a militia captain argued "that no power existed but the president of the United States" to order him and his troops out, Jackson replied angrily that the captain's position was "calculated to sow seeds of sedition & disobedience." He reminded the captain that his company was called into the service of the United States by Maj. Gen. Thomas Pinckney and that Jackson commanded all the troops in Tennessee in the service of the United States. He expected the captain and his men to organize and march immediately.[25]

Governor Blount had called out 5,000 militia, and General Pinckney augmented Jackson's force by assigning the Thirty-ninth Regiment of regulars. By early March 1814, Jackson had a large force, carefully disciplined, to move again into Indian country. With the addition of about 1,000 friendly Indians, he approached the strongly fortified main enemy encampment on the Tallapoosa River known as Horseshoe Bend. On March 27, after placing General Coffee's force across the river behind the enemy, Jackson's army assaulted the main enemy fortifications. The combination of attacks from the front and rear eventually broke the Creek resistance, and Jackson won a major victory. His army suffered 49 killed and 153 wounded, but somewhere between 800 and 900 of the Indians were killed. Although Coffee's Tennessee Volunteers and the regulars of the Thirty-ninth Regiment were critical to victory, Jackson related in his battle report to General Pinckney that "the militia of the venerable Genl. [George] Doherty accompanied them in the charge, with a vivacity & firmness which would have done honor to Regulars." In a proclamation to the Tennessee troops a few days after the battle, Jackson praised the militiamen, declaring that they had "redeemed the character of Tennessee, & of that description of troops of which the greater part of the army was composed."[26]

By the end of April the various forces fighting the Creeks joined at the junction of the Coosa and Tallapoosa Rivers in a meeting that signaled the end of Indian resistance. As happened so often during the war, there were problems of seniority caused by the reluctance of the regular officers to defer to Jackson, the senior militia officer. The arrival of General Pinckney to take command resolved that issue, however. In time, Jackson's contribution to the Creek War was recognized. In late May he was appointed to the regular army to command the Seventh Military District in place of General Flournoy, who had resigned. Jackson was to be a brigadier general with a brevet major general, but the resignation of General Harrison allowed the government to give Jackson the rank of major general.[27]

After negotiating a harsh treaty at Fort Jackson with the defeated Creeks in August 1814, Jackson turned his attention to his district. There were reports that the British were inciting Indians along the Gulf in Spanish-held Florida. Even more disturbing was the news that a British force had arrived in Pensacola in mid-August with Spanish acquiescence. In late August, Jackson learned that the British were planning an invasion of Mobile and probably also of New Orleans. He immediately urged Governor Willie Blount to call out the Tennessee militia to meet this threat.[28]

Jackson also asked the Mississippi Territory in late July to give him 500 troops for the defense of New Orleans. Governor David Holmes pledged his support, but he cautioned that there was a shortage of tents and camp equipage of every kind. Since the fall of Fort Mims, he said, the Mississippi Territory had put a large force in the field; but none had been paid and nothing had been heard on that subject from the War Department. "This circumstance," he declared, "will make it difficult to procure many volunteers." On September 19, Holmes wrote Jackson that he was doing all he could to forward the movement of troops, but he was "greatly embarrassed for the want of equipments." Ten days later, Holmes informed Jackson that Maj. Thomas Hinds would lead a battalion of cavalry "partly armed with muskets, and as well furnished in other respects as our means would permit."[29]

In early September a British attack launched from Pensacola upon Mobile was repulsed by American regulars commanded by Maj. William Lawrence at Fort Bowyer. Jackson decided to attack Pensacola to deprive the British of this place as a staging base. He assembled a force of approximately 4,100 men, about two-thirds militia, including battle-tested volunteers, and the remainder regulars and Indians. On November 6, Jackson arrived at Pensacola and demanded that the Spanish surrender. The Spanish, who had only about 500 men, vacillated. Jackson did not hesitate and invaded the city the next day. Pensacola was captured with little resistance. The British withdrew to their vessels in Pensacola Bay, blew up two forts guarding the entrance, and sailed out into the Gulf. They continued to hover off the coast to lend aid to the Indians in the area.[30]

Having accomplished his object, Jackson turned his attention to Mobile and New Orleans. His dilemma was whether to focus his efforts on the defense of the former, which he believed the most likely British target, or the latter, which his government was urging him to defend. Belatedly, he received intelligence that the British intended to assault New Orleans. He turned over the defense of Mobile to Gen. James Winchester and hurried to New Orleans, where he arrived on December 1.[31]

In New Orleans, little had been done to prepare the city's defenses. Louisiana governor William C.C. Claiborne wrote Acting Secretary of War James Monroe on October 25 that while about two-thirds of the local militiamen were well armed (an exaggeration), "the militia in the interior of the State are almost wholly destitute of arms; they are," he added, "very pressing in their demands on me, and it is with regret I find myself without the means of arming them." Another problem was that citizens of French and Spanish descent who had been summoned for militia duty "absolutely refused to be marched," insisting that they were subjects of France or Spain.[32]

Jackson's energetic activities, however, soon spurred the people to action. Jackson scouted the various approaches to the city and prepared defenses. He also set about raising a military force to meet the invaders. Obviously the city militia would not be adequate. Jackson therefore called for volunteers from Tennessee, the Mississippi Territory, and even Kentucky, which was not within his military district.[33]

Governor Holmes informed Claiborne that he had ordered out his Mississippi Territory militia for the protection of Louisiana. Holmes declared, perhaps correctly, "Since the commencement of the war, we have constantly had upon the Eastern frontier, in proportion to the number of our Inhabitants, more troops in service than any state or territory in the Union." In late December, Holmes wrote General Jackson that he was sending between 400 and 500 troops. Only 200 muskets were available, so the remaining militiamen had to be armed with rifles and shotguns. As usual, Holmes charged the expenses to the War Department.[34]

One interesting and extremely valuable addition to Jackson's force were pirates from Barataria Bay, led by Jean Laffite. About 1,000 in number, they brought with them not only intelligence about the enemy but also arms, ammunition, powder, flints, and other supplies. Jackson also added free black militia companies to his force. Governor Claiborne had been daring enough to consider organizing the thousand or so free blacks in and around New Orleans into militia companies. The legislature had balked at the idea before, but perhaps because of the declaration of war, it authorized a corps of "free men of colour" in September 1812. The act decreed that the commander must be white, that no more than four companies could be organized, and that eligibility would be limited to those holding landed property of at least $300.[35]

While Jackson was preparing defenses, Commodore Daniel T. Patterson, the naval commander, asked the Louisiana legislature to suspend the writ of habeas corpus to allow the impressment of seamen. A joint committee recommended against suspension, but Jackson, after learning of the British capture of American gunboats on Lake Borgne, ended the discussion by declaring martial law on December 16. Two days earlier, he had ordered Governor Claiborne to hold the Louisiana militia in readiness.[36]

Despite Jackson's best efforts, not all approaches to New Orleans were obstructed, and the British found their way to the Mississippi River by means of Villeré's Canal on December 23. Jackson wasted no time and rushed 1,750 men, including 800 of Gen. John Coffee's Tennessee volunteers, about 400 Louisiana militia, and the remaining regulars, to Villeré's plantation, where he attacked the British two hours after dark. The nighttime attack, while not entirely "highly honorable to our arms," as Jackson noted, at least delayed the British attack on New Orleans. Jackson was given critical time to prepare his defenses along the Rodriguez Canal about two miles up the Mississippi from the Villeré plantation.[37]

Jackson was still assembling his force. Unfortunately, many of the drafted militiamen either failed to appear at rendezvous or quickly deserted. Claiborne complained to Jackson, who was too busy to go after these deserters, about the "base and wilful neglect of duty" of many militiamen. Jackson reported to Secretary Monroe that he had about 3,000 effectives, although they were very deficient in arms, accouterments, and flints.[38] (Unfortunately, arms enroute from Pittsburgh and traveling by way of the Ohio and Mississippi Rivers since November 8 failed to arrive in New Orleans until January 26.)

As of December 29, the Kentucky militia still had not arrived in New Orleans. On January 2, 1815, Gen. John Adair, adjutant general of the Kentucky militia, appeared in Jackson's camp ahead of his troops, who arrived a couple of days later. As Jackson reported to Monroe, however, of the approximately 2,300 Kentuckians, not more than a third were armed, "& *those* very indifferently." He wondered whether he could make any useful disposition of them. Many were also ill clothed and suffering from exposure. The legislature and citizens of New Orleans provided blankets, which were then made by the women of the city into clothes for the ill-clad troops. Jackson took muskets from the city militiamen and armed 400 of the Kentuckians. He also ordered a search of every house and store in New Orleans for muskets, bayonets, cartridge boxes, spades, shovels, pickaxes, and hoes. To augment his forces further, Jackson ordered that every man under fifty belonging to fire companies or others legally exempted from militia duty be enrolled immediately in a volunteer company.[39]

While Jackson had built a fortification line along the Rodriguez Canal that was capable of withstanding a strong artillery bombardment, he had taken few precautions to prepare a defensive line on the right (or west) bank. The main position on the west bank was about three miles below the city. There Commodore Patterson established a battery of guns capable of firing on the flanks of an enemy attacking Jackson's line on the opposite side. While the main attack of the British was made on January 8 on Jackson's line, the enemy also attacked on the west bank. The British plan was to assault the west bank position prior to the main attack, but because of delays in getting troops across the river, the main attack was actually made first.

The British commander on the west bank was Col. William Thornton. His objective was to knock out Patterson's batteries and possibly to turn these guns upon Jackson's flank. The American line was unprepared. Only about 200 yards of the line extending from the river (about one-tenth) was fortified when the attack occurred. The remainder of the line was a shallow ditch, lightly defended. The defense was commanded by Maj. Gen. David B. Morgan, who had about 500 Louisiana militiamen under his command. In addition, Jackson ordered 400 Kentucky militiamen under Col. John Davis to reinforce Morgan. Unbeknownst to Jackson, however, only about 260 crossed the river; the others returned to camp rather than go over unarmed.[40]

Thornton's force was roughly equal to Morgan's, but there was a vast difference in the quality of the soldiers. Not only were Morgan's troops inferior, but they were also badly deployed. About 120 Louisiana militiamen were placed about a mile in advance of the line to contest the enemy landing. When the British landed, however, as General Morgan later recounted, the "corps retreated in a most shameful and dastardly manner without even firing a gun, and in lieu of retreating to my lines . . . , they ran precipitately into the woods, since which time I have not received any intelligence." Colonel Davis's small force of Kentuckians, also placed in advance of the line, upon their first contact with the British fired off about two rounds and then broke and ran. General Morgan was critical of their precipitate flight also: "It was a complete flight in place of a retreat, they were in the utmost disorder, one running after another, or in other words every man for himself."[41]

The Kentuckians regrouped behind the American lines and were assigned to defend the far right flank close to the woods. Almost immediately they were assaulted by the British and were flanked, so that another retreat occurred with a rippling effect. The officers could not stop the withdrawal, which quickly turned into a general rout. The cannon placed behind the lines could not be used without firing into the retreating militia. The retreat left the cannon untenable. They were spiked and the ammunition thrown into the river. The militiamen did not stop their flight until Morgan was able to form a new line about a mile and a half upriver. Most of the militia, however, had scattered and could not be found.[42]

The conduct of the militiamen on the right bank was the source of a great deal of controversy for many years thereafter. Jackson was furious at the militiamen. In the immediate aftermath of the battle he told the troops that "no words can express the mortification I felt at witnessing the scene Exhibited on the opposite bank." He added, "The want of Discipline, the want of Order, a total disregard to Obedience, and a Spirit of insubordination, not less destructive than Cowardice itself, this appears to be the cause which led to the disaster." Jackson clearly blamed the Kentucky militia. In his official report of the Battle of New Orleans, Jackson described the events on the right bank and stated, "The Kentucky reinforcements, ingloriously fled, drawing after them, by their example, the remainder of the forces; and thus yielding to the enemy that most fortunate position."[43]

A court of inquiry mostly exonerated the Kentucky militia on the right bank because of a lack of arms and poor troop placement. Gen. John Adair, who commanded the Kentuckians on the right bank, sought to get Jackson to withdraw his harsh judgment of the Kentuckians. Jackson, however, refused to concede Adair's point, and this triggered an angry response in the press in Kentucky that lasted many years and was dredged up again during Jackson's presidential campaigns in 1824, 1828, and 1832.[44]

While the militia on the right bank failed utterly to perform its duty, albeit under difficult circumstances, the militia on the left bank won great glory on January 8. Here, however, the militia was behind a firmly entrenched line facing an enemy assault head-on. Moreover, Jackson's militiamen included many veterans of the Creek War, particularly those in William Carroll's and John Coffee's brigades, who performed creditably in this battle. It should be noted, however, that contemporary evidence, as well as common sense, suggests the greatest damage done to the British was by the American artillery manned by the Baratarian pirates and not the muskets and rifles of militia.[45]

The mythmaking about the militia in the Battle of New Orleans began almost immediately. Jackson himself was one of the most potent mythmakers. He wrote to Gen. James Winchester on January 19, for example, that his effective force on the left bank amounted to only 3,000, and of the 550 regulars, two-thirds were "not better than raw militia." Yet with this force he had "defeated this Boasted army of Lord Wellingtons—double my numbers at least." He also wrote to Senator James Brown of Louisiana on January 27, declaring that "3200 effectives met on the line 9500 of the choice of Wellingtons army two thirds of whom . . . were destroyed since the[y] landed." Jackson's figures are low. He had between 4,000 and 5,000 troops on his line, with about 3,000 in reserve (but mostly unarmed). Moreover, many, if not most, of Coffee's Volunteers and Carroll's Tennessee Volunteers (about 2,000) were veterans of the Creek War and were as well-disciplined as any regulars. Jackson also had with him many able and experienced officers.[46]

Jackson's feelings about militia were indicated in his letter to Secretary Monroe on January 25. After reporting that the enemy had decamped, he asked for "not less than 5000" regulars, "the only description of troops upon which reliance can be placed." While the militiamen had shown themselves worthy, "it is only for purposes thus temporary that they can be considered as valuable." Noting their short terms, he remarked that "they are so strongly recalled to their families & home [which] render them a very unequal match, in continued warfare, for men . . . following arms as a profession."[47]

Indeed, as soon as news of a peace treaty reached New Orleans, Jackson was besieged with requests to release the militiamen to return to their homes. Jackson was concerned that until the treaty was officially ratified he must keep up his guard. He even refused a request from Governor Claiborne to allow the Louisiana militia, called out en masse, to return to their homes. Regardless of Jackson's concern, the militiamen no longer saw an emergency, and desertions became common. One officer informed Jackson on February 24 that unless serious steps were taken to stop the desertions at Camp Chef Menteur, he would "in a few days . . . be left without a private to command."[48]

Jackson persisted in his war of wills with the militia. When two privates from the Louisiana militia were sentenced to death by a court-martial for desertion, a petition from citizens of Louisiana pleaded for

Andrew Jackson, by Ralph W. Earl. Courtesy of the National Portrait Gallery, Smithsonian Institution.

mercy on the grounds that the news of peace placed their offense in a different light. Jackson waited until the day of the execution to pardon them. When 137 militiamen secured certificates of citizenship from the French consul to gain release from the militia, Jackson responded by ordering all French subjects having certificates "to repair to the interior not short of Baton Rouge."[49]

One militia officer informed Jackson that his command at Camp Navy Yard "was almost abandoned" because of "a malignant disease . . . in consequence of which many of our brethren in arm[s] are consigned to the solitary mansions of the grave." He added that "there are many who have a[b]sented without leave and deserted I am persuaded in consiquence [*sic*] of the disease that visited us in so unfriendly a manner with other Causces [*sic*]." Jackson's position was plain: he intended to maintain martial law. "We must be prepared for defence, we must be vigilant and ready to act on the shortest notice—Or our brave expulsion of the Enemy may ultimate in disgrace and surprise."[50]

Jackson's firmness led to a messy dispute with Dominick A. Hall, judge of the federal district court. Before it was over, Jackson had jailed not only Hall but also the federal district attorney and another federal judge. He also ordered Judge Hall and the French consul to be banished from New Orleans. Eventually, Judge Hall convicted Jackson in March 1815 for contempt and fined him $1,000.[51]

Jackson's rather bizarre actions during this period did not diminish his place among American heroes of the war. Moreover, the militia had its image refurbished. Jackson continued to foster the militia myth. In dismissing the Louisiana militia on March 7, 1815, he stated grandly, "The Commanding General in parting with the Militia, is enabled in all the Simplicity of truth, to say, by these men the invincibles of Wellington were foiled, the Conquerors of Europe Conquered."[52]

Jackson's leadership of the militia during the Battle of New Orleans showed once again that, under the right circumstances, given proper leadership, discipline, training, and arms and equipment, American militiamen were capable of fighting. Jackson's force, drawn up behind defensive lines, as with William Henry Harrison's men at Fort Meigs, could hold off superior numbers. The example on the right bank, however, as critics pointed out, revealed the weaknesses of the militia that were amply demonstrated at Bladensburg. Once drawn from behind barricades, the militia was no match for professional soldiers. Defenders of the militia, however, pointed to the example of New Orleans as proof that the militiamen were truly the bulwark of liberty in the War of 1812.

Chapter 10

The War's End and the Decline of the Militia

The end of the war coincided with the news of the victory at New Orleans. Some critics of the militias now turned to praise them. The *Philadelphia Aurora*, for example, declared that the British, "on the very threshold of a spot which they had selected as the weakest and most disaffected portion of the union . . . , have been met, beaten, and disgraced, with the loss of their most valued and distinguished commanders, by a raw militia, hastily collected together from the adjoining country, and commanded by farmers and planters." The *Boston Yankee* similarly exclaimed, "His veterans fall before the undisciplined militia of our country like snow before the sun." Hezekiah Niles was more restrained. He noted that regulars had won glory on the Niagara and the militiamen at New Orleans and Plattsburgh. The latter two victories, he added, "spunges off the stain" of the debacle at Washington. He expressed the hope a peace establishment would be kept that retained the "*experience* derived in the war."[1]

Congress had sought for months by numerous expedients to fill the regular army and avoid calling on the militia. Now, ever adaptable, politicians shifted to accolades for the citizen soldier and to refurbishing the militia myth. George M. Troup hailed "the farmers of the country triumphantly victorious over the conquerors of the conquerors of Europe." He added, "The men of Europe, bred in camps, trained to war, with all the science and all the experience of modern war, are not a match for the men of America taken from the closet, the bar, the courthouse, and the plough." Troup took exception to the wording of a Senate resolution giving thanks to Gen. Andrew Jackson and his troops. It was obvious, Troup declared, that it was a "triumph of militia over regular troops," but the Senate resolution gave the impression that regular troops were the principal force and the militiamen the auxiliary. He moved to amend the resolution to correct that impression. The Senate, however, disagreed with the House amendment. The House insisted, and the Senate adhered to its disagreement. The point of difference was whether the credit belonged principally to the drafted militiamen *or* to the regulars, volunteer militia, *and* drafted militiamen. The House asked for a conference on February 22 to clear up the "unfortunate disagreement." The compromise that was worked out added to the resolution thanking Jackson and his officers and soldiers of the regular army, militia, and the volunteers the phrase "the greater proportion of which troops consisted of militia and volunteers suddenly collected together."[2]

With the war now at an end, Congress turned its attention to reduction of the regular army. On February 22, Troup reported a bill from his committee to fix a peacetime establishment of 10,000. When the bill was taken up in the Committee of the Whole on February 25, Troup stated that several factors had been considered, including questions of the security of the country, the interest of the country, and the just claims of the army. He cautioned against unilateral reductions. Wisdom and prudence suggested that the reduction should be "moderate, limited, and gradual." Although the administration proposed a force of 20,000, the committee had recommended 10,000, and he did not think the House should go any lower. Left unspecified was the role that the militias would play in providing for national security. Joseph Desha, who had declared earlier during the debate on the volunteer bill that the militia was inefficient and expensive and that "we must rely principally on regulars," now reversed his position and argued that the militia was "a better security than ten, or even fifty thousand regulars." Accordingly, he moved to insert 6,000 for the regular force. He also declared, "It is proven that the militia of the country are capable at all times at least of defensive operations. . . . We have boasted that a well organized militia was the bulwark of our liberty, and recent circumstances have proved it to be a fact."[3]

Desha's motion was supported generally by Federalists and southern Republicans. John Jackson, a Republican from Virginia, declared that he "would rather rely on the militia to repel sudden invasion than keep up a force enervated by the inactivity of a camp in time of peace—a moth on the public treasury." Samuel M. Hopkins (N.Y.) argued, however, that those who objected to an adequate force for fear it would become a standing army should "reflect that they were creating a military host by resorting to militia, and that danger to our civil institutions was much more likely to arise from making every man in the country a soldier, than from keeping up an efficient Peace Establishment." John C. Calhoun also argued that "it is easier to keep soldiers than to get them—to have officers of skill and renown in your possession, than to make them." Thomas Grosvenor of New York surprised his Federalist friends by supporting the larger force, citing the maxim, "to be sure of peace you must be prepared for war." Nevertheless, Desha's motion was sustained in the committee of the whole by nineteen votes.[4]

The question was not whether a regular force was necessary but how large a force the circumstances warranted. Obviously, many still considered 6,000 a sizable peacetime army. In response to concerns that the militia was not completely reliable, the Old Republican, Nathaniel Macon (N.C.), declared that "the true way to make our militia efficient, is to let them know that the safety of the nation depends on them." He added, "History almost universally proves, that in proportion as you rely on regulars, militia lost their efficiency and utility." Albert Cuthbert (Ga.) denied, however, that militiamen were "calculated for garrison duty." Nor were they "fit to contest a regular campaign . . . [or] to sustain an equal conflict with regular troops." Desha's motion was approved by ten votes, and the bill passed easily on March 1.[5]

The debate on the size of the regular force to be retained and the efficacy of relying upon militias for national defense was also waged in the newspapers. One correspondent, "E," called for the retention of a decent military force, particularly the "services of qualified meritorious officers." Another writer, "Crisis," maintained, astonishingly, that an army of 25,000 was needed to retain military genius. He added that the people should not fear a standing army. "A Militia-Man" declared in the *Daily National Intelligencer* that "experience appears to lose all effect upon us." A militia force was not adequate in an emergency, he continued, and he added, "we appeal to the experience of other nations as well as our own, and, if a particular instance is required, we will point to the ruins of our capitol." Moreover, militiamen were much more expensive than regulars. As for New Orleans, he noted that every general was not a Jackson; that the battle was fought in an ideal defensive posture, and even Jackson admitted "that he durst not venture out and expose himself to the skill of the enemy, which would not have been the case with disciplined troops."[6]

In the Senate, the House bill was amended to insert 15,000 in lieu of 6,000. The Senate approved other amendments, including retention of two major generals instead of one, and the bill was passed on March 3. The House rejected the Senate amendments, and when the Senate insisted, the House asked for a conference. The conference committee recommended 10,000, which both houses accepted. The House accepted two major generals but rejected the other Senate amendments. The bill was approved by both houses and was signed into law on March 3.[7]

The new peacetime army was substantially larger than the authorized force prior to the war. It consisted of eight regiments of infantry and riflemen, one light artillery regiment, and eight battalions of artillery. Although there was no provision for a commanding general, Maj. Gen. Jacob Brown commanded the northern division, and Maj. Gen. Andrew Jackson the southern. Four brigadier generals and other staff officers were apportioned among the two divisions. Separate Ordnance, Medical, Pay, and Purchasing Departments were established.[8] Overall, in terms of personnel and organization, the new army was a vast improvement over the regular army prior to the war.

Nevertheless, there were critics, such as "Wallace" in the *Albany Argus*, who declared that the new military establishment fell short of public expectations. He feared army reduction would lose the military experience gained. The country would again be forced to rely on militia for defense, with "masses of citizens being thrown together in camp, ignorant of the rudiments of discipline, and deficient in every principle of camp police." "Wallace" estimated that ten militiamen "perished by disease . . . where one has by the sword"; militia operations, "in most instances, terminate[d] in disaster." Even at Plattsburgh the militiamen faced no sterner test than skirmishing, while at New Orleans they fought behind entrenched defenses, and on the other bank of the Mississippi the militiamen "fled ingloriously without firing a single shot." He quoted George Washington, who said at the end of the Revolution, "if called upon to declare under oath whether *militia* had been more serviceable or *prejudicial* to the American cause, I should subscribe to the latter!" The experience in the War of 1812, "Wallace" declared, "confirmed the wisdom of the above remark." Breaking up the army was not only impolitic but unjust. A "decent sized army" was needed to deter Britain from aggression. "In war it would prevent a long train of disasters, which inevitably attend military operations with militia and would save a prodigal waste of life and treasure." He concluded, "It would impart energy to the federal system, which is daily becoming more necessary, from the increasing centrifugal propensities of the bodies which compose it."[9]

Despite the persistence of the militia myth, the concept of the militia as a main defense force was eroded during the war, as "Wallace's" critique suggests. Contrary to expectations, whether intended or not, the Army Reduction Act of 1815 was a positive step toward a professional army. The militia was relegated to a secondary role in national defense.

The Army Reduction Act was an early indication of a growing disenchantment with the idealized but inefficient and unreliable militia. The *Albany Argus*, in fact, declared that the creation of a standing army represented the "predominance of popular feeling."[10] The reorganization of the regular army carried out in the spring of 1815 retained officers and soldiers in the service who were highly meritorious and provided a higher degree of professionalism than ever before.

The growing professionalism of the regular army portended a neglect of the militia by the federal government. This new attitude was reflected in correspondence between Brig. Gen. Edmund P. Gaines and Secretary of War John C. Calhoun in September 1818. Reporting hostilities by Seminoles in Florida, Gaines stated that he would have called for two militia regiments "had I not been taught by painful experience that the *good* to be expected from a force of drafted militia falls too far short of the common calculations." Calhoun agreed and urged Gaines to use the regular army and avoid "the expense and vexation attending militia requisitions."[11] This correspondence clearly indicates that a genuine reliance on the militia in the pre–War of 1812 era was giving way to a verbal reliance in the postwar era.

In fact, the government had a problem determining the availability of militia, as state officials failed to submit their militia returns promptly. Benjamin Ruggles of Ohio, chairman of the Senate Committee on Militia, solicited suggestions from Secretary Calhoun in 1819 on ways to compel returns, even to withholding arms from those that failed to comply. Calhoun noted that such a measure would only increase the expense of the arsenals of the United States, which would now have to preserve the arms, but he could offer no solution to the problem. Returns for 1820 showed none from Delaware since 1810, from South Carolina and Maryland since 1811, from Mississippi since 1812, and the Arkansas Territory had never made a return. Many states were over a year late. The adjutant for Delaware wrote in 1820 that its law of February 2, 1816, repealed militia fines for nonattendance at training. "The consequences naturally flowing from that law," he wrote, "have been a total neglect of every appearance of militia duty."[12]

When the effects of the panic of 1819 reduced government income and forced retrenchment, an antiarmy faction moved to reduce the authorized strength of the regular army from 10,000 to 6,000. Much of the debate in the Sixteenth Congress over army reduction revolved around the ability of the militiamen to support the regular army during wartime. Proarmy supporters argued that reduction of the regular force would leave the nation without an effective defense. Claiming the mantle of Republican orthodoxy, the antiarmy faction asserted that the militia was the only safe and reliable defense for the nation, while a standing army was not only dangerous but expensive and burdensome to the people. The antiarmy forces prevailed, and on March 2, 1821, the regular army was reduced to 6,000.[13]

By the 1820s the militia was fast declining in public favor. In 1823, William H. Sumner, the adjutant general of Massachusetts, complained about "the open manner in which the militia has been assailed . . . ; sentiments are openly promulgated respecting it, which no man, who valued his popularity, would have dared to express, even five years ago." Sumner's point was echoed by a writer in the *North American Review* in 1826 who declared, "The time has past [*sic*] in the United States, when any just fears are entertained of such a standing army, as may be required by the present system of general defence."[14]

Secretary of War James Barbour convened a board of regular and militia officers in fall 1826 to review the organization of the state militias, which were universally believed to be "both defective and onerous." Barbour sent a circular letter to the governors of every state and territory asking nineteen questions touching on virtually all aspects of militia existence. Among other things, the secretary was interested in the relationship of volunteer militia to regular militia. Other questions dealt with organization, arming, and the value of militia musters for training. About fifty responses—many quite lengthy—were received from twenty states. Virtually all lamented the sad state of the militia. These documents were laid before the board of officers, chaired by Maj. Gen. Winfield Scott.[15]

The board report, dated November 28, 1826, noted various defects including that the current militia law enrolled an excessive number for militia duty; that the training musters placed a heavy burden upon the working class; and that, despite the law, only a small portion of the militia was armed. The board proposed changing the age of enrollment to twenty-one (from eighteen) and to twenty-nine or thirty (instead of forty-five); forcing states to have a uniform organization; distributing training manuals to every militia officer at federal expense; and assigning an adjutant general for militia to the War Department to act as liaison with the state militias.

More controversial proposals included extending tours of duty from three months to twelve and creating ten-day camps of instruction for militia officers that would be conducted by regular army officers or graduates of the U.S. Military Academy. The report was well received by the public, and it continued to be printed and cited for many years.[16] In Congress, however, the report had little impact, and no effort was made to enact the recommendations of the board.

Fines for nonattendance were gradually reduced over the years, and this was general practice all over the Union. The low fines predictably resulted in low attendance at drill days. Brig. Gen. John McCalla of the Third Brigade of the Kentucky militia complained in 1826 that his state laws were "little better than an order to disband the militia altogether. In consequence of our fine for absence only amounting to one dollar, currency, I have seen my regiment, which enrolls upwards of 1,000 men, parade less than 110."[17]

A continuing problem was that militiamen attended musters with no firearms. Most states imposed fines for not appearing at training with weapon and equipment in proper order. States also had provisions exempting firearms and equipment from any tax lien or judgments against an individual's property, however. Poverty exemptions for those unable to afford weapons were included in many laws. Some states allowed courts-martial to remit fines on these individuals, while others required the towns or militia units to provide public arms for such individuals.[18]

Still other states assessed no fines, but individuals were required to appear even without weapons. General McCalla griped that because Kentucky exempted "a militiaman from parading with a gun if *he does not actually own one*, I have seen regiments parade in which not more than one in forty or fifty have a gun at all." Similarly, Daniel Elmer of Cumberland County, New Jersey, noted in 1826 that his brigade enrolled 2,000 men, but that no more than 325 stand of arms were fit for service.[19]

There was general agreement that virtually no training took place during these musters. No less a supporter of the militia than Gen. William Henry Harrison declared in 1817, "The late war repeatedly exhibited the melancholy fact, of large corps of militia going into the field of battle without understanding a single elementary principle, and without being able to perform a single evolution." An increasingly serious problem was a lack of individuals willing to command a militia company. More than a dozen states exempted officers who served for a certain number of years, ranging from four to ten years but averaging about five. To get a militia officer to stay on for even this period, however, was a problem. Ebenezer Huntington estimated in 1826 that the Connecticut legislature, for various reasons, had to issue about 300 new commissions each year.[20]

With more than 2 million enrolled militia in the states by the 1830s, complaints multiplied about the excessive number of militia, the time lost (or wasted) in training, and the unnecessary expense and waste of public property. The average number of musters gradually declined from six per year after the War of 1812 to three by 1830 and to one in another fifteen years. In addition, states began to compromise the length of militia obligation. At least nine states adopted laws excusing those thirty-five to forty-five years old from militia training. In two cases a nominal fee was levied for this exemption. Four states—New Jersey (1829), Vermont (1837), Ohio (1843), and Michigan (1846)—exempted men who were eighteen to twenty-one. Some states experimented with their own classification schemes. Louisiana between 1834 and 1835, and Indiana between 1840 and 1844, divided their militiamen into two classes.[21]

Despite the fact that most states had fines for disorderly conduct, insubordination, firing of weapons at parade without permission, and so on, there were many examples of contempt by muster participants, and many made a mockery of the system. One way to show contempt was in the election of militia officers. A Pennsylvania regiment in 1824 elected the town fool as colonel. A board of officers voided the election and ordered a new one, but the regiment reelected the "colonel," who was not confirmed. Nevertheless, the regiment raucously paraded in outlandish uniforms with "ponderous imitations of weapons" before the colonel, who delivered a speech to the regiment and proclaimed his willingness to fight. In Albany, New York, in 1831, privates from two regiments conducted burlesque parades "in the most ludicrous and fantastic costumes imaginable."[22]

Not surprisingly, state laws began to appear in the 1830s to counter such activity. In July 1834 New Hampshire provided for fines or arrest for any militiaman "appearing in a grotesque or unusual dress, or by affected awkwardness and ignorance of his duty attempt to disturb the order of parade and to bring ridicule upon his officers and company or upon the military service." Similar laws were passed in Vermont (1834), Maine (1838), Rhode Island (1840), and Louisiana (1850).[23]

Despite efforts to maintain the dignity of militia training, George W. Bowman, the adjutant general of Pennsylvania, wrote to Governor Francis R. Shunk on December 22, 1845, "In almost every town the effort to bring [the militia] into contempt, by means of fantastical parades, has been more or less successful; and, in some places, public opinion is so wholly averse to them, that no officer will undertake to do more than call the men out at six o'clock in the evening, read over the roll, and dismiss them."[24]

Many states, in lieu of the regular militia, encouraged volunteer militia, by reducing the service obligation for officers and privates to five to fourteen years except in case of invasion. The volunteers had separate and more frequent musters, and fines for missing musters were usually higher. Obviously some men were attracted to the volunteer service. They wore different uniforms and generally had more spirit and pride in their units. Volunteer companies were really private clubs. They drew up charters, obtained authorization from the state, and established their own membership rules. They were responsible for their own support, although they did receive occasional arms and equipment from state governments. Volunteer companies showed a tendency to select wealthy citizens as officers, because such individuals usually contributed liberally to the company funds and expenses. Suffice it to say that this method often resulted in inefficient officers. Volunteer units adopted elaborate uniforms, often more for show than for active, practical use, and their training tended to concentrate more on the manual of arms and drilling for pageantry and parade than on practical matters like rifle practice, camping, maneuvers, and general tactics. One authority on the militia declared that the compulsory militia by 1850 "was little more than a vehicle for registering men eligible for military service and . . . the volunteers had come to more closely resemble a men's social club than a bona fide military organization."[25]

Faced by a growing opposition to the universal training provisions of the federal law, states moved with public opinion and progressively weakened their enforcement efforts. State authorities became increasingly negligent about making the required annual returns of militia. The most notable fact about these reports is their irregularity. Western states were notoriously lax, owing no doubt to their imperfect organizations, which made it nearly impossible to find out how many were enrolled. One study charting the returns between 1802 and 1862 found that states reported an average of only slightly over 39 percent of the time.[26] Such reports as were filed were unreliable and would have been of little use in case of mobilization.

Some states and even militia officers adopted resolutions imploring the federal government to reform the militia system but to no avail. Secretary of War Lewis Cass noted in 1835 that calls for militia reform had been communicated to Congress by the executive branch "no less than thirty-one times." No doubt the failure to act was due to a certain delicacy about the federal government's interference in a state responsibility, but in truth there was a complex of motives. Proarmy advocates did not want to "waste" money training militiamen when funds could be better spent on the regular army. States' rights advocates feared federal involvement would lead to federal control over state militia. There were some who did not want an efficient militia, fearing that it would pose as much of a threat as a regular standing army. Still others held that regular discipline enervated and stilled the love of liberty in soldiers, and they vowed that militiamen should never have to undergo such training.[27]

The militia system established in the law of 1792 continued, unchanged, until 1903, but the system envisioned by the authors of the law was dead by the 1850s. Compulsory militia training was effectively abolished by Delaware in 1829. Massachusetts followed in 1840; Rhode Island in 1843; Maine, Vermont, and Ohio in 1844; Michigan and New York in 1846; Connecticut and Missouri in 1847; Pennsylvania in 1849; and Louisiana and New Hampshire in 1850. Although 12,601 militiamen were used during the Mexican War, they comprised only 12 percent of the total force, compared to 88 percent in the War of 1812. Attempts after the Mexican War in several states to reorganize the militia, most notably in Massachusetts and New York, were short-lived and largely ineffectual.[28]

That the militia system was maintained as long as it was attests to the persistence of the concept of the citizen soldier. Whether the militia system was a good idea in the first place is debatable, but the American people and its leaders wanted it. It was a substitute for a standing army, but at best it gave the federal government only a more readily accessible pool of manpower in the event of war. Americans were not a martial people, and save for occasional Indian problems and the Mexican War, the nation was not threatened in the first half of the nineteenth century. It should be noted that while the militia declined, the regular army did not necessarily prosper. Army strength was set at 12,927 in 1850, but actual strength in the 1850s was usually less, and appropriations were small.[29]

It might be argued that the survival of the militia enabled states to mobilize men to conduct the Civil War and that it would have been better if the decline of the militia had been more complete. Confirmation of this point was made by Arkansas governor Henry M. Rector, who urged his legislature on November 15, 1860, to revise the militia code. "Life and liberty," he wrote, "may soon, in each slaveholding state, find protection only behind the breastworks of the citizen soldiery."[30]

Strikes and violence in the 1870s and 1880s prompted industrialists to campaign to rejuvenate the militia, and a new corps called the national guard was created.[31] Thus revived, the guard eventually evolved into a respectable and reliable reserve force for our national defense, approximating the intent of our Founding Fathers and preserving their idea of citizen soldiers.

Notes

Abbreviations

Annals   *Annals of Congress: Debates and Proceedings in the Congress of the United States, 1789-1824*, 42 vols., Washington, D.C., 1834-1856.
ASPIA   *American State Papers: Indian Affairs*, 2 vols., Washington, D.C., 1832-1834.
ASPMA   *American State Papers: Military Affairs*, 7 vols., Washington, D.C., 1832-1861.
BEHS   Buffalo and Erie Historical Society, Buffalo, N.Y.
JAH   *Journal of American History*
LC   Library of Congress, Washington, D.C.
MA   *Military Affairs*
MDAH   Mississippi Department of Archives and History, Jackson, Miss.
MHS   Massachusetts Historical Society, Boston, Mass.
NEQ   *New England Quarterly*
NYHS   New-York Historical Society, New York, N.Y.
NYPL   New York Public Library, New York, N.Y.
PMHB   *Pennsylvania Magazine of History and Biography*
RSUS   Records of the States of the United States
WD/LR   U.S. Department of War, Letters Received by the Secretary of War, Registered Series, 1801-1870 (Microfilm, M222), National Archives, Washington, D.C.
WD/LS   U.S. Department of War, Letters Sent by the Secretary of War Relating to Military Affairs, 1800-1889 (Microfilm, M6), National Archives, Washington, D.C.
WMQ   *William and Mary Quarterly*, 3d ser.
WPHM   *Western Pennsylvania Historical Magazine*

Introduction

1. Donald R. Hickey, *The War of 1812: A Forgotten Conflict* (Urbana, 1989), 322. The actual number of participants in the militia cannot be determined with any accuracy. Emory Upton, *The Military Policy of the United States* (1904; reprint, New York, 1968), 137, cites information from the Adjutant General's Office and the rolls of the Pension Office to arrive at a figure of 458,463 militia, 56,032 regulars, 10,110 volunteers, and 3,049 rangers. These figures, however, undoubtedly represent many soldiers (militia and regulars alike) who served more than one tour of duty.

2. Art. 1, sec. 8.

3. Quoted in J.C.A. Stagg, *Mr. Madison's War: Politics, Diplomacy, and Warfare in the Early Republic, 1783-1830* (Princeton, 1983), 138.

4. Ibid., 10-11.

Chapter 1

1. See Daniel J. Boorstin, *The Americans: The Colonial Experience* (New York, 1958), 345-372.

2. Willard M. Wallace, *Appeal to Arms: A Military History of the American Revolution* (1951; reprint, Chicago, 1964), 115 (first quotation); John K. Mahon, *The American Militia: Decade of Decision, 1789-1800* (Gainesville, 1960), 5 (second quotation). Wallace, *Appeal to Arms*, 48-55, 271.

3. Lawrence D. Cress, *Citizens in Arms: The Army and Militia in American Society to the War of 1812* (Chapel Hill, 1981), 78-92; Richard H. Kohn, *Eagle and Sword: The Federalists and the Creation of the Military Establishment in America, 1783-1802* (New York, 1975), 42-53.

4. See Martin Shapiro, ed., *The Constitution of the United States and Related Documents* (1966; reprint, Northbrook, Ill., 1973). The Articles of Confederation are at 84-96, and article 6 is at 87-88.

5. Art. 1, sec. 8.

6. Cress, *Citizen in Arms*, 100. See also Cecelia M. Kenyon, ed., *The Antifederalists* (Indianapolis, 1966), 22-23, 37, 57-58, 228-229, 243, 248-249, 310.

7. Historians have generally been critical of the Uniform Militia Act. Richard Kohn entitled his chapter dealing with it "The Murder of the Militia System." Kohn, *Eagle and Sword*, 128-138. While Emory Upton declared that "its foundations were built on the sands," he nevertheless praised two features: it "laid down the truly democratic doctrine that every able-bodied male citizen owed military service to his country, and likewise provided for a system of enrollment and territorial recruiting." Emory Upton, *The Military Policy of the United States* (1904; reprint, New York, 1968), 85. For legislation increasing the regular army's strength and providing for the organization of state militia, see Acts of April 30, 1790, March 3, 1791, and March 5, 1792, I *U.S. Statutes at Large* 119, 222, 241.

8. Knox's proposal, submitted on Jan. 21, 1790, is found in many places, most conveniently in *ASPMA*, Doc. 2, I, 6-13. See also *Annals*, 1st Cong., 2d sess. (House), 2088-2107. The 1790 and 1791 debates are in ibid., 1058, 1544, 1546, 1658; ibid., 3d sess., 1804-1828, 1837, 1840.

9. Act of May 8, 1792, I *U.S. Statutes at Large* 271. Knox to Speaker of the House, Dec. 10, 1794, *ASPMA*, Doc. 21, I, 70-71.

10. Wayne to Knox, Aug. 28, 1794, *ASPIA*, Doc. 52, I, 491-492. Thomas P. Slaughter, *The Whiskey Rebellion: Frontier Epilogue to the American Revolution* (New York, 1986), 213-214 [quoting William Findley, *History of the Insurrection in the Four Western Counties of Pennsylvania in the Year MDCCXCIV* (Philadelphia 1796), 41]. *ASPMA*, Doc. 21, I, 70.

11. Mahon, *Decade of Decision*, 22. Knox report, Jan. 18, 1790, *ASPMA*, Doc. 2, 7.

12. James D. Richardson, ed., *A Compilation of the Messages and Papers of the Presidents, 1789-1897*, 10 vols. (Washington, D.C., 1900), I, 140, 166, 184, 204, 212.

13. *ASPMA*, Doc. 15, I, 66. *Annals*, 3d Cong., 2d sess. (House), 1214. The issue of militia reform was debated earlier on Jan. 9, 1795 (ibid., 1067-1071), and culminated in the appointment of the Giles Committee. Prominent members of the committee included Theodore Sedgwick of Massachusetts, Samuel Smith of Maryland,

and Jonathan Dayton of New Jersey. For the debate, see *Annals*, 3d Cong., 2d sess. (House), 1214-1220, 1236-1237.

14. *Annals*, 4th Cong., 2d sess. (House), 1677-1678 (Harper), 1679-1680 (Henderson, who estimated that it would cost between $3 million and $4 million), 1681-1682 (Rutherford).

15. Ibid., 1683-1684 (Harper), 1685-1687, 1691, 2099, 2223-2224.

16. Nisbet, quoted in Kohn, *Eagle and Sword*, 122. See Kohn's discussion on 279-283.

17. Adams's message is in Richardson, ed., *Messages and Papers*, I, 238. On the maneuvering for the provisional army, see Kohn, *Eagle and Sword*, 221-229, and Cress, *Citizens in Arms*, 137, 143-146. See also C. Joseph Bernardo and Eugene H. Bacon, *American Military Policy: Its Development Since 1775* (Harrisburg, 1955), 85-87.

18. James McHenry to H.G. Otis (Chairman, Committee of Defence), Jan. 31, 1800, *ASPMA*, Doc. 40, I, 142.

19. Richardson, ed., *Messages and Papers*, I, 323, 329.

20. Richardson, ed., *Messages and Papers*, I, 385. Jefferson also called for revision of the militia laws in his second annual message, ibid., I, 345.

21. Theodore J. Crackel, *Mr. Jefferson's Army: Political and Social Reform of the Military Establishment, 1801-1809* (New York, 1987), 36-53; Upton, *Military Policy*, 89. *ASPMA*, Doc. 50, I, 63. See also Jefferson to House of Representatives, Jan. 5, 1803, *ASPMA*, Doc. 48, I, 160-162.

22. *ASPMA*, Doc. 57, I, 189.

23. Crackel, *Mr. Jefferson's Army*, 163.

24. Upton, *Military Policy*, 91.

25. The Act of April 22, 1808, is in II *U.S. Statutes at Large* 490. The committee estimate is in *ASPMA*, Doc. 62, I, 198. In a report in 1830, Col. George Bomford (Ordnance) informed Secretary of War John H. Eaton (Feb. 26, 1830) that the average number of arms distributed by the government in the fourteen years from 1816 to 1830 was 14,214 muskets per year. *ASPMA*, Doc. 442, IV, 301.

26. J.C.A. Stagg, *Mr. Madison's War: Politics, Diplomacy, and Warfare in the Early Republic, 1783-1830* (Princeton, 1983), 139 (citing War Department Report to House Speaker, Jan. 17, 1810).

27. See Madison's messages dated Nov. 29, 1809, and Jan. 3, 1810, in Richardson, ed., *Messages and Papers*, I, 476, 478-479. See also *ASPMA*, Doc. 90, I, 248. Smith's report is in *ASPMA*, Doc. 95, I, 256.

28. *Annals*, 11th Cong., 2d sess. (House), 1381 (Dana), 1382, 1384, 1385.

29. Ibid., 1471-1478, 1478-1479, 1479.

30. Ibid., 1499, 1499-1501.

31. Ibid., 1502-1503 (Bacon), 1503-1506 (Key, quotation is on 1503-1504), 1507-1508 (Lyon's comment is on 1507).

32. Ibid., 1508-1510, 1510-1512, 1512-1513, 1513-1514. Ross's statement is on 1510.

33. Ibid., 1517-1520, 1577-1580. The Hufty motion is on 1576, and the Moseley quotation is on 1578.

34. Ibid., 1586-1595, 1604-1605; (Senate), 675.

35. Ibid. (House), 1609-1616 (Randolph resolution), 1863 (Macon's amendment), 1863-1864 (Nelson), 1876 (McKim), 1874-1875 (McKee), 1878 (Dana).

36. Ibid., 1950-1951, 1933-1934, 1950-1954, 1957-1986, 1989-1996, 2007-2016. Seven frigates were laid up by the Jefferson administration and were not in service. See Leonard D. White, *The Jeffersonians: A Study in Administrative History, 1801-1829* (New York, 1951), 267.

37. Richardson, ed., *Messages and Papers*, I, 486. Eustis to President of Senate, Dec. 13, 1810, ibid., *Annals*, 11th Cong., 3d sess. (Senate), 20-21.
38. *Annals*, 11th Cong., 3d sess. (Senate), 356; ibid. (House), 1101, 1108, 1113.

Chapter 2

1. Resolution of North Carolina, Dec. 16, 1811, Governor's Letterbooks, 13-14, RSUS, Executive Records, North Carolina, reel 7. Kentucky Resolution, *ASPMA*, Doc. 110, I, 318.
2. Richardson, ed., *Messages and Papers*, I, 494. *Annals*, 12th Cong., 1st sess. (Senate), 44-45 (Giles), 55-58 (Anderson), 68-77.
3. *Annals*, 12th Cong., 1st sess. (House), 596-597, 603, 616. For the entire debate, see 595-606, 608-609, 611-617, 619-635, 636-664, 665-691, 700, 701-718. The law is in I *U.S. Statutes at Large* 671.
4. Giles's speech is in *Annals*, 12th Cong., 1st sess. (Senate)(appendix), 1693-1712. The Volunteer Act of Feb. 6, 1812, is in I *U.S. Statutes at Large* 676.
5. *Annals*, 12th Cong., 1st sess. (House), 1058-1069.
6. Ibid., 1004.
7. Huntington was responding to a query from Benjamin Tallmadge of Connecticut, a member of the House Committee on the Militia. Tallmadge to Huntington, Dec. 18, 1809, Huntington to Tallmadge, Jan. 5, 1810, *ASPMA*, Doc. 98, I, 263-265.
8. The defeated motions are in *Annals*, 12th Cong., 1st sess. (House), 1007-1010. Tallmadge's speech is in ibid., 1015-1018.
9. *Annals*, 12th Cong., 1st sess., 1004, 1007-1010, 1019-1020, 1021. John Taliaferro (Va.) changed his vote and voted against the bill. Three votes were picked up by supporters of the bill, which failed to offset the nine absentees. Three opponents of the bill were absent on the final vote, but Taliaferro's negative vote, along with that of Thomas Newton (Va.), who had not voted earlier, made the difference.
10. *Annals*, 12th Cong., 1st sess. (House), 1032, 1046-1047, 1048-1082, 1084-1085. Ibid., (Senate), 128, 185, 193-194, 195. Ibid., (House), 1298.
11. Bernardo and Bacon, *American Military Policy*, 115.
12. Monroe to Chairmen, Military Committees (David R. Williams and Joseph Anderson), Dec. 23, 1812, *Annals*, 12th Cong., 2d sess. (appendix), 1757-1762.
13. Ibid., (House), 461-464.
14. Ibid., 482-485.
15. Ibid., 538-539, 580.
16. Ibid., 607-608, 616.
17. Ibid., 618, 629-630.
18. Ibid., 799.
19. Ibid., 823, 843-844; ibid. (Senate), 63; I *U.S. Statutes at Large* 794.
20. *Daily National Intelligencer*, Jan. 28, 1813.
21. *Annals*, 12th Cong., 2d sess. (House), 923-926.
22. Ibid., 926-928.
23. Ibid., 942.
24. Ibid., 944-945, 946. Varnum's motion is in *Annals*, 12th Cong., 2nd sess. (Senate), 110; *Daily National Intelligencer*, March 12, 1813.
25. *Annals*, 13th Cong., 1st sess. (House), 135.
26. Ibid., 135-136. *Annals*, 13th Cong., 2d sess., 1230.
27. *Annals*, 13th Cong., 1st sess., 158-159, 159-160, 160-161.
28. Ibid., 161-162 (Fisk), 162-163 (Webster), 163 (Calhoun). The Troup committee report, with details on arms distributed, appears in ibid., 400-403.
29. Armstrong to Smith, June 10, 1813, National Archives, RG107, Reports to

Congress from the Secretary of War, Vol. 1 (Letterbooks, Feb. 3, 1803–April 13, 1818), 270 (microfilm), reel 1.

30. Ibid., 271-272.

31. Ibid., 13th Cong., 2d sess. (House), 815-816, 1432 (quotation), 1696-1697.

32. Armstrong to George M. Troup (Committee on Military Affairs), Jan. 1, 1814, WD/Reports to Congress; Armstrong to Madison, Dec. 5, 1813, Madison Papers, LC. *Annals*, 13th Cong., 2d sess. (House), 1099, 1103-1106 (quotations are on 1104-1106).

33. *Annals*, 13th Cong., 2d sess. (House), 1160-1162, 1167-1168.

34. Ibid., 1230-1231, 1471.

35. Ibid., 1926-1928, 1930-1931. The Act of April 18, 1814, may be found in ibid. (appendix), 2847-2850.

36. Gaines to Cushing, Jan. 2, 1813, *Daily National Intelligencer,* March 6, 1813.

37. Jackson to Rhea, Oct. 10, 1814, in Moser, ed., *Jackson Papers*, III, 156-157.

38. Jackson to Monroe, Nov. 20, 1814, ibid., III, 193.

39. "Spirit of the Times," *Daily National Intelligencer,* Sept. 23, Oct. 5, Oct. 19, 1814.

40. "Jackson," ibid., Oct. 7, 1814.

41. Ibid., Oct. 27, 1814. The average wage cited appears in Hickey, *War of 1812*, 76-77.

42. Richardson, ed., *Messages and Papers*, I, 549-550. J.C.A. Stagg, "Enlisted Men in the United States Army, 1812-1815: A Preliminary Survey," *WMQ* 43 (Oct. 1986), 615-645, concluded that the number of men who enlisted in the army "was greater than has been recognized." While this statement may be true, Congress and the nation believed that there was a shortage of troops.

43. Monroe to Giles, Oct. 17, 1814, *Annals*, 13th Cong., 3d sess. (House), 483-491. German's proposal is in Annals, 13th Cong., 3rd sess. (Senate), 30.

44. *Annals*, 13th Cong., 3d sess. (Senate), 38, 41-42, 45; ibid., (House), 723-729, 733-742.

45. *Annals*, 13th Cong., 2d sess. (House), 753, 756, 1837-1838.

46. *Annals*, 13th Cong., 3d sess. (Senate), 58-70.

47. Ibid., 70-75.

48. Ibid., 78-91, 96-102.

49. Ibid., 103-108, 109.

50. "Americanus," *Daily National Intelligencer,* Nov. 18, 1814.

51. Noble E. Cunningham, Jr., ed., *Circular Letters of Congressmen to Their Constituents, 1789-1829*, 3 vols. (Chapel Hill, 1978), II, 961. "Memorandum," n.d. [Nov. 1814], Timothy Pickering Papers, MHS (microfilm), reel 55. In his papers there is a copy of a speech he gave against the conscription bill. It was not recorded in the *Annals of Congress*, and the exact date on which he gave it is not certain. He charged that the purpose was to turn the militia into regulars, and he called it unconstitutional and arbitrary. He urged the House to "contrive . . . practicable & constitutional plans to save the country." Speech on Giles Bill, n.d. [Dec. 1814], ibid.

52. *Annals*, 13th Cong., 3d sess. (House), 705-712, 712.

53. Ibid., 771, 775.

54. Ibid., 775-799.

55. Speech against conscription bill, Dec. 9, 1814, Daniel Webster Papers, Dartmouth College (Microfilm), reel 2. Webster wrote his brother that upon reflection he had decided not to publish his speech (Webster to Ezekiel Webster, Dec. 22, 1814, ibid.), and to a friend (Webster to Jacob McGaw, Dec. 31, 1814, ibid.) he wrote, "I said nothing worth everybody's reading." Webster, perhaps, considered his remarks a little too extreme.

56. *Annals*, 13th Cong., 3d sess. (House), 808-819 (quotation is on 817, 818, and 819).

57. Ibid., 841, 863-864.

58. Ibid., 882-883, 883-884, 897-898, 900, 901-902.

59. Ibid., 904-913 (quotation is on 911 and 913).

60. Ibid., 928-929; ibid. (Senate), 131-132; ibid. (House), 972-976, 992-994; ibid. (Senate), 141. Webster to Ezekiel Webster, Jan. 9, 1815, Webster Papers, reel 3. The Maryland House of Delegates passed a resolution thanking King for killing the conscription bill. He acknowledged the resolution but noted that he had voted for "supplies of men and money, and for other important measures within the pale of the Constitution, that are deemed necessary, to revive the public credit, to protect the several states against invasion, and to defend, & save from dismemberment, the Territory and Sovereignty of the Nation." See Resolution of House of Delegates (Md.), Jan. 6, 1815, and King to Henry Chapman (House of Delegates, Md.), Jan. 8, 1815, Rufus King Papers, NYHS, Vol. 14.

61. "Franklin," *Daily National Intelligencer,* Oct. 25, 1814.

62. *Annals*, 13th Cong., 3d sess. (House), 482, 519, 520, 521.

63. Ibid., 541, 715.

64. Ibid. (Senate), 146, 148, 150, 161-162; (House), 1066, 1071-1072, 1074, 1075, 1084, 1086. III *U.S. Statutes at Large* 193.

65. *Annals*, 13th Cong., 3d sess. (House), 1125-1128 (Rich quotation is on 1127), 1128 (Webster), 1128 (Fisk), 1129-1130 (Troup), 1154.

Chapter 3

1. *Annals*, 12th Cong., 1st sess. (Senate), 283.

2. Message of Gov. Return J. Meigs, Dec. 9, 1812, *Niles' Weekly Register* 3 (Jan. 9, 1813), 289-290.

3. Order of Adj. Gen. T.H. Cushing (U.S.), March 19, 1813, encl. in Maj. Gen. Thomas Pinckney to Gov. William Hawkins, June 11, 1813, Governor's Letterbooks, 256, RSUS, Executive Records, North Carolina, reel 7.

4. Message of Gov. Alston, Nov. 23, 1813, *Niles' Weekly Register* 5 (Dec. 18, 1813), 262; Message of Gov. Barbour, Dec. 6, 1813, ibid., 261. Message of Gov. Snyder, Dec. 10, 1813, *Daily National Intelligencer,* Dec. 15, 1813.

5. Annual Message, Oct. 18, 1814, Executive Journals, 83-86, RSUS, Executive Records, Georgia, reel 11. The legislature, on Nov. 23, 1814, gave the executive authority to reorganize the militia, prescribing 90 privates, 5 officers, 5 sergeants, 4 corporals, and 2 musicians per company. General Order, Dec. 19, 1814, Executive Journals, 170-171, RSUS, Executive Records, Georgia, reel 11.

6. Annual Message, Dec. 5, 1815, Executive Journals, 276, RSUS, Executive Records, Kentucky, reel 2.

7. The Act of Feb. 28, 1795, I *U.S. Statutes at Large* 424, established the three-month tour. The six-month duty was prescribed by the Act of April 10, 1812, II *U.S. Statutes at Large* 705. Many states, such as Tennessee, retained the three-month tour. Ohio was an example of a state that established a six-month tour for state service. See Act of Feb. 9, 1813 (chap. 39), *Laws Passed at the First Session of the Eleventh General Assembly of the State of Ohio* (Chillicothe, 1812 [1813?]), 136, RSUS, Session Laws, Ohio, reel 2. General Order, June 3, June 25, 1814, Minutes of Executive Department, 17, 26, RSUS, Georgia, reel 11. See also Early to Maj. Isham Fannin, May 31, 1814, Governor's Letterbooks, 5, RSUS, Executive Records, Georgia, reel 2. Early to Capt. Richard H. Long, Sept. 26, 1814, Governor's Letterbooks, 31, RSUS, Georgia, reel 2.

8. Early to Thomas, Oct. 20, 1814, Governor's Letterbooks, 42; Early to Floyd, Oct. 20, Nov. 17, Dec. 1, 1814, Governor's Letterbooks, 42-43, 53, 53-54; Early to Buford, Jan. 7, 1815, Governor's Letterbooks, 65; Early to Floyd, Feb. 1, 1815, Governor's Letterbooks, 87, all in RSUS, Georgia, reel 2. Early's message to the legislature is in Executive Journals, 83-86, RSUS, Executive Records, Georgia, reel 11. In his message to the legislature on Nov. 8, 1815, Early complained, "There are many remnants through the State, who in point of fact are complete exempts from the public service." He recommended that they be thrown by law back into the line and "none suffered to remain in the character of volunteers any longer than they shall preserve their full complement of men." Ibid., 313.

9. Paul Le Roy, *Some Social Aspects on the Life and Organization of the Soldier in the War of 1812* (Columbus, Ohio, 1958), 1.

10. Act of Jan. 7, 1812 (chap. 182), *Laws Made and Passed by the General Assembly of the State of Maryland* (Annapolis, 1812), 189, 191-192, RSUS, Session Laws, Maryland, reel 5. See, for an example of the last provision, Act of March 28, 1814 (chap. 189), *Acts of the General Assembly of the Commonwealth of Pennsylvania* (Philadelphia, 1814), 347, RSUS, Session Laws, Pennsylvania, reel 6.

11. Act of Feb. 9, 1813 (chap. 39), *Laws Passed at the First Session of the Eleventh General Assembly of the State of Ohio* (Chillicothe, 1812 [1813?]), 147, RSUS, Session Laws, Ohio, reel 2; Act of Jan. 3, 1814 (chap. 1), *Acts of Assembly of the Indiana Territory* (Madison, 1814), 54-55, RSUS, Session Laws, Indiana, reel 1; Act of Feb. 3, 1813 (chap. 90), *Acts . . . of the Twenty-first General Assembly for the Commonwealth of Kentucky* (Frankfort, Ky., 1813), 102, RSUS, Session Laws, Kentucky, reel 2; Act of Feb. 12, 1814, *Public Acts of the Thirty-eighth General Assembly of the State of New Jersey*, 83, RSUS, Session Laws, New Jersey, reel 5b.

12. Act of Nov. 9, 1812 (chap. 149), *Acts and Laws Passed by the Legislature of the State of Vermont* (Danville, 1812), 207, RSUS, Session Laws, Vermont, reel 2. Act of March 28, 1814 (chap. 149), *Acts of the General Assembly of the Commonwealth of Pennsylvania* (Philadelphia, 1814), 321, RSUS, Session Laws, Pennsylvania, reel 6; Act of May 29, 1813 (chap. 19), *Laws Made and Passed by the General Assembly of the State of Maryland* (Annapolis, 1813), 20-21, RSUS, Session Laws, Maryland, reel 5; Act of Feb. 9, 1813 (chap. 39), *Laws Passed at the First Session of the Eleventh General Assembly of the State of Ohio* (Chillicothe, 1812 [1813?]), 133, RSUS, Session Laws, Ohio, reel 2; Act of Feb. 3, 1813 (chap. 90), *Acts . . . of the Twenty-first General Assembly for the Commonwealth of Kentucky* (Frankfort, Ky., 1813), 102, RSUS, Session Laws, Kentucky, reel 2; Act of Feb. 12, 1814, *Public Acts of the Thirty-eighth General Assembly of the State of New Jersey* (Trenton, 1814), 83, RSUS, Session Laws, New Jersey, reel 5b; Act of Jan. 18, 1815, *Acts Passed at a General Assembly of the Commonwealth of Virginia* (Richmond, 1815), 41-48, RSUS, Session Laws, Virginia, reel 5.

13. Perry LeRoy, *The Weakness of Discipline and Its Consequent Results in the Northwest During the War of 1812* (Columbus, 1958), 3, 5-7.

14. Presidential Proclamation, Oct. 8, 1812, quoted in ibid., 5.

15. Act of Feb. 3, 1813 (chap. 90), *Acts . . . of the Twenty-first General Assembly of the Commonwealth of Kentucky* (Frankfort, Ky., 1813), 101, RSUS, Session Laws, Kentucky, reel 2. Act of Dec. 24, 1814, *Acts Passed at the Second Session of the Eighth General Assembly of the Mississippi Territory* (Natchez, 1814), 50-51, RSUS, Session Laws, Mississippi, reel 2; Act of Jan. 18, 1815 (chap. 6), *Acts Passed at a General Assembly of the Commonwealth of Virginia* (Richmond, 1815), 49, ibid., Virginia, reel 5. Vermont stated simply that failure to rendezvous was "deemed desertion" and would be "punished as such." Act of Nov. 9, 1812 (chap. 149), *Acts and Laws Passed by the Legislature of the State of Vermont* (Danville, [1812]), 205-206, RSUS, Session

Laws, Vermont, reel 2. Act of Dec. 25, 1813 (chap. 1), *Laws of the State of North Carolina* (Raleigh, 1814), 4, RSUS, Session Laws, North Carolina, reel 4. Ohio fined privates from $100 to $200 and required them to serve the next tour of duty. Non-commissioned officers could be fined from $150 to $250, reduced in rank, and forced to serve the next tour as a private. Act of Feb. 9, 1813 (chap. 39), *Laws Passed at the First Session of the Eleventh General Assembly of the State of Ohio* (Chillicothe, 1812 [1813?]), 142-143, RSUS, Session Laws, Ohio, reel 2. See also Pennsylvania ($48 fine), Act of March 28, 1814 (chap. 189), *Acts of the General Assembly of the Commonwealth of Pennsylvania* (Philadelphia, 1814), 342, RSUS, Session Laws, Pennsylvania, reel 6; Indiana Territory ($100 to $150 fine), Act of Jan. 3, 1814 (chap. 1), *Acts of Assembly of the Indiana Territory* (Madison, 1814), 49, RSUS, Session Laws, Indiana, reel 1; and New Jersey (up to $100 fine and two months' imprisonment), Act of Feb, 18, 1815, *Public Acts of the Thirty-ninth General Assembly of the State of New Jersey* (Trenton, 1815), 57, RSUS, Session Laws, New Jersey, reel 5b.

16. Message of Gov. Meigs, Dec. 7, 1813, *Daily National Intelligencer,* Dec. 21. 1813.

17. Gov. Levin Winder to Col. Henry Ashton, May 28, 1813, Letterbooks of the Governor and Council, RSUS, Executive Records, Maryland, reel 3; Act of May 29, 1813, *Laws Made and Passed by the General Assembly of the State of Maryland* (Annapolis, 1813), 22-23, RSUS, Session Laws, Maryland, reel 5. Act of Nov. 23, 1814, *Laws of Georgia* (Milledgeville, 1814), 10-11, RSUS, Session Laws, Georgia, reel 4. Holmes to Brig. Gen. Ferdinand Claiborne, Oct. 6, 1812, Governor's Letterbooks, 233-234, RSUS, Executive Records, Mississippi, reel 2. Connecticut stated that any non-commissioned officer, musician, or private refusing to march would be "conducted to the place of rendezvous." Act of Oct. Session (chap. 5), *The Public Statute Laws of the State of Connecticut* (n.p., n.d.), 99, RSUS, Session Laws, Connecticut, reel 2.

18. Act of Sept. 24, 1813, *Acts and Resolutions of the General Assembly of the State of South Carolina* (Columbia, 1813), 8, RSUS, Session Laws, South Carolina, reel 6. States and territories with fines of twenty dollars per month included Connecticut, Rhode Island, Ohio, and the Indiana Territory. See Act of May 1814 Session (chap. 24), *The Public Statute Laws of the State of Connecticut* (n.p., n.d.), 167, RSUS, Session Laws, Connecticut, reel 2; Act of Sept. 16, 1814, *Public Laws of the State of Rhode Island and Providence Plantations* (Newport, [1840?]), 183-184, RSUS, Session Laws, Rhode Island, reel 7; Act of Feb. 9, 1813 (chap. 39), *Laws Passed at the First Session of the Eleventh General Assembly of the State of Ohio* (Chillicothe, 1812 [1813?]), 143, 147, RSUS, Session Laws, Ohio, reel 2; Act of Jan. 3, 1814 (chap. 1), *Acts of Assembly of the Indiana Territory* (Madison, 1814), 50, 54-55, RSUS, Session Laws, Indiana, reel 1. The average wage is cited in Hickey, *War of 1812,* 76-77. Connecticut imprisoned militiamen from thirty to sixty days if the fine was not paid. Act of May 1814 Session (chap. 24), cited above. States imposing confinement at five dollars per month were Pennsylvania and Virginia. See Act of March 28, 1814 (chap. 189), *Acts of the General Assembly of the Commonwealth of Pennsylvania* (Philadelphia, 1814), 338, RSUS, Session Laws, Pennsylvania, reel 6; Act of Feb. 14, 1814 (chap. 4), *Acts Passed at a General Assembly of the Commonwealth of Virginia* (Richmond, 1814), 27, RSUS, Session Laws, Virginia, reel 5. Act of Sept. 16, 1814, *Public Laws of the State of Rhode Island and Providence Plantations* (Newport, [1840?]), 183-184, RSUS, Session Laws, Rhode Island, reel 7.

19. General Orders, March 1, 1814, Governor's Letterbooks, 432-433, RSUS, Executive Records, Mississippi, reel 2.

20. Act of Nov. 9. 1812 (chap. 149), *Acts and Laws Passed by the Legislature of the State of Vermont* (Danville, [1812]), 208-209, RSUS, Session Laws, Vermont, reel 2; Act of Feb. 15, 1813 (chap. 3), *Acts Passed at a General Assembly of the Commonwealth*

of Virginia (Richmond, 1813), 17, RSUS, Session Laws, Virginia, reel 4; Act of Feb. 14, 1815 (chap. 54), *Acts Passed at the First Session of the Thirteenth General Assembly of the State of Ohio* (Chillicothe, 1814 [1815?]), 219, RSUS, Session Laws, Ohio, reel 2.

21. LeRoy, *Weakness of Discipline*, 5-7. Anne Castrodale Golovin, "William Wood Thackara, Volunteer in the War of 1812," *PMHB* 91 (July 1967), 308.

22. LeRoy, *Weakness of Discipline*, 5-6, 9.

23. As quoted in James Wallace Hammack, Jr., *Kentucky and the Second American Revolution: The War of 1812* (Lexington, Ky., 1976), 30-31.

24. LeRoy, *Weakness of Discipline*, 7.

25. "Papers on the Defence of Boston and Other Places," Feb. 27, 1813, Doc. 4, 11, RSUS, Legislative Documents, Massachusetts, reel 2.

26. Act of Jan. 7, 1812 (chap. 189), *Laws Made and Passed by the General Assembly of the State of Maryland* (Annapolis, 1812), 178-179, RSUS, Session Laws, Maryland, reel 5; Act of June 18, 1812 (chap. 9), ibid., 8.

27. Message of Gov. Plumer, Nov. 18, 1812, *Niles' Weekly Register* 3 (Dec. 5, 1812), 209-211.

28. Act of Jan. 29, 1812 (chap. 297), *Acts . . . of the Twentieth General Assembly for the Commonwealth of Kentucky* (Frankfort, Ky., 1812), 7-8, RSUS, Session Laws, Kentucky, reel 2; Act of Feb. 3, 1813 (chap. 90), *Acts . . . of the Twenty-first General Assembly for the Commonwealth of Kentucky* (Frankfort, Ky., 1813), 101-103, RSUS, Session Laws, Kentucky, reel 2. Act of Oct. Session, 1812 (chap. 1), *The Public Statute Laws of the State of Connecticut* (n.p., n.d.), 95-97, RSUS, Session Laws, Connecticut, reel 2; Act of Oct. 26, 1812 (chap. 46), *Acts and Laws Passed by the Legislature of the State of Vermont* (Danville, [1812]), 52-53, RSUS, Session Laws, Vermont, reel 3; Act of Dec. 22, 1814, *Acts Passed at the Second Session of the Eighth General Assembly of the Mississippi Territory* (Natchez, 1814), 16-17, RSUS, Session Laws, Mississippi, reel 2.

29. Act of Oct. 19, 1812 (chap. 28), *Acts Passed at the Second Session of the Ninth General Assembly of the State of Tennessee* (Nashville, 1812), 27, RSUS, Session Laws, Tennessee, reel 2; Act of Sept. 16, 1814, *Public Laws of the State of Rhode Island and Providence Plantations* (Newport, [1840?]), 182-183, RSUS, Session Laws, Rhode Island, reel 7.

30. Tisdale to Hawkins, June 1, 1813, Hawkins to Tisdale, June 12, 1813, Governor's Letterbooks, 236, 246, RSUS, Executive Records, North Carolina, reel 7; Act of 1814 (chap. 1), *Laws of the State of North Carolina* (Raleigh, 1815), 3, RSUS, Session Laws, North Carolina, reel 4.

31. Act of Dec. 16, 1814, *Acts Passed at the Second Session of the First Legislature of the State of Louisiana* (New Orleans, 1815), 14-16, RSUS, Session Laws, Louisiana, reel 2.

32. Claiborne to Col. Tousard, Oct. 13, 1812, Governor's Letterbooks, 212, RSUS, Executive Records, Louisiana, reel 2. Holmes to Morgan, April 23, 1814, Governor's Letterbooks, 6-9, RSUS, Executive Records, Mississippi, reel 2.

33. Act of June 1814, *Public Laws of the State of Rhode Island and Providence Plantations* (Newport, [1840?]), 24, RSUS, Session Laws, Rhode Island, reel 8; Act of Oct. 18, 1814 (chap. 69), *Laws of the Commonwealth of Massachusetts* (Boston, 1814-1815), 568-569, RSUS, Session Laws, Massachusetts, reel 6; Act of Nov. 9, 1812 (chap. 149), *Acts and Laws Passed by the Legislature of the State of Vermont* (Danville, [1812]), 208, RSUS, Session Laws, Vermont, reel 2; Act of Dec. 17, 1812, *The Public Laws of the State of New Hampshire* (Concord, 1812), 34, RSUS, Session Laws, New Hampshire, reel 2, and Act of June 14, 1814, *Public Laws of the State of New Hampshire* (Concord, 1814), 28-29, RSUS, Session Laws Act of Feb. 19, 1813, *Public Acts of the Thirty-seventh General Assembly of the State of New Jersey* (Trenton, 1813), 50, RSUS, Session Laws, New Jersey, reel 5b. The Pennsylvania provision was enacted

several times. See Act of March 29, 1813 (chap. 203), *Acts of the General Assembly of the Commonwealth of Pennsylvania* (Philadelphia, 1813), 254, RSUS, Session Laws, Pennsylvania, reel 6, and Act of March 28, 1814 (chap. 189), 348, ibid.

34. Act of Feb. 27, 1813 (chap. 70), *Acts of the General Assembly of the Commonwealth of Pennsylvania* (Philadelphia, 1813), 95-96, RSUS, Session Laws, Pennsylvania; Act of Feb. 2, 1813 (chap. 27), *Laws Passed at the First Session of the Eleventh General Assembly of the State of Ohio* (Chillicothe, 1812 [1813?]), 59-60, RSUS, Session Laws, Ohio, reel 2; Act of Jan. 29, 1813 (chap. 57), *Acts . . . of the Twenty-first General Assembly of the Commonwealth of Kentucky* (Frankfort, Ky., 1813), 53, RSUS, Session Laws, Kentucky, reel 2. Debate on bill to regulate militia of Pennsylvania, March 11, 1813, *Journal of the Twenty Third House of Representatives of the Commonwealth of Pennsylvania . . .* (Harrisburg, 1812 [1813?]), 516-517, 530-532, RSUS, Session Laws, Pennsylvania, reel 12.

35. See Hawkins to Adj. Gen. Calvin Jones, April 27, 1812, Lenoir to Hawkins, May 22, 1812, Governor's Letterbooks, 129-133, 199-200, RSUS, Executive Records, North Carolina, reel 7. Hawkins to Eustis, June 3, 1812, Eustis to Hawkins, June 8, 1812, Governor's Letterbooks, 170-171, 202, ibid.

36. Early to Carruth, Dec. 14, 1814, March 3, 1815, April 7, 1815, Governor's Letterbooks, 58-59, 95, 105, RSUS, Executive Records, Georgia, reel 2. On merchants' refusal to forward supplies, see, for example, William H. Harrison to William Eustis, Aug. 28, 29, 1812, Harrison Papers, LC. *Daily National Intelligencer,* Jan. 19, 1813 (figures on frostbite).

37. Paul John Woehrmann, *The American Invasion of Western Upper Canada, September-October, 1813* (Columbus, 1962), 18, 15.

38. Le Roy, *Social Aspects of Soldiers in the War of 1812,* 4-5.

39. Samuel R. Brown, *Views of the Campaigns of the North-Western Army, &c. . . .* (Burlington, Vt., 1814), 113-115. Reports dated Nov. 6, 8, 11, 1812, in *New York Evening Post,* Nov. 25, 1812, in Ernest Cruikshank, ed., *The Documentary History of the Campaign on the Niagara Frontier,* 9 vols. Welland, Canada, 1902-1908) (reprint, 4 vols., New York, 1971), pt. 2, I, 218-220; Statement of David Harvey, undated, ibid., pt. 2, I, 249.

40. Elias Darnall, *A Journal, Containing an Accurate and Interesting Account of the Hardships, Sufferings, Battles, Defeat and Captivity of those Heroic Kentucky Volunteers and Regulars Commanded by General James Winchester in the Years 1812-1813. . .* (Frankfort, Ky., 1814), 25. See also Robert Breckinridge McAfee, *History of the Late War in the Western Country . . .* (Lexington, Ky., 1816), 183-184.

41. "Journal of the Northwestern Campaign of 1812-13 under Major General W.H. Harrison; by E.D. Wood," in George W. Cullum, *Campaigns of the War of 1812-1815 . . .* (New York, 1879), 402-403.

42. McAfee, *History of the Late War,* 302.

43. Cameron to Hawkins, Aug. 21, 1813, Governor's Letterbooks, 393-394, RSUS, Executive Records, North Carolina, reel 7; King to Hawkins, Oct. 28, 1813, Governor's Letterbooks, 466, ibid.

44. Dudley to Miller, Jan. 13, 1815, Governor's Letterbooks, 39-40; Croom to Miller, Dec. 26, 1814, Governor's Letterbooks, 29-30; Miller to Croom, Jan. 13, 1815, Governor's Letterbooks, 38-39. Blount to Miller, Jan. 24, 1815, Governor's Letterbooks, 53, all in RSUS, Executive Records, North Carolina, reel 7.

45. McDonald to Miller, Jan. 16, 1815, Governor's Letterbooks, 42-43; Atkinson to Miller, Feb. 1, 1815, Governor's Letterbooks, 69-70, in RSUS, Executive Records, North Carolina, reel 7.

46. (From the *Richmond Enquirer*), in the *Daily National Intelligencer,* Jan. 19, 1815.

47. Ernest A. Cruikshank, ed., *Documents Relating to the Invasion of Canada and the Surrender of Detroit, 1812* (Ottawa, 1912), 204. Golovin, "William Wood Thackara," *PMHB* 91 (1967), 306, 310.

48. Quoted in James T. Doyle, *The Organization and Operational Administration of the Ohio Militia in the War of 1812* (Columbus, 1958), 31. LeRoy, *Weakness of Discipline*, 1. Taul's account as quoted in Hammack, *Kentucky and the War of 1812*, 26-27.

49. Jackson to Rachael Jackson, Jan. 28, 1814, Harold D. Moser et al., *The Papers of Andrew Jackson*, 5 vols. to date (Knoxville, 1991), III, 20-21.

50. Golovin, "William Wood Thackara," *PMHB* 91 (1967), 314.

51. Report of Gen. Samuel Hopkins to Gov. Isaac Shelby, [Oct.], Nov. 27, 1812, *Niles' Weekly Register* 3 (Nov. 28, Dec. 26, 1812), 204-205, 264-265.

52. Winder to Armstrong, Aug. 7, 1813, Letterbooks of the Governor and Council, RSUS, Executive Records, Maryland, Reel 3.

53. James Grant Forbes, *Report of the Trial of Brig. General William Hull; Commanding the Northwestern Army of the United States . . .* (New York, 1814), 118.

54. Doyle, *Organization of Ohio Militia*, 26-27.

55. Golovin, "William Wood Thackara," *PMHB* 91 (1967), 307-308.

56. McAfee, *History of the Late War*, 149-151.

57. Quoted in *Daily National Intelligencer*, Jan. 17, 1814.

58. "Journal of E.D. Wood," Cullum, *Campaigns of the War of 1812-1815*, 378, 383.

59. McClure to Armstrong, Dec. 10, 1813, *Annals*, 13th Cong., 2d sess. (appendix), 2474-2475.

60. Jackson to Willie Blount, Jan. 2, 1814, Jackson to Robert Hays, Jan. 4, 1814, Jackson to Hugh Lawson White, Jan. 6, 1814, Moser, ed., *Jackson Papers*, III, 5-6, 7-8, 9. See also Marquis James, *Andrew Jackson: Border Captain* (Indianapolis, 1938), 173-176; Frank Lawrence Owsley, Jr., *Struggle for the Gulf Borderlands: The Creek War and the Battle of New Orleans, 1812-1815* (Gainesville, 1981), 68-71.

61. Patton, Harris, and Pickens to Jackson, Feb. 3, 1814, Moser, ed., *Jackson Papers*, III, 24-26.

Chapter 4

1. Hammack, *Kentucky and the War of 1812*, 14-15, 19-20. The other congressmen were Richard M. Johnson, who organized a regiment of mounted volunteers; John Simpson and William P. Duvall, who served as captains in the militia; and Samuel McKee and Thomas Montgomery, who served as lowly privates. *Daily National Intelligencer*, June 11, 1812.

2. *Niles' Weekly Register* 2 (June 13, 27, Aug. 15, 1812), 256, 286, 392. Other reports are found in the *Daily National Intelligencer*, June 2, 1812.

3. A.Y. Nicoll to Eustis, June 6, 1812, *Annals*, 12th Cong., 1st sess. (appendix), 2111-2112; Eustis to Anderson, June 8, 1812, ibid., 2113. Eustis to Anderson, June 6, 1812, ibid., 2110; Act of April 10, 1812, ibid., 2267-2269.

4. Mullany to Gen. Peter B. Porter, July 12, 1812, Augustus A. Porter Papers, BEHS, reel 2.

5. Capt. William Jack and Lt. Robert Layson to Claiborne, June 12, 1813, J.F.H. Claiborne Collection, Box 14, Mississippi Department of Archives and History.

6. (From the *Virginia Patriot*), *Daily National Intelligencer*, June 2, 1812. *Niles' Weekly Register* 3 (Oct. 17, 1812), 103-104.

7. The *Daily National Intelligencer* account in the *Baltimore Patriot*, Aug. 19, 1813, mentions only one apprentice, Daniel Wells. The Baltimore-based *Niles' Weekly*

Register 5 (Sept. 18, 1813), 47-48, adds more information and lists another apprentice, John Pocock.

8. *Daily National Intelligencer,* Sept. 8, 1813, April 1, 1814; *Niles' Weekly Register* 6 (April 16, 1814), 120.

9. *Niles' Weekly Register* (Supplement), 7 (Feb. 15, 1815), 96.

10. Ibid., 8 (March 18, 1815), 46.

11. The quotas were: Massachusetts, 10,000; New Hampshire, 3,500; Connecticut, 3,000; Vermont, 3,000, and Rhode Island, 500. *ASPMA,* Doc. 111, I, 319. A good general discussion of state command versus federal command appears in Donald R. Hickey, "New England's Defense Problem and the Genesis of the Hartford Convention," *NEQ* 50 (Dec. 1977), 587-604. The relevant documents are conveniently gathered in *Message of His Excellency Governour Griswold to the General Assembly, at their Special Session, August 25, 1812* (New Haven, 1812), RSUS, Executive Records, Governor's Messages, Connecticut, reel 1. Documents cited in the text are: Eustis to Griswold, June 12, 1812; Griswold to Eustis, June 17, 1812; Dearborn to Griswold, June 22, 1812; Griswold to Council, June 29, 1812; Council to Griswold, June 29, 1812.

12. Lt. Gov. John Cotton Smith (Acting Governor) to Dearborn, July 2, 1812; Smith to Eustis, July 2, 1812; Eustis to Smith, July 14, 1812; Dearborn to Smith, July 17, 1812; Council Report, Aug. 4, 1812, *Message of His Excellency Gouvernour Griswold to the General Assembly,* RSUS, Executive Records, Governor's Messages, Connecticut, reel 1.

13. Griswold to Eustis, Aug. 13, 1812, Proclamation of Governor, Aug. 6, 1812, *Message to His Excellency Gourvernour Griswold to the General Assembly,* RSUS, Executive Records, Governor's Messages, Connecticut, reel 1. See *Report of the Committee of the General Assembly at their Special Session, August 25, 1812, on that Part of His Excellency, the Governour's Speech, which relates to his Correspondence with the Secretary of War, &c.* (New Haven, 1812), RSUS, Executive Records, Governor's Messages, Connecticut, reel 1.

14. *Speech of His Excellency the Governor of the Commonwealth of Massachusetts . . . in January, 1812* (Boston, 1811 [?]), 19, RSUS, Legislative Documents, Massachusetts, reel 1. According to Gerry, even former president John Adams had received a threat upon his life.

15. *ASPMA,* Doc. 115, I, 324. The three justices were Theophilus Parsons, Samuel Sewall, and Isaac Parker.

16. Strong to Eustis (enclosing Supreme Court opinion), Aug. 5, 1812, ibid., 323.

17. *Answer of the House of Representatives, to His Excellency the Governor's Speech* (n.p., 1812), 38, RSUS, Legislative Documents, Massachusetts, reel 1; *Answer of the Senate, to the Governor's Speech . . . in October, 1812* (Boston, 1812), 4-6, ibid.

18. Minutes of the Council of War, Aug. 12, 1812, 1-2, RSUS, Executive Records, Proceedings of Extraordinary Executive Bodies, Rhode Island, reel 1. *ASPMA,* Doc. 142, I, 621. Minutes of the Council of War, Sept. 24, 1812, 3-4, RSUS, Executive Records, Proceedings of Extraordinary Executive Bodies, Rhode Island, reel 1.

19. [John Lowell,] *Perpetual War, the Policy of Mr. Madison. . .* (Boston 1812), 11, 73, 89.

20. Ibid., 96.

21. Message of Gov. Plumer, Nov. 18, 1812, in *Niles' Weekly Register* 3 (Dec. 5, 1812), 209-211; ibid. 3 (Dec. 19, 1812), 256. The vote was 7-5 in the New Hampshire Senate and 93-77 in the New Hampshire House. Ibid., 3 (Oct. 24, 1812), 115-116.

22. The two letters, entitled "The Militia of the Union," are in the *Daily National Intelligencer,* May 29, June 7, 1813. For the Gales editorial, see ibid., June 7, 1813.

23. Resolutions of House of Delegates (Md.), *Niles' Weekly Register* 3 (Dec. 19, 1812), 248; Resolutions of Dec. 24, 1812, ibid. (Jan. 2, 1813), 273; Senate Resolutions (Md.), ibid. (Jan. 16, 1813), 305. Niles noted the Senate resolutions replied to the former set of House resolutions of Dec. 22. Either Niles misstated the date or his Dec. 19 issue was printed later than the publication date.

24. Message of Gov. Barbour, *Daily National Intelligencer,* Nov. 30, 1812; Message of Gov. Middleton, Aug. 24, 1812, *Niles' Weekly Register* 3 (Sept. 24, 1812), 50.

25. Richardson, comp., *Messages and Papers,* I, 516.

26. Message of Gov. Plumer, June 6, 1812, *Niles' Weekly Register* 2 (June 27, 1812), 274; Message of Gov. Galusha, ibid., 3 (Oct. 24, 1812), 115-116.

27. Report of House Committee, Oct. sess., 33-34, RSUS, Session Laws, Rhode Island, reel 7; Message of Gov. Jones, Feb. 16, 1813, Feb. sess., 3-4, ibid.; Message of Gov. Jones, June 29, 1813, June sess., 3, ibid.

28. Senate committee report, n.d., Doc. 4, 4-6, 6-7, 10-11, 13-14, 16, RSUS, Legislative Documents, Massachusetts, reel 2; *Public Documents of the Legislature of Massachusetts . . .* (Boston, 1813), Doc. 8, 68-69, ibid.

29. Tompkins to Dearborn, June 28, 1812, in Cruikshank, ed., *Documentary History,* pt. 1, I, 83-84. See also the message of Gov. Arthur Middleton (S.C.), Aug. 24, 1812, in *Niles' Weekly Register* 3 (Sept. 26, 1812), 50.

30. Annual Message, Dec. 3, 1812, *Journal of the Senate,* vol. 23 (Harrisburg, 1812), 16-19, RSUS, Legislative Records, Pennsylvania, reel 7.

31. Message of Dec. 8, 1813, Letterbooks of the Governor and Council, RSUS, Executive Records, Maryland, reel 3. Act of Feb. 2, 1811 (chap. 157), *Laws of the State of Delaware* (Dover, 1811), 443-444, RSUS, Session Laws, Delaware, reel 2. On May 25, 1812, however, Delaware reinstituted fines. The number of drills was not prescribed, but companies had to be mustered on or before the first Monday of August to be classed. Company captains failing to comply would forfeit their commissions and pay a fine of fifty dollars. Act of May 25, 1812 (chap. 217), ibid., 582-586.

32. Hawkins to Eustis, June 3, 1812, Eustis to Hawkins, June 8, 1812, Governor's Letterbooks, 170-171, 202, RSUS, Executive Records, North Carolina, reel 7. Annual Message, Nov. 18, 1812, ibid., 371. See also Maj. Nathan Tisdale to Adj. Gen. Calvin Jones, Sept. 8, 1812, ibid., 307.

33. Pinckney to Hawkins, July 4, 1812, ibid., 221; Major General Thomas Brown to Hawkins, Aug. 1, 1812, ibid., 261; Pinckney to Hawkins, Aug. 27, Sept. 19, 1812, ibid., 267, 321; Major Nathan Tisdale to Adj. Gen. Calvin Jones, Sept. 8, 1812, ibid., 307, ibid.; General Orders, Nov. 4, 1812, by James Ferguson (aide-de-camp to Pinckney), ibid., 357-358.

34. General Orders, Jan. 7, 1812, Executive Journals, 271, RSUS, Executive Records, Georgia, reel 10; Mitchell to Brig. Gen. John Floyd, March 29, 1812, Governor's Letterbooks, 58, RSUS, Executive Records, Georgia, reel 2. Mitchell to Brig. Gen. Thomas Flournoy, Sept. 21, 1812, 73, RSUS, Executive Records, Georgia, reel 2.

35. Annual Message, Nov. 2, 1812, Executive Journals, 37-38, RSUS, Executive Records, Georgia, reel 10; Mitchell to Jones, March 26, 1813, Governor's Letterbooks, 98-99, RSUS, Executive Records, Georgia, reel 2.

36. Mitchell to Gen. Thomas Flournoy, Sept. 21, 1812, Governor's Letterbooks, 73-74, RSUS, Executive Records, Georgia, reel 2. Mitchell to Maj. Gen. John McIntosh, Sept. 1, 1813, ibid., 150.

37. Holmes to Eustis, June 15, 1812, Holmes to Wilkinson, July 22, 1812, Governor's Letterbooks, 173-174, 195, RSUS, Executive Records, Mississippi, reel

2. Holmes to Eustis, Sept. 29, 1812, Governor's Letterbooks, 230, ibid.. Holmes to Wilkinson, Oct. 6, 1812, Governor's Letterbooks, 231, ibid.

38. Details of the insurrection may be found in Gov. Claiborne to Major St. Armand, Jan. 9, 1811, Claiborne to Major Bullingney, Jan. 9, 1811, Claiborne to Secretary of State, n.d., Claiborne to Secretary of State, Jan. 11, 12, 1811, Claiborne to Colonel André, Jan. 13, 1811, Claiborne to Secretary of State, Jan. 16, 1811, Claiborne to Judge St. Martin, Jan. 19, 1811, Claiborne to John N. Detrehan, Jan. 19, 1811, Claiborne to Major Dubourg, Jan. 21, 1811, Official Letters, 18, 19-20, 20, 21, 22, 23, 25, 26-27, 32-33, 38, RSUS, Executive Records, Louisiana, reel 2. Claiborne's Message to Legislature, Jan. 29, 1811, gives a succinct official version of the events, Official Letters, 61-62, ibid. See also Herbert Aptheker, *American Negro Slave Revolts* (1943; reprint, New York, 1969), 249-251. Claiborne to Ballinger, Jan. 20, 1811, Claiborne to André, Jan. 14, 1811, Official Letters, 39, 25, RSUS, Executive Records, Louisiana, reel 2.

39. Message to Legislature, Jan. 29, 1811, Official Letters, 63-64, RSUS, Executive Records, Louisiana, reel 2. Act of April 29, 1811, *Acts Passed at the Second Session of the Third Legislature of the Territory of Orleans* . . . (New Orleans, 1811), chap. 34, RSUS, Session Laws, Louisiana, reel 2. Claiborne to Eustis, May 31, 1811, Official Letters, 286, RSUS, Executive Records, Louisiana, reel 2.

40. Message to Legislature, July 30, 1812, Official Letters, 155, RSUS, Executive Records, Louisiana, reel 2. The veto is in Message to Legislature, Sept. 5, 1812, Claiborne to Wilkinson, Sept. 22, 1812, ibid., 190-191, 199. The legislature also passed a resolution requesting a loan from the national government of 4,000 stand of arms as well as other equipment. Resolution, Sept. 7, 1812, *Acts Passed at the First Session of the First General Assembly of the State of Louisiana* . . . (New Orleans, 1812), chap. 23, 84, RSUS, Session Laws, Louisiana, reel 1.

Chapter 5

1. Robert S. Lambert, "The Conduct of Militia at Tippecanoe: Elihu Stout's Controversy with Colonel John P. Boyd, January 1812," *Indiana Magazine of History* 51 (Sept. 1955), 237-250.

2. "Resolutions of Militia Officers of St. Clair County," Feb. 7, 1812; "Statement of Militia Officers of St. Clair County," Feb. 7, 1812; Edwards to Eustis, March 3, 1812; Eustis to Edwards, March 11, 1812; Eustis to Edwards and Gov. Charles Scott (Ky.), May 2, 1812, in Clarence Edwin Carter, ed., *The Territorial Papers of the United States: Vol. 16, The Territory of Illinois, 1809-1814* (Washington, D.C., 1948), 188-189, 189-190, 193-194, 197-198, 217.

3. McAfee, *History of the Late War*, 49-52. Forbes, *Trial of Brig. General William Hull*, 124, 105, 124-125.

4. Cass to Eustis, Sept. 10, 1812. Forbes, *Trial of Brig. General William Hull*, app. 2, 28.

5. William Hull, *Defence of Brigadier General W. Hull* . . . (Boston, 1814), 52. Forbes, *Trial of Brig. General William Hull*, 21, 124-125, 153.

6. Hull, *Defence*, 54, 89-92.

7. Ibid., 92-93. Alec R. Gilpin, *The War of 1812 in the Old Northwest* (East Lansing, Mich., 1958), 79-80; McAfee, *History of the Late War*, 64.

8. Forbes, *Trial of Brig. General William Hull*, 67, 70. McAfee, *History of the Late War*, 73-75. Hull, *Defence*, 107, 137.

9. Hull, *Defence*, 94, 82, 100. Forbes, *Trial of Brig. General William Hull*, 123.

10. Hull, *Defence*, 165.

11. McAfee, *History of the Late War*, 106-108. Hammack, *Kentucky and the War of 1812*, 30-34.

12. McAfee, *History of the Late War*, 151. Campbell is quoted in John H. Niebaum, "The Pittsburgh Blues," *WPHM* 4 (1921), 117-118. See also Gilpin, *War of 1812 in the Old Northwest*, 153-154; McAfee, *History of the Late War*, 177-181.

13. Hammack, *Kentucky and the War of 1812*, 46-47. Gilpin, *War of 1812 in the Old Northwest*, 161-164.

14. McAfee, *History of the Late War*, 204-207. Darnall, *Journal*, 29.

15. The most extensive account of this episode is in McAfee, *History of the Late War*, 204-227. See also Hammack, *Kentucky and the War of 1812*, 47-54, and Gilpin, *War of 1812 in the Old Northwest*, 163-169.

16. Ibid., 174-176. See also Emanuel Hallaman, *The British Invasions of Ohio— 1813* (Columbus, Ohio, 1958), 1-2.

17. Armstrong served as aide-de-camp to Gen. Horatio Gates and later as minister to France. A controversial choice, he was grudgingly approved to head the War Department because of his authorship of the Newburgh Addresses, written at the end of the Revolutionary War. In France, Armstrong studied the military campaigns of the French army, and he was believed to have a good military mind. In 1812, Madison appointed him a brigadier general and placed him in charge of the defense of New York City. Armstrong also found time to publish a short book, *Hints to Young Generals*, a distillation of the concepts of the French military writer Maj. Gen. Antoine H. Jomini. A good judge of military talent, Armstrong advanced the careers of many young military leaders who influenced the U.S. Army until the Civil War. See C. Edward Skeen, *John Armstrong, Jr., 1758-1843: A Biography* (Syracuse, 1981). His appointment is discussed on 121-125; his conduct of the War Department on 127-143. Armstrong to Duane, April 29, 1813, *Historical Magazine* 4 (Aug. 1868), 62.

18. Armstrong to Harrison, March 5, 7, May 4, 1813, Logan Esarey, ed., *Messages and Letters of William Henry Harrison*, 2 vols. (Indianapolis, 1922), II, 379-380, 380-381, 430-431. See also Armstrong to Capt. Thomas S. Jesup, March 9, 1813, WD/LS, VI, 310.

19. Harrison to Armstrong, March 27, 1813, Esarey, ed., *Harrison Letters*, II, 400-404.

20. Harrison to Armstrong, March 28, 1813, ibid., II, 404-406.

21. Harrison to Shelby, April 9, 1813, ibid., II, 416-417; Harrison to Armstrong, April 17, 1813, ibid., II, 418-419. Shelby is quoted in Hammack, *Kentucky and the War of 1812*, 59.

22. Armstrong to Huntington, April 1, 1813, WD/LS, VI, 343-344.

23. A good, succinct account is Hallaman, *British Invasions of Ohio*, 2-17. See also McAfee, *History of the Late War*, 258-277.

24. For accounts of the siege and battle on May 5, see McAfee, *History of the Late War*, 259-277; Hammack, *Kentucky and the War of 1812*, 62-68; Gilpin, *War of 1812 in the Old Northwest*, 183-190.

25. Quoted in Hallaman, *British Invasions of Ohio*, 15. General Orders, May 9, 1813, *Daily National Intelligencer*, May 22, 1813. Harrison to Armstrong, May 13, 1813, *Niles' Weekly Register* 4 (May 22, 1813), 192.

26. *Niles' Weekly Register* 4 (May 22, 1813), 190.

27. Armstrong to Harrison, April 11, 1813, Harrison to Armstrong, May 13, 1813, Esarey, ed., *Harrison Letters*, II, 417, 442-447. See also Meigs to Armstrong, April 11, 1813, Worthington to Armstrong, April 10, 1813, McArthur and Cass to Armstrong, March 31, 1813, Owings to Armstrong, May 2, 1813, Cass to Armstrong, April 18, May 8, June 16, 1813, Harrison to Armstrong, May 26, 1813, McArthur to Armstrong, June 30, 1813, WD/LR.

28. Owings to Armstrong, April 17, 1813, WD/LR.

29. Johnson to Armstrong, April 13, 1813, WD/LR. See also Armstrong to Ninian Edwards, May 4, 1813, WD/LS, VIII, 146. Armstrong to Johnson, May 5, 1813, WD/LS, VIII, 148; Johnson to Armstrong, May 12, 1813, WD/LR.

30. Harrison to Armstrong, May 23, 1813, Esarey, ed., *Harrison Letters*, II, 458-459. Johnson to Armstrong, June 4, 1813, WD/LR; Johnson to Harrison, June 14, 1813, WD/LR. Johnson to Harrison, July 4, 1813, Esarey, ed., *Harrison Letters*, II, 482. See also Harrison to Meigs, June 23, 1813, ibid., 476; Harrison to Armstrong, June 24, July 2, 1813, ibid., 478, 480-482; McAfee, *History of the Late War*, 293-307.

31. Armstrong to Harrison, July 14, 1813, Esarey, ed., *Harrison Letters*, II, 491-492. See also Harrison to Armstrong, July 9, 12, 1813, ibid.; Johnson to Harrison, July 9, 1813, ibid.

32. Harrison to Armstrong, July 6, 1813, ibid., II, 484; Harrison to Shelby, July 20, 1813, ibid., II, 492-493; Harrison to Meigs, Aug. 6, 1813, ibid., II, 517.

33. Harrison to Armstrong, July 23, July 24, 1813, ibid., II, 494-495, 496.

34. Gilpin, *War of 1812 in the Old Northwest*, 205-208; Hallaman, *British Invasions of Ohio*, 28-35; Harrison to Armstrong, Aug. 4, 1813, Croghan to Harrison, Aug. 5, 1813, *Daily National Intelligencer*, Aug. 12, 1813; Niebaum, "The Pittsburgh Blues," *WPHM* 4, pt. 2 (1921), 184-185.

35. Harrison to Armstrong, Aug. 11, 1813, Esarey, ed., *Harrison Letters*, II, 523. Harrison to Armstrong, Aug. 22, 29, 1813, Sept. 8, 1813, Esarey, ed., *Harrison Letters*, II, 525-526, 531, 537.

36. Perry to Harrison, Sept. 10, 1813, ibid., 539; Harrison to Armstrong, Sept. 15, 1813, ibid., 541; Perry to Secretary of the Navy William Jones, Sept. 23, 1813, ibid., 546; Harrison to Armstrong, Sept. 27, 1813, ibid., 551.

37. Harrison to Armstrong, Sept. 30, 1813, ibid., 556. Harrison to Armstrong, Oct. 9, 1813, ibid., 558-565. Accounts of the battle are in Woehrmann, *American Invasion of Western Upper Canada*, 37-45, and McAfee, *History of the Late War*, 362-398.

38. *Daily National Intelligencer*, Oct. 28, 1813.

39. *Niles' Weekly Register* 5 (Dec. 18, 1813), 263-264.

40. Harrison to Armstrong, Feb. 13, 1814, quoted in Freeman Cleaves, *Old Tippecanoe* (New York, 1939), 218.

41. Armstrong to Harrison, March 2, 1814, in Esarey, ed., *Harrison Letters*, II, 631. Armstrong to Harrison, April 25, 1814, in ibid., II, 645; Armstrong to Holmes, April 25, 1814, WD/LS, VII, 172; Croghan to Harrison [n.d.], McAfee, *History of the Late War*, 449-452.

42. Cleaves, *Old Tippecanoe*, 222. See also Harrison to Madison, May 11, 1814, in Esarey, ed., *Harrison Letters*, II, 647-648.

43. Skeen, *Armstrong*, 142-143. *Daily National Intelligencer*, Sept. 3, 1814. See also Gilpin, *War of 1812 in the Old Northwest*, 242-245.

44. McArthur to Armstrong, July 31, Aug. 8, 1814, WD/LR.

45. Shelby to Armstrong, Aug. 13, 1814, ibid.

46. McArthur Report, Nov. 18, 1814, *Daily National Intelligencer*, Dec. 22, 1814.

Chapter 6

1. Asa Stanard, John Selay, and Blenact Field to Porter, April 15, 1812, Augustus A. Porter Papers, BEHS, reel 2.

2. Tompkins to Porter, May 11, 1812, Porter Papers, BEHS, reel 2; Swift and Barton to Porter, June 24, 1812, in Cruikshank, ed., *Documentary History*, pt. 1, I, 71-73. Tompkins to Porter, June 20, 1812, Porter Papers, BEHS, reel 2; Wadsworth

to Tompkins, June 28, 1812, in Cruikshank, ed., *Documentary History*, pt. 1, I, 77-78. Tompkins to Peter B. Porter, July 8, 1812, Porter Papers, BEHS, reel 2.

3. Hall to Tompkins, July 4, 1812, Porter Papers, BEHS, reel 2. See also John M. O'Connor to Peter B. Porter, July 1, 1812, and Augustus Porter to Peter B. Porter, July 2, 1812, ibid.

4. Van Rensselaer to Tompkins, July 23, 1812, in Cruikshank, ed., *Documentary History*, pt. 1, I, 142.

5. Van Rensselaer to Dearborn, Aug. 28, Aug. 31, Sept. 1, 1812, ibid., I, 219, 227, 230. Dearborn to Van Rensselaer, Sept. 1, Sept. 2, 1812, ibid., I, 231, 232.

6. Solomon Van Rensselaer to Maj. Gen. Morgan Lewis, Sept. 11, 1812, ibid., I, 254. Van Rensselaer's anger with Porter almost resulted in a duel, but Gen. Van Rensselaer forbade the duel. See Solomon Van Rensselaer to Porter, Sept. 14, 1812, ibid., I, 262.

7. Oliver Phelps, Freeman Attwater, and J. Howley to Gov. Tompkins, Oct. 4, 1812, ibid., pt. 2, I, 32.

8. Van Rensselaer to Dearborn, Oct. 14, 1812, in *Daily National Intelligencer,* Oct. 29, 1812. See, for example, Hickey, *War of 1812*, 87. Statement of Lt. Col. Thompson Mead, Seventeenth Regiment, Detached Militia, Nov. 18, 1812, in Cruikshank, ed., *Documentary History*, pt. 2, I, 90-93. Accounts of the Battle of Queenston may be found in *Daily National Intelligencer,* Oct. 27, Nov. 7, 1812; *Niles' Weekly Register* 3 (Oct. 31, 1812), 140-141. See also Theodore Crackel, "The Battle of Queenston Heights, 13 October 1812," in Charles Heller and William Stofft, eds., *America's First Battles, 1776-1965* (Lawrence, Kans., 1986), 33-56.

9. Smyth to Van Rensselaer, Sept. 29, 1812, in Cruikshank, ed., *Documentary History*, pt. 1, I, 300; Van Rensselaer to Smyth, Sept. 30, 1812, ibid., pt. 1, I, 305-306.

10. Van Rensselaer to Dearborn, Oct. 8, 1812, ibid., pt. 1, I, 40-42. Van Rensselaer to Eustis, ibid., pt. 1, I, 81.

11. Van Rensselaer to Smyth, Oct. 10, 11, and 12, 1812, ibid., pt. 1, I, 59-60, 66, 68. Smyth to Editor of *Daily National Intelligencer,* Nov. 8, 1812, published in ibid., Nov. 26, 1812.

12. Tompkins's Message to the New York Legislature, Nov. 3, 1812, ibid., Nov. 17, 1812.

13. Inspection reports of Capt. William King, enclosed in Gen. Smyth to Langdon Cheves (Speaker of the House of Representatives), Feb. 8, 1814, in *Annals,* 13th Cong., 2d sess. (appendix), Docs. 3 and 4, 2482-2483, 2483-2484.

14. Ibid., Doc. 9, 2486, Doc. 11, 2487; Doc. 18, 2491-2492.

15. John Lovett to Joseph Alexander, Nov. 4. 1812, in Cruikshank, ed., *Documentary History*, pt. 2, I, 181; Livingston to Smyth, Nov. 4, 1812, ibid., pt. 2, I, 180.

16. On the executions, see statement of David Harvey, undated, ibid., pt. 2, I, 249. Smyth's statement appears in ibid., pt. 2, I, 232-233.

17. Smyth to Dearborn, Nov. 9, 1812, ibid., pt. 2, I, 186-188.

18. Snyder to Brigade Inspectors, Aug. 25, 1812, ibid., pt. 1, I, 208. Smyth to Dearborn, Nov. 9, 1812, ibid., pt. 2, I, 186-188. Smyth to Tannehill, Nov. 21, 1812, ibid., pt. 2, I, 225. Tannehill to Smyth, Nov. 22, 1812, ibid., pt. 2, I, 225-226.

19. Proclamation, Nov. 10, 1812, ibid., pt. 2, I, 194. Josiah Robinson to Col. Solomon Van Rensselaer, Dec. 2, 1812, ibid., pt. 2, I, 266. See also the report in the *Buffalo Gazette,* Dec. 1, 1812, ibid., pt. 2, I, 259.

20. Smyth to George McClure, Lewis Birdsall, John Griffin, and William B. Rochester, Dec. 3, 1812, in Cruikshank, ed., *Documentary History*, pt. 2, I, 270-271.

21. Statement of Bill Sherman, Dec. 3, 1812, ibid., pt. 2, I, 247. See also the reports

in the *New York Gazette*, Dec. 15, 1812, ibid., pt. 2, I, 281; *New York Evening Post*, Dec. 13, 1812, ibid., pt. 2, I, 281-282; and *Niles' Weekly Register* 3 (Dec. 19, 1812), 252.

22. Porter Address, "To the Public," *Buffalo Gazette*, Dec. 15, 1812, in Cruikshank, ed., *Documentary History*, pt. 2, I, 303-308.

23. Smyth to Editors of *Daily National Intelligencer*, Jan. 28, 1813, in Cruikshank, ed., *Documentary History*, pt. 2, I, 308-310.

24. Accounts of the Buffalo riot may be found in Abel M. Grosvenor to his brother, Nov. 25, 1812, published in the *New York Evening Post*, Dec. 10, 1812, ibid., pt. 2, I, 238, and a letter from an unknown person to Col. Solomon Van Rensselaer, Dec. 6, 1812, in the *New York Evening Post*, Dec. 24, 1812, ibid., pt. 2, I, 282-284.

25. Tannehill to Smyth, Dec. 7, 1812, ibid., pt. 2, I, 285-286; General Order, Dec. 8, 1812, ibid., pt. 2, I, 291; *Buffalo Gazette*, Dec. 22, 1814, ibid., pt. 2, I, 335.

26. Secretary of War Eustis to Gen. Dearborn, Dec. 19, 1812, ibid., pt. 2, I, 330.

27. Allan S. Everest, *The War of 1812 in the Champlain Valley* (Syracuse, 1981), 91-92.

28. *Daily National Intelligencer*, Dec. 22, 1812.

29. A. C. Clarke to Porter, May 10, 1813, Porter Papers, BEHS, reel 2.

30. Skeen, *Armstrong*, 145.

31. Ibid., 154-155; Brown to Armstrong, June 1, 1813, *Niles' Weekly Register* 4 (June 19, 1813), 261. See also Brown to Tompkins, June 1, 1813, in Cruikshank, ed., *Documentary History*, pt. 1, II, 283-287. There is an obituary for Colonel Mills in *Military Monitor* 1 (June 28, 1813), 350.

32. This account is based on a memorandum (undated) in Peter B. Porter Papers, BEHS, reel 2; Porter to Dearborn, July 11, 1813, ibid.; Porter to Dearborn, July 13, 1813, in Cruikshank, ed., *Documentary History*, pt. 2, II, 223-225.

33. Porter is the subject of three doctoral dissertations: I. Frank Mogavero, "Peter B. Porter, Citizen and Statesman" (Ottawa University, 1950); Joseph Anthony Grande, "The Political Career of Peter Buell Porter, 1797-1829" (University of Notre Dame, 1971); and Daniel Dean Roland, "Peter Buell Porter and Self Interest in American Politics" (Claremont Graduate School, 1990).

34. Porter to Armstrong, July 27, 1813, copy enclosed in Porter to Tompkins, July 27, 1813, in Cruikshank, ed., *Documentary History*, pt. 2, II, 282-285. Boyd to Porter, July 21, 1813, Porter Papers, BEHS, Reel 4.

35. Porter to Boyd, July 22, 1813, Cruikshank, ed., *Documentary History*, pt. 2, II, 262-264. Boyd to Porter, Aug. 1, 1813, ibid., pt. 2, II, 297-298.

36. Porter to Boyd, Aug. 5, 1813, ibid., pt. 2, II, 311-312. See also Erastus Granger to Boyd, Aug. 6, 1813, ibid., pt. 2, II, 315-316. Boyd to Porter, Aug. 8, 1813, ibid., pt. 2, II, 322.

37. Boyd to Porter, Aug. 13, 1813, Cruikshank, ed., *Documentary History*, pt. 3, II, 14; Boyd to Armstrong, Aug. 15, 17, 1813, ibid., pt. 3, II, 23-24, 30-31. Porter to Boyd, Aug. 28, 30, 1813, Porter Papers, BEHS, reel 2.

38. General Orders, Aug. 25, 1813, Cruikshank, ed., *Documentary History*, pt. 3, II, 69; Tompkins to McClure, Aug. 27, 1813, ibid., pt. 3, II, 77-78. McClure to Tompkins, Sept. 10, 1813, ibid., pt. 3, II, 112-113; "Address of Brigadier General McClure to his Brigade," *Buffalo Gazette*, Sept. 28, 1813, ibid., pt. 3, II, 113-115.

39. McClure Proclamation, Oct. 2, 1813, ibid., pt. 3, II, 184-186; Advertisement in *Buffalo Gazette*, Oct. 5, 1813, ibid., pt. 3, II, 186.

40. McClure to Tompkins [Nov. 1813], ibid., pt. 1, III, 164-165; Harrison to Tompkins, Nov. 1, 1813, ibid., pt. 1, III, 116-117.

41. Armstrong to Harrison, Nov. 3, 1813, ibid., pt. 1, III, 127-128; Harrison to Armstrong, Nov. 8, 11, 1813, in Esarey, ed., *Harrison Letters*, II, 596-598; McClure to Harrison, Nov. 15, 1813, in Cruikshank, ed., *Documentary History*, pt. 1, III, 181;

Harrison to McClure, Nov. 15, 1813, ibid., pt. 1, III, 190-191. The quotation is in an excerpt from a letter, dated Nov. 14-15, 1813, in the *New York Evening Post,* Nov. 29, 1813, ibid., pt. 1, III, 179.

42. McClure to Tompkins, Nov. 21, 1813, ibid., pt. 1, III, 222; Armstrong to McClure, Nov. 25, 1813, ibid., pt., 1 III, 235; Armstrong to Tompkins, Nov. 26, 1813, ibid., pt. 1, III, 238-239; Tompkins to Hall, Nov. 28, 1813, ibid., pt. 1, III, 240-241.

43. General Order, Nov. 30, 1813, ibid., pt. 1, III, 244-245. McClure to Tompkins, Dec. 6, 1813, ibid., pt. 1, III, 253-254.

44. McClure to Armstrong, Dec. 10, 1813, ibid., pt. 1, III, 262-263.

45. Armstrong to [McClure], Oct. 4, 1813, ibid., pt. 3, II, 193; Madison to Armstrong, Dec. 29, 1813, Congressional Ed., *Letters and Other Writings of James Madison,* 4 vols. (Philadelphia, 1865), III, 395. Three officers under McClure (John A. Rogers, Captain, Twenty-fourth U.S. Infantry, John Wilson, Brigadier Major of Militia, and Donald Fraser, Lieutenant, Thirteenth Infantry) wrote the editor of the *Buffalo Gazette,* Dec. 21, 1813, in Cruikshank, ed., *Documentary History,* pt. 2, III, 9-10, explaining and justifying McClure's action. They asserted that the act was not only authorized but "necessary for the protection of our frontier."

46. On Dec. 25, McClure wrote Armstrong that the loss of Fort Niagara was due to its commander, Captain Leonard. It was a "notorious fact," he wrote, that Leonard was not at the fort but was instead at home "much intoxicated." McClure to Armstrong, Dec. 25, 1813, *Annals,* 13th Cong., 2d sess. (appendix), 2478.

47. Hopkins to Tompkins, Dec. 20, 1813, in Cruikshank, ed., *Documentary History,* pt. 2, III, 24-25; McClure to Tompkins, Dec. 20, 1813, ibid., pt, 2, III, 25-26. McClure to Armstrong, Dec. 25, 1813, *Annals,* 13th Cong., 2d sess. (appendix), 2478.

48. Spencer to Tompkins, Dec. 26, 1813, in Cruikshank, ed., *Documentary History,* pt. 2, III, 52-54.

49. McClure to Granger, Dec. 25, 28, 1813, ibid., pt. 2, III, 46, 61.

50. McClure to Armstrong, Dec. 25, 1813, *Annals,* 13th Cong., 2d sess. (appendix), 2478.

51. Hall to Tompkins, Dec. 26, 1813, in Cruikshank, ed., *Documentary History,* pt. 2, III, 54-55; Hall to McClure, Dec. 29, 1813, ibid., pt. 2, III, 64. Hall to Tompkins, Jan. 4, 6, 1814, pt. 2, III, 79-80, 95-96.

52. Cass to Armstrong, Jan. 12, 1814, ibid., pt. 2, III, 109. *Manlius Times,* Jan. 8, 1814, ibid., pt. 2, III, 83; *New York Evening Post,* Jan. 19, 1814, ibid., pt. 2, III, 84.

53. Camp to editor of *Buffalo Gazette,* Jan. 29, 1814, ibid., pt. 2, III, 156-157.

54. Wadsworth to Tompkins, Jan. 6, 1814, ibid., pt. 2, III, 97.

55. Ibid., pt. 2, III, 116-117.

56. Everest, *War of 1812 in the Champlain Valley,* 129-130.

57. The Chittenden affair is discussed in *Niles' Weekly Register* 5 (Nov. 13, 27, Dec. 4, 11, 1813), 181-184, 212, 230, 251.

58. Quoted in *Daily National Intelligencer,* Nov. 25, 1813. Message of Gov. Pennington, ibid., Nov. 9, 1813; Resolutions of N.J. Legislature, Feb. 12, 1814, *Niles' Weekly Register* 6 (March 5, 1814), 11. The Pennsylvania legislature also expressed their "astonishment and high disapprobation" of Chittenden's proclamation. *Niles' Weekly Register* 5 (Feb. 26, 1814), 423. In Massachusetts, Harrison Gray Otis introduced a resolution in his legislature supporting Vermont in "their constitutional rights," but the resolution was tabled. Hickey, *War of 1812,* 267.

59. *Annals,* 13th Cong., 2d sess. (House), 859-861.

60. Ibid., 129-130; Hampton to Armstrong, Oct. 4, 1813, *Annals,* 13th Cong., 2d sess. (appendix), 2407.

61. Skeen, *Armstrong,* 163-166.

62. Ibid., 176-177.

63. Hickey, *War of 1812,* 267. Cited in Everest, *War of 1812 in the Champlain Valley,* 144.

64. Macomb's characterization is in his General Orders, Sept. 14, 1814, in *Niles' Weekly Register* 7 (Oct. 1, 1814), 44. See also Macomb to Secretary of War, Sept. 15, 1814, *Daily National Intelligencer,* Oct. 1, 1814.

65. Everest, *War of 1812 in the Champlain Valley,* 163. The correspondence between Chittenden and Macomb and Newell is in *Niles' Weekly Register* 7 (Supplement), 101-105.

66. Macomb to Secretary of War, Sept. 15, 1814, *Daily National Intelligencer,* Oct. 1, 1814; General Orders, Sept. 8, 1814, *Niles' Weekly Register* 7 (Oct. 15, 1814), 70.

67. Everest, *War of 1812 in the Champlain Valley,* 175.

68. General Order of Sept. 14, 1814, *Niles' Weekly Register* 7 (Oct. 1, 1814), 44. Macomb to Secretary of War, Sept. 12, 15, 1814, in *Daily National Intelligencer,* Sept. 20, Oct. 1, 1814.

69. General Orders of Sept. 13, 1814, in *Niles' Weekly Register* 7 (Oct. 15, 1814), 70.

70. Chittenden's Proclamation is in *Daily National Intelligencer,* Oct. 6, 1814. Committee report and resolution, *Niles' Weekly Register* 7 (Supplement), 105-106.

71. Message of Governor Tompkins, Jan. 31, 1814, in *Niles' Weekly Register* 5 (Feb. 12, 1814), 392, 394, 396. See also Message of Governor Tompkins, Jan. 25, 1814, *Daily National Intelligencer,* Feb. 4, 1814. A printed copy of the broadside, dated March 25, 1814, is in Porter Papers, BEHS, reel 2.

72. McClure to Porter, April 1, 1814, ibid. See also the Rev. Simeon R. Jones (Elmira), April 2, 1814, and Joshua Hathaway (Rome), April 4, 1814, ibid. See Maj. Samuel Hill to Porter, April 11, 1814, ibid.; R. Coffin to Porter, April 12, 1814, ibid.; John Campbell and James McNair to Porter, May 15, 1814, ibid., reel 3. Rochester to Porter, April 22, 1814, ibid.

73. Capt. Richard M. Skinner to Porter, May 16, 1814, ibid. Porter to Tompkins, May 3, 1814, in Cruikshank, ed., *Documentary History,* pt. 1, IV, 13-14. See also Erastus Granger to Porter, May 28, 1814, and Gen. Winfield Scott to Porter, May 29, 1814, Porter Papers, BEHS, reel 3.

74. Tompkins to Porter, May 17, 1814, ibid. Porter to Tompkins, July 3, 1814, in Cruikshank, *Documentary History,* pt. 1, IV, 26.

75. Porter to Col. Elisha Jenkins, June 19, 1814, Porter Papers, BEHS, reel 3; Porter to Tompkins, July 3, 1814, Cruikshank, ed., *Documentary History,* pt. 1, IV, 26.

76. Brown to Armstrong, July 7, 1814, ibid., pt. 1, IV, 38-42.

77. Porter to Brown, [July 1814], draft in Porter Papers, BEHS, reel 3. Porter to W.L. Stone, May 26, 1840, Cruikshank, ed., *Documentary History,* pt. 1, IV, 358-368, quotation is on 365. Draft of letter to W.L. Stone, May 26, 1840, Porter Papers, BEHS, reel 4.

78. Draft of letter, Porter to W.L. Stone, May 26, 1840, Porter Papers, BEHS, reel 4.

79. Stone to Tompkins, July 25, 1814, in Cruikshank, ed., *Documentary History,* pt. 1, IV, 74. British and American Indians, by mutual consent, withdrew from participation in the war. The American Indians promised to return if the British Indians reappeared on the field. Porter to W.L. Stone, May 26, 1840, in ibid., IV, 367-368.

80. Porter to Brown, July 26, 1814, Porter Papers, BEHS, reel 3; Brown to Armstrong, Aug. 7, 1814, in Cruikshank, ed., *Documentary History,* pt. 1, IV, 100.

81. Porter to Tompkins, July 29, 1814, in ibid., pt. 1, IV, 103-103. Brigade Orders of July 31, 1814 consolidated the volunteers into three companies, roughly 300 men, Porter Papers, BEHS, reel 3.

82. Tompkins to Porter, Aug. 13, 1814, Porter Papers, BEHS, reel 3.

83. Brown to Tompkins, Aug. 1, 1814, in Cruikshank, ed., *Documentary History*, pt. 1, IV, 103-104.

84. Lt. Edward MacMahon to William Jarvis, Aug. 22, 1814, ibid., IV, 166-168. Porter to Gaines, Aug. 15, 1814, Porter Papers, BEHS, reel 4; Gaines to Armstrong, Aug. 23, 1814, Cruikshank, ed., *Documentary History*, pt. 1, IV, 155.

85. Gaines to Porter, Aug. 16, 1814, Porter Papers, BEHS, reel 3; Brigade Orders, Aug. 16, 1814, ibid.; Jacob Dox to Porter, Aug. 25, 1814, ibid.; Jacob Brown to Porter, Aug. 25, 1814, ibid. McClure to Porter, Aug. 26, 1814, ibid. General Order, Sept. 1, 1814, ibid.; Lt. Col. George Fleming to Porter, Sept. 4, 1814, ibid.; Maj. Benajah Mallory to Porter, Sept. 2, 1814, ibid.

86. Yates to Tompkins, Sept. 3, 1814, in Cruikshank, ed., *Documentary History*, pt. 1, IV, 192; Lt. Col. James R. Mullany to Porter, Sept. 15, 1814, Porter Papers, BEHS, reel 3.

87. Matteson to Ripley, Sept. 5, 1814, Porter Papers, BEHS, reel 3; Matteson to Porter, Sept. 6, 1814, Porter Papers, BEHS, reel 3; General Order, Sept. 6, 1814, in Cruikshank, ed., *Documentary History*, pt. 1, IV, 194.

88. Brown to Porter, Sept. 8, 1814, in Cruikshank, ed., *Documentary History*, pt. 2, IV, 450; Brown to New York Militia, Sept. 9, 1814, in ibid. Brown to Izard, Sept. 11, 1814, in ibid., pt. 1, IV, 198.

89. British accounts of the battle are found in Maj. Gen. DeWatteville to Sir Gordon Drummond, Sept. 19, 1814, in ibid., pt. 1, IV, 203-204, and Lt. Gen. Drummond to Sir George Prevost, Sept. 19, 1814, in ibid., pt. 1, IV, 204-206. See also Brown to Secretary of War, Sept. 18, 1814, in ibid., pt. 1, IV, 206-207. Porter to Brown, Sept. 23, 1814, in ibid., pt. 1, IV, 208-211; Brown to Tompkins, Sept. 20, 1814, in ibid., pt. 1, IV, 207.

90. A report of this incident in the *Ontario Messenger* was published in *Niles' Weekly Register* 7 (Oct. 29, 1814), 124.

91. Draft of speech [Oct. 1814], Porter Papers, BEHS, reel 2. The date is fixed as late October because Porter's force was discharged by general order on Oct. 22, 1814, ibid. See also Porter to Izard, Oct. 23, 1814, thanking him for the "highly complimentary" order on the discharge of his troops, and Porter's General Order, Oct. 24, 1814, ibid., for the troops to march to Batavia for discharge.

92. Richardson to Porter, Oct. 28, 1814, Porter Papers, BEHS, reel 3; General Orders, Nov. 2, 1814, ibid. See, for example, solicitations for Porter's aid for claims against the government from one of his former officers, H.W. Dobbin, Feb. 26, 1818, ibid.; Oct. 27, 1824, ibid., reel 4; Dec. 18, 1830, ibid.

93. See the correspondence relating to this subject: Alexander J. Dallas (acting secretary of war) to Joseph Hopkinson (president, Philadelphia Academy of Fine Arts), May 25, 1815, copy in ibid., reel 3; Dallas to Porter, June 3, 1815, ibid.; Porter to Hopkinson, July 6, 1815, ibid.; Hopkinson to Porter, July 16, 1815, ibid.; George Graham (acting secretary of war) to Porter, Nov. 19, 1817, ibid.; Hopkinson to Porter, Jan. 14, 1821, ibid.; John C. Calhoun (secretary of war) to Porter, Dec. 3, 1824, ibid.; Calhoun to Porter, Jan. 3, 1825, ibid.; Porter to Calhoun, Jan. 17, 1825, ibid.

Chapter 7

1. One account claimed that every house was burned in Fredericktown and Georgetown. Only a church at the latter place was spared. See *General View of the*

Late War (n.p., n.d., 1815?), 52-54. The damage to property at Fredericktown was set at $15,871 and $35,626 for property at Georgetown. "Spirit and Manner in Which the War is Waged by the Enemy," Doc. 122, *ASPMA*, I, 358-367, 375-382. *Daily National Intelligencer,* May 14, 17, July 13, 1813.

2. Winder to Armstrong, March 20, 1813, Letterbooks of the Governor and Council, RSUS, Executive Records, Maryland, reel 3. Winder to Committee of Town of Easton, March 29, 1813, ibid.

3. Winder to Madison, April 26, 1813, ibid.

4. Message to Legislature, May 17, 1813, ibid.

5. Winder to Madison, May 20, 1813, ibid.; William B. Martin and Walter Dorsey to Winder, May 25, 1813, ibid.; Armstrong to Martin and Dorsey, May 22, 1813, ibid. Winder to Forman, June 1, 1813, ibid.

6. Lt. Col. H. Beatty to Brig. Gen. Robert Taylor, June 25, 1813 in (Jacob Elder?), *Events of the War Between the United States of America and Great Britain, During the Years 1812 and 1813: Both Military and Naval* (Harrisburg, 1814), 177-178. See also Hickey, *War of 1812,* 153-154. Col. S. Crutchfield to Gov. James Barbour, June 28, 1813, Elder, *Events of the War,* 172-176; *ASPMA*, I, 375-382.

7. Pinckney to Hawkins, Oct. 6, 1812, Governor's Letterbooks, 336, RSUS, Executive Records, North Carolina, reel 7; Hawkins to Turner and Stone, June 11, 1813, ibid., 242, enclosing petitions from Beaufort, May 18, 1813, and Wilmington, May 19, 1813, Governor's Letterbooks, 209-213, 217-218, ibid.

8. Hawkins to Etheridge, July 1, 1813, Governor's Letterbooks, 272-273, ibid.

9. Banks to Hawkins, July 19, 1813, Governor's Letterbooks, 318-319, ibid., Bryan to Hawkins, Governor's Letterbooks, 326-329.

10. Cameron to Hawkins, July 23, 1813, Governor's Letterbooks, 345, ibid.

11. Hawkins to Maj. Gen. Thomas Brown, July 29, 1813, Governor's Letterbooks, 356-357, ibid. Pasteur to Hawkins, Aug. 12, 1813, Governor's Letterbooks, 384.

12. Morris to Secretary of the Navy William Jones, Sept. 20, 1814, in *Daily National Intelligencer,* Sept. 30, 1814; Hickey, *War of 1812,* 194.

13. *Daily National Intelligencer,* Aug. 24, 1814.

14. Ibid., July 16, 1813. Report of House Committee on the "Capture of Washington," *Annals,* 13th Cong., 3d sess., 1518-1738, Van Ness Statement, 1685. Armstrong Statement, *Annals,* 13th Cong., 3d sess., 1565.

15. Armstrong Statement, 1565.

16. Memorandum of the Cabinet meeting of July 1, 1814, Madison Papers, LC; John Armstrong, *Notices of the War of 1812,* 2 vols. (New York, 1840), II, 128.

17. Winder statement, *Annals,* 13th Cong., 3d sess., 1577-1578, 1601. Armstrong to Winder, July 12, 1814, quoted in Edward D. Ingraham, *A Sketch of the Events which preceded the Capture of Washington by the British on the twenty-fourth of August, 1814* (Philadelphia, 1849), 12. Winder to Armstrong, July 16, 1814, Winder Statement, *Annals,* 13th Cong., 3d sess., 1579.

18. Madison to Barbour, June 16, 1814, Madison Papers, LC.

19. Winder to Armstrong, July 23, 1814, Winder Statement, *Annals,* 13th Cong., 3d sess., 1582.

20. Ibid., 1581, 1603.

21. Winder to Van Ness, Aug. 2, 1814, *Daily National Intelligencer,* Aug. 6, 1814.

22. Stull to Thomas L. McKenney, Jan. 16, 1847, in Thomas L. McKenney, *Reply to Kosciuszko Armstrong's Assault upon Col. McKenney's Narrative of the Causes that Led to General Armstrong's Resignation of the Office of Secretary of War in 1814* (New York, 1847), app. A, 24-26.

23. Winder to Armstrong, July 27, 1814, Winder Statement, *Annals,* 13th Cong., 3d sess., 1585. Winder to Armstrong, Aug. 13, 1814, ibid., 1586. Ibid., 1606.

24. Winder to Armstrong, July 23, Aug. 13, 1814, ibid., 1581, 1586.

25. District Orders, Aug. 13, 1814, *Daily National Intelligencer,* Aug. 16, 1814.

26. Winder to Armstrong, Aug. 19, 1814, Winder Statement, *Annals,* 13th Cong., 3d sess., 1588.

27. Armstrong to Winder, Aug. 19, 22, 1814, ibid., 1592, 1587; Armstrong, *Notices,* app. 29, II, 232-236.

28. Madison to Monroe, Aug. 21, 1814, Madison Papers, LC. Winder Statement, *Annals,* 13th Cong., 3d sess., 1609-1610, 1622.

29. Ibid., 1614-1615. Minor Statement, *ASPMA,* Doc. 137, I, 568-579. Minor alleged the delay was occasioned by the absence of Col. Henry Carberry (Thirty-sixth Regiment, U.S. Infantry), who was in charge of the arsenal. Carberry, in a letter to Richard M. Johnson, head of the congressional committee (Dec. 16, 1814), *ASPMA,* Doc. 137, I, 597, disputed Minor's statement and cited an opinion that Minor's troops had sufficient time to get their arms and reach the battlefield.

30. Madison Memorandum, Aug. 24, 1814, in Gaillard Hunt, ed., *The Writings of James Madison,* 9 vols. (New York, 1900-1910), VIII, 295. *Baltimore Patriot,* in *Daily National Intelligencer,* Aug. 31, 1814.

31. Winder Statement, *Annals,* 13th Cong., 3d sess., 1614. Henry Adams, *History of the United States During the Administrations of Jefferson and Madison,* 9 vols. (New York, 1890), VIII, 153. See also Irving Brant, *James Madison, Commander in Chief, 1812-1836* (Indianapolis, 1961), 301. Monroe to George Hay, Sept. 7, 1814, Monroe Papers, NYPL. Armstrong's statement is in Armstrong, *Notices,* II, 148.

32. *ASPMA,* Doc. 137, I, 529.

33. A relatively detailed account of the battle appears in the congressional committee report that investigated this affair. See *ASPMA,* Doc. 137, I, 529-530.

34. Hickey, *War of 1812,* 198.

35. *Niles' Weekly Register* 6 (Aug. 27, 1814), 443.

36. Account of Henry Crease (Acting Commander of the *Menelaus*), Sept. 1, 1814, *Maryland Gazette* (Annapolis), Dec. 22, 1814; *Daily National Intelligencer,* Sept. 6, 1814.

37. Stricker to Smith, Sept. 15, 1814, *Maryland Gazette,* Sept. 22, 1814.

38. British Account of Battle of Baltimore, *Maryland Gazette,* Nov. 3, 1814. Another British account of the Battle of Baltimore by Colonel Brooke called the British attack a great victory, as did Admiral Cochrane's account, *Maryland Gazette,* Dec. 6, 1814.

Chapter 8

1. *Proceedings of a General Court Martial for the Trial of Lieut. Col. Louis Bache . . .* (Philadelphia, 1815), 6-7.

2. Ibid., 7-9.

3. Ibid., 9-10, 19.

4. Ibid., 20, 26-27.

5. Ibid., app., doc. H, 7. Gaines's statement is on 13.

6. Ibid., 46.

7. Ibid., 47-50, 56-57.

8. Ibid., 66.

9. Barbour to Armstrong, May 29, 1813, WD/LR. *Niles' Weekly Register* 4 (June 5, 1813), 219-220.

10. Skeen, *Armstrong,* 131-134.

11. Early to McIntosh, May 18, 1814, Governor's Letterbooks, 248, RSUS, Executive Records, Georgia, reel 2.

12. Annual Message, Dec. 8, 1813, Letterbooks of the Governor and Council, RSUS, Executive Records, Maryland, reel 3. Winder to General Assembly, Dec. 23, 1813, ibid.

13. Martin to General Assembly, Dec. 10, 1814, ibid.

14. Message of Gov. Rodney, Jan. 18, 1814, *Niles' Weekly Register* 5 (Feb. 5, 1814), 371. Armstrong to Cheves, Jan. 24, 1814, ibid., 5 (Jan. 29, 1814), 362-363; Armstrong to Cheves, Jan. 28, 1814, ibid., 5 (Feb. 5, 1814), 379.

15. Governor's message, Dec. 20, 1814, Governor's Letterbooks, XXI, 3-4, RSUS, Executive Records, North Carolina, reel 8. Miller's Address to Assembly, Dec. 20, 1814, XXI, 3-4, ibid.; Miller to William Britton, May 1, 1815, XXI, 165, ibid.; Miller to James Graham, Sept. 6, 1815, XXI, 239, ibid. Sarah McCulloh Lemmon, *North Carolina and the War of 1812* (Raleigh, 1971), 14.

16. Shelby to Armstrong, Aug. 13, 1814, WD/LR. See Robert Brent (paymaster of the United States) to Armstrong, Aug. 19, 1814, Madison Papers, LC.

17. Early to Floyd, June 29, 1814, Governor's Letterbooks, 9-10, RSUS, Executive Records, Georgia, reel 2.

18. Ibid.; Early to Senate and House of Representatives, Nov. 9, 1814, Governor's Letterbooks, 135, ibid.

19. Holmes to Monroe, Feb. 20, March 13, June 2, 1815, Governor's Letterbooks, 161, 169-170, 185-187 (quotation at 187), ibid., Mississippi, reel 2; Report of House Committee on Militia Claims, Jan. 11, 1816, 14th Cong., 1st sess., *ASPMA*, Doc. 143, I, 624.

20. *Niles' Weekly Register* 4 (Aug. 21, 1813), 407.

21. Hickey, "New England's Defense Problem," *NEQ* 50 (1977), 594-596.

22. Ibid., 591-593. Correspondence relating to this affair is conveniently gathered in *Annals*, 13th Cong., 3d sess. (appendix), 1777-1789.

23. Hickey, "New England's Defense Problem," *NEQ* 50 (1977), 596-598.

24. Ibid., 598-599.

25. Strong to Secretary of War, Sept. 7, 1814, Monroe to Strong, Sept. 17, 1814, *Annals*, 13th Cong., 3d sess. (appendix), 1769-1770, 1772-1773. A similar letter was sent to Governor Smith of Connecticut.

26. Report of Committee on the Governor's Message, Oct. 15, 1814, Doc. 20, 3-8, RSUS, Legislative Records, Massachusetts, reel 2.

27. Senate Minority Report, Oct. 15, 1814, and Protest of the Minority of the House of Representatives, [Oct. 1814], in *Daily National Intelligencer*, Oct. 27, 1814.

28. For the Hartford Convention resolutions, see ibid., Jan. 11, 1815. See also *Proceedings of a Convention of Delegates . . . Convened at Hartford . . . December 15, 1814*, 3d ed. (Boston, 1815), Doc. 34, 6-12, RSUS, Legislative Records, Massachusetts, reel 2.

29. Act of Oct. sess., 1812 (chap. 1), *The Public Laws of the State of Connecticut* (n.p., n.d.), 95-97, RSUS, Session Laws, Connecticut, reel 2; Speech of Gov. John Cotton Smith, *Daily National Intelligencer*, May 22, 1813. Niles was commenting on an article by "A Constitutionalist" from the *Boston Daily Advertiser*. See *Niles' Weekly Register* 5 (Nov. 20, 1813), 199.

30. Act of Oct. sess., 1814 (chap. 2), *The Public Laws of the State of Connecticut*, 170, RSUS, Session Laws, Connecticut, reel 2; Act of Oct. 26, 1812 (chap. 46), *Acts and Laws Passed by the Legislature of the State of Vermont* (Danville, [1812]), 51-53, RSUS, Session Laws, Vermont, reel 3; Act of June 1814, *Public Laws of the State of Rhode Island and Providence Plantations* (Newport, [1840?]), 24-25, ibid., Rhode Island, reel 7; Act of Oct. 20, 1814 (chap. 77), *Laws of the Commonwealth of Massachusetts* (Boston, 1814-1815), 575-578, ibid., Massachusetts, reel 6.

31. Message of Gov. Tompkins, Sept. 27, 1814, *Daily National Intelligencer*, Oct.

5, 1814; Message of Gov. Tompkins, Sept. 30, 1814, *Niles' Weekly Register* 7 (Oct. 27, 1814), 97-98.

32. "Legislature of New York," *Niles' Weekly Register* 7 (Oct. 29, 1814), 123.

33. See the critique and objection to the New York law by Chancellor James Kent, Minutes of the Council of Revision, Oct. 24, 1814, 363-366, RSUS, Executive Records, Miscellany, New York, reel 9. *An Address to the Citizens of Oneida, on the Subject of the Late Law of this State for Raising 12,000 Men, by Classification of the Militia. By an Exempt.* (Utica, 1814), 5-6, 9.

34. *Niles' Weekly Register* 3 (Jan. 9, 1813), 300. Snyder to Mead, Feb. 4, 1814, in Cruikshank, ed., *Documentary History*, pt. 2, III, 164. Message of Gov. Snyder, Dec. 10, 1814, *Journal of the Senate*, vol. 25 (Harrisburg, 1814), 20-21, RSUS, Session Laws, Pennsylvania, reel 9. The draft of the act is in the appendix, 50-57.

35. Message of Gov. Pennington, Jan. 14, 1814, *Daily National Intelligencer,* Feb. 4, 1814. Message of Gov. Pennington, Oct. 1814, *Niles' Weekly Register* 7 (Nov. 19, 1814), 161.

36. Act of Jan. 31, 1815 (chap. 114), *Laws Made and Passed by the General Assembly of the State of Maryland* (Annapolis, 1815), 126-129, RSUS, Session Laws, Maryland, reel 5.

37. Act of Feb. 15, 1813 (chap. 3), *Acts Passed at a General Assembly of the Commonwealth of Virginia* (Richmond, 1813), 13-18, RSUS, Session Laws, Virginia, reel 4; Monroe to Barbour, March 21, 1813, *Niles' Weekly Register* 4 (May 29, 1813), 207; Armstrong to Barbour, March 22, 1813, ibid., 208; Barbour to Monroe, March 24, 1813, ibid., 207-208; Message of Gov. Barbour, May 17, 1813, ibid., 206-207; Act of May 26, 1813 (chap. 3), *Acts Passed at a General Assembly of the Commonwealth of Virginia* (Richmond, 1813), 4, RSUS, Session Laws, Virginia, reel 5.

38. Message of Gov. Barbour, Oct. 10, 1814, *Daily National Intelligencer,* Oct. 22, 1814. See also *Daily National Intelligencer,* Oct. 25, 1814.

39. Act of Jan. 18, 1815 (chap. 6), *Acts Passed at a General Assembly of the Commonwealth of Virginia* (Richmond, 1815), 40-51, RSUS, Session Laws, Virginia, reel 5.

40. Message of Gov. Hawkins, Nov. 23, 1814, *Niles' Weekly Register* 7 (Supplement), 121-122; Act of Dec. 20, 1814, *Acts and Resolutions of the General Assembly of the State of South Carolina* (Columbia, 1815), 27-33, RSUS, Session Laws, South Carolina, reel 6.

41. Message of Gov. Return J. Meigs, Dec. 9, 1812, *Niles' Weekly Register* 3 (Jan. 9, 1813), 289-290. Message of Gov. Worthington, *Daily National Intelligencer,* Jan. 14, 1815.

42. Message of Gov. Shelby, Jan. 25, 1815, RSUS, Executive Documents, Kentucky, reel 2.

43. Smith's speech is in *Niles' Weekly Register* 7 (Supplement), 95.

44. Worthington to Dallas, Jan. 4, Feb. 8, 1815, Governor's Letterbooks, 7-8, RSUS, Executive Records, Ohio, reel 1. See also Hickey, *War of 1812*, 277, 279.

45. Gov. Williams to Dallas, Dec. 22, 1814, Thomas Lee (Comptroller General of South Carolina) to Dallas, Dec. 21, 1814, *Niles' Weekly Register* 7 (Jan. 14, 1815), 318, 318-319; Dallas to Williams, Dec. 29, 1814, Dallas to Lee, Dec. 29, 1814, *Niles' Weekly Register* 7 (Supplement), 192. For a chart showing direct taxes for 1815, see *Niles' Weekly Register* 7 (Jan. 28, 1815), 348.

46. *Daily National Intelligencer,* Dec. 12, 1814.

47. Message of Governor Strong, Jan. 18, 1815, *Niles' Weekly Register* 7 (Supplement), 98.

48. Monroe to Senate Committee, Feb. 11, 1815, *ASPMA*, Doc. 142, I, 605-607.

49. Ibid., 604. Brant, *Madison, Commander-in-Chief,* 49. See also *Martin v. Mott,* 12 Wheaton 19.

Chapter 9

1. Claiborne to Wilkinson, Dec. 28, 1812, Official Letters, 231, RSUS, Executive Records, Louisiana, reel 2. Act of Feb. 12, 1813, *Acts Passed at the Second Session of the First Legislature of the State of Louisiana* . . . (New Orleans, 1813), 40-84, RSUS, Session Laws, Louisiana, reel 2.

2. Claiborne to Brown and Fromentin, May 19, June 10, 1813, Official Letters, 247-248, 257, RSUS, Executive Records, Louisiana, reel 2.

3. Claiborne to Flournoy, June 17, 1813, ibid., 260.

4. Armstrong to Claiborne, June 22, 1813, ibid., 28-29; Claiborne to Flournoy, Sept. 17, 1813, ibid., 54; Claiborne to Fromentin, Sept. 17, 1813, ibid., 56.

5. Col. Joseph Carson to Brig. Gen. Ferdinand L. Claiborne, July 30, 1813, *Daily National Intelligencer*, Sept. 20, 1813. Owsley, *Gulf Borderlands*, 30-41.

6. Holmes to Flournoy, Aug. 12, 1813, Governor's Letterbooks, 320, RSUS, Executive Records, Mississippi, reel 2; Holmes to Armstrong, Aug. 30, 1813, Governor's Letterbooks, 327, ibid.

7. Holmes to Toulmin, Sept. 3, 1813, Governor's Letterbooks, 329, ibid. Holmes to Flournoy, Sept. 12, 1813, Governor's Letterbooks, 339-340, ibid.; Holmes to Armstrong, Sept. 14, 1813, Governor's Letterbooks, 343. Holmes to Flournoy, Nov. 3, 1813, Holmes to Maj. Thomas Hinds, Nov. 9, 1813, Holmes to Harry Toulmin, Nov. 10, 1813, Governor's Letterbooks, 389-392, 394, 397, ibid.

8. Skeen, *Armstrong*, 171-172, 173.

9. Owsley, *Gulf Borderlands*, 45.

10. For Hinds's command, see Flournoy to Claiborne, Oct. 28, Nov. 5 (quotation), 7, 9, 10, 1813, J.F.H. Claiborne Collection, Box 14, MDAH. Flournoy to Claiborne, Nov. 7, 9, 1813, ibid.

11. Claiborne to Armstrong, Jan. 1, 1814, ibid. Owsley, *Gulf Borderlands*, 46-48.

12. Claiborne to Armstrong, Jan. 24, 1814, J.F.H. Claiborne Collection, Box 14, MDAH.

13. Holmes to Flournoy, March 6, 1814, Holmes to Lt. Col. Nixon, March 21, 1814, Holmes to Armstrong, March 26, 1814, Governor's Letterbooks, 434, 438-439, 441, RSUS, Executive Records, Mississippi, reel 2.

14. Armstrong to Governors Blount and Mitchell, July 13, 1813, WD/LS, VII, 14; Mitchell to Armstrong, Aug. 9, 24, 1813, Governor's Letterbooks, 137-138, 244, RSUS, Executive Records, Georgia, reel 2; General Orders, Aug. 19, 1813, Executive Journals, 237, RSUS, Executive Records, reel 10.

15. Mitchell to Armstrong, Aug. 31, 1813, Governor's Letterbooks, 140, RSUS, Executive Records, reel 2; Mitchell to Cook, Sept. 7, 1813, Governor's Letterbooks, 152, ibid. Mitchell to Floyd, Sept. 17, 1813, Governor's Letterbooks, 158-159, ibid.

16. Mitchell to Armstrong, Sept. 14, 1813, ibid., 157.

17. Owsley, *Gulf Borderlands*, 52-55.

18. Ibid., 57-59.

19. Early to Armstrong, Nov. 18, 1813, Jan. 12, 1814, Governor's Letterbooks, 178, 195-196, RSUS, Executive Records, Georgia, reel 2; Early to Troup, Jan. 12, 1814, Governor's Letterbooks, 196, ibid.

20. Early to Pinckney, Feb. 6, Feb. 7, 1814, Governor's Letterbooks, 204, ibid.; Early to Gen. McIntosh, Feb. 8, 1814, Governor's Letterbooks, 206, ibid.

21. Early to Pinckney, Sept. 30, 1814, Governor's Letterbooks, 34, ibid.

22. Coffee to Jackson, Nov. 4, 1813, *Niles' Weekly Register* 5 (Nov. 27, 1813), 218-219. Owsley, *Gulf Borderlands*, 62-66; Jackson to Gov. Willie Blount, Nov. 11, 1813, *Niles' Weekly Register* 5 (Dec. 18, 1813), 267; Jackson to Armstrong, Nov. 20, 1813, John Spencer Bassett, ed., *Correspondence of Andrew Jackson*, 6 vols. (Washington, D.C., 1926), I, 355-357.

23. Owsley, *Gulf Borderlands*, 66-67. Moser, ed., *Jackson Papers*, III, 37-39, 43, 146, 245.

24. Owsley, *Gulf Borderlands*, 68-70, 72. Jackson to Pinckney, Jan. 29, 1814, *Daily National Intelligencer*, Feb. 19, 1814; Bassett, ed., *Jackson Correspondence*, I, 447-454. See also Jackson to Rachael Jackson, Jan. 28, 1814, in Moser, ed., *Jackson Papers*, III, 17-22, 21.

25. Jackson to Capt. Eli Hammond, Feb. 1, 1814, Moser, ed., *Jackson Papers*, III, 22.

26. Jackson to Pinckney, March 28, 1814, Moser, ed., *Jackson Papers*, III, 52-54. See also Jackson to Rachael Jackson, April 1, 1814, ibid., 54-55. The most complete account of the battle is Owsley, *Gulf Borderlands*, 78-82. Moser, ed., *Jackson Papers*, III, 57.

27. For the controversy surrounding this appointment, see Skeen, *Armstrong*, 142-143.

28. Owsley, *Gulf Borderlands*, 92-94.

29. Holmes to Jackson, Aug. 15, 1814, Governor's Letterbooks, 33-35, RSUS, Executive Records, Mississippi, reel 2. Holmes to Jackson, Sept. 19, Sept. 29, 1814, Governor's Letterbooks, 57, 71-72, ibid.

30. Hickey, *War of 1812*, 205-206. Owsley, *Gulf Borderlands*, 112-119.

31. Owsley, *Gulf Borderlands*, 120-126.

32. Claiborne to Monroe, Oct. 25, 1814, Governor's Letterbooks, 5, RSUS, Executive Records, Louisiana, reel 2. The quoted statement appears in Hickey, *War of 1812*, 206.

33. The Battle of New Orleans is well covered by historians. An excellent account is Robin Reilly, *The British at the Gates: The New Orleans Campaign in the War of 1812* (New York, 1974). Also useful are Owsley, *Gulf Borderlands*, and Adams, *History*, VIII, 311-385. Wilburt S. Brown, *The Amphibious Campaign for West Florida and Louisiana, 1814-1815* (University, Ala., 1969), is ably reasoned. Two useful but not always reliable contemporary accounts are A. Lacarriere Latour, *Historical Memoir of the War in West Florida and Louisiana in 1814-15* (1816; reprint, Gainesville, 1964); and George R. Gleig, *The Campaigns of the British Army at Washington and New Orleans* (1827; reprint, Totowa, N.J., 1972).

34. Holmes to Claiborne, Oct. 3, 1814, Governor's Letterbooks, 74, RSUS, Executive Records, Mississippi, reel 2. Holmes to Jackson, Dec. 26, Dec. 30, 1814, Governor's Letterbooks, 118, 114, ibid.

35. Owsley, *Gulf Borderlands*, 131. Act of Sept. 6, 1812 (chap. 23), *Acts Passed at the First Session of the First General Assembly of the State of Louisiana* (New Orleans, 1812), 72, RSUS, Session Laws, Louisiana, reel 2. On organizing free blacks, see Claiborne to Eustis, Aug. 31, 1811, Official Letters of the Governor, 396, RSUS, Executive Records, Louisiana, reel 2. On use of the "coloured militia," see Claiborne to Jackson, Oct. 24, Oct. 28, Official Letters of the Governor, 4-5, 8, ibid.

36. General Orders, Dec. 16, 1814, in Moser, ed., *Jackson Papers*, III, 206-207.

37. Jackson to Gov. David Holmes, Dec. 25, 1814, in Moser, ed., *Jackson Papers*, III, 218-220. In a private note to Col. Robert Hays, Jackson stated his suspicion that the British had gained their foothold on the Mississippi through the treachery of Louisiana militia. See Jackson to Hays, Dec. 26, 1814, in ibid., III, 221-222.

38. Claiborne to Jackson, Oct. 28, 1814, Governor's Letterbooks, 10, RSUS, Executive Records, Louisiana, reel 2. Jackson to Monroe, Dec. 29, 1814, in Moser, ed., *Jackson Papers*, III, 224-225.

39. Jackson to Monroe, Jan. 3, 1815, in ibid., III, 228-229. Reilly, *British at the Gates*, 287-288. Edward Livingston to Nicholas Girod, Dec. 29, 1814, in Moser, ed., *Jackson Papers*, III, 225.

40. Owsley, *Gulf Borderlands*, 155.

41. "General David B. Morgan's Defense of the Conduct of the Louisiana Militia in the Battle on the Left Side of the River, January 8, 1815," *Louisiana Historical Quarterly* 9 (Jan. 1926), 18, 19.

42. Ibid., 20-21.

43. Jackson's Address to his Troops on the Right Bank," Jan. 8, 1815, in Bassett, ed., *Jackson Correspondence*, II, 135-136. Jackson to Monroe, Jan. 9, 1815, in ibid., II, 136-138.

44. Adair to Jackson, March 20, 1815, Jackson to Adair, April 2, 1815, in ibid., II, 192-195, 200-201.

45. See the discussion by John William Ward, *Andrew Jackson: Symbol for an Age* (New York, 1955), 18-27. Owsley, *Gulf Borderlands*, 163-164, noted that cannon fire "broke the British ranks," but he attributed the greatest damage to musket fire.

46. Jackson to Winchester, Jan. 19, 1815, in Moser, ed., *Jackson Papers*, III, 252. Jackson to Brown, Jan. [27], 1815, ibid., III, 259. Owsley, *Gulf Borderlands*, 158-159, 162-163.

47. Jackson to Monroe, Jan. 25, 1815, in Moser, ed., *Jackson Papers*, III, 255.

48. Claiborne to Jackson, Feb. 24, 1815, Jackson to Claiborne, Feb. 25, 1815, in ibid., III, 286-287, 287. Brigadier General Robert McCausland to Jackson, Feb. 24, 1815, in ibid., III, 287.

49. Citizens of Louisiana to Jackson, Feb. 27, 1815, in ibid., III, 291. Order to the French Citizens of New Orleans, Feb. 28, 1815, in ibid., III, 294.

50. John Wright to Jackson, March 3, 1815, Jackson to Philemon Thomas, March 4, 1815, in ibid., III, 294-296, 296-297.

51. See Robert V. Remini, *Andrew Jackson and the Course of American Empire, 1767-1821* (New York, 1977), 308-315.

52. General Orders, "To the Louisiana Militia," March 7, 1815, in Moser, ed., *Jackson Papers*, III, 303-304.

Chapter 10

1. Both newspapers are quoted in *Daily National Intelligencer,* Feb. 16, 1815. *Niles' Weekly Register* 8 (March 4, 1815), 417, 419.

2. *Annals,* 13th Cong., 3d sess. (House) 1155-1157, 1167, 1174, 1184-1185, 1191, 1194; ibid. (Senate), 233-234, 238-239, 239-241, 241-243, 250, 253, 258-259, 274. The resolution, dated Feb. 27, is in ibid. (appendix), 1966-1967.

3. Ibid. (House), 538, 1200-1201. Desha served as a major general of volunteers under Gen. William Henry Harrison during the Battle of the Thames.

4. Ibid., 1208, 1212, 1216, 1221, 1223.

5. Ibid., 1230-1231, 1233-1234, 1251-1252, 1254.

6. *Daily National Intelligencer,* Feb. 24, 28, 1815. "A Militia-Man," ibid., March 3, 1815.

7. *Annals,* 13th Cong., 3d sess. (Senate), 287, 291-292, 297-298; ibid. (House), 1266, 1267, 1271-1272, 1272-1273.

8. The Act of March 3 is in III Stat. 224. Details of the reorganization are found in Department of the Army, *American Military History, 1607-1953* (Washington, D.C., 1956), 150-151.

9. "Wallace," *Daily National Intelligencer,* April 1, 1815.

10. *Albany Argus,* March 7, 1815.

11. Gaines to Calhoun, Sept. 20, 1818, Calhoun to Gaines, Sept. 23, 1818, in W. Edwin Hemphill, ed., *The Papers of John C. Calhoun, 1817-1818,* 23 vols. to date (Columbia, S.C., 1963), II, 144, 152. See also Carlton B. Smith, "Congressional

Attitudes Toward Military Preparedness During the Monroe Administration," *Military Affairs* 40 (Feb. 1976), 22-25.

12. Calhoun to Ruggles, Feb. 18, 1819, Hemphill, ed., *Calhoun Papers*, III, 587. The returns for 1820 are in *ASPMA*, Doc. 191, II, 134-137; W. Kennedy (Adjutant, Del.) to Daniel Parker (Adjutant and Inspector General, United States), Dec. 22, 1820, ibid., Doc. 208, II, 320.

13. Examples of proarmy speeches are Alexander Smyth (Va.), *Annals*, 16th Cong., 2d sess. (House), 735, 744-756; Eldred Simpkins, ibid., 758-767. Examples of antiarmy speeches are Lewis Williams (N.C.), ibid., 767-779; Charles Fisher (N.C.), ibid., 816-821; and Newton Cannon (Tenn.), ibid., 824-841. See Act of March 2, 1821, ibid., 1789-1799. For an in-depth analysis of army reduction, see C. Edward Skeen, "Calhoun, Crawford, and the Politics of Retrenchment," *South Carolina Historical Magazine* 73 (July 1972), 141-155.

14. William H. Sumner, *An Inquiry into the Importance of the Militia to a Commonwealth* . . . (Boston, 1823), 4, 13. *North American Review* 23 (Oct. 1826), 274.

15. "Annual Report of the Secretary of War . . . and Report of the Board of Officers on the Organization of the Militia," in *ASPMA*, Doc. 334, III, 330-488. Barbour's cover letter, dated Nov. 28, 1826, is on 330-331, and the circular letter, dated July 11, 1826, is on 393-394. The other members of the board were Maj. Gen. Thomas Cadwalader, First Division, Pennsylvania militia; William H. Sumner, Adjutant General of Massachusetts; Beverly Daniel, Adjutant of North Carolina; Lt. Col. Abram Eustis, Fourth Artillery; Lt. Col. Zachary Taylor; Lt. Col. Enos Cutler, Third Infantry; and Capt. Charles J. Nourse. An in-depth analysis of the report is John K. Mahon, "A Board of Officers Considers the Condition of the Militia in 1826," *MA* 15 (Summer 1951), 85-94.

16. The board report is in *ASPMA*, Doc. 334, III, 388-392. At about the same time, Maj. Gen. Edmund P. Gaines, after touring the United States to assess the military situation, rendered a report concerning the militia. See "General Remarks Concerning the Militia of the United States," Dec. 2, 1826, *ASPMA*, Doc. 407, IV, 134-140. Maj. Gen. Jacob Brown did not forward the report to the Secretary of War. This report was found in Brown's office after his death in March 1828, and it was not submitted to Congress until Feb. 27, 1829. Gaines proposed an elaborate classification scheme and active duty training of three to four months on a rotating basis. The estimated cost of training one-tenth of the disposable force every two years was $3 million annually, which perhaps explains why Brown did not forward the report. Gaines argued that it was less than was "annually expended by the militia of the United States under the present defective system, taking into view the value of their time lost and expenses incurred in attending musters, trainings, courts-martial, &c. . . . incurred without the attainment of any useful knowledge . . . but often with the loss of health and morals." The board report was republished in 1833. See "Militia of the United States," *Military and Naval Magazine of the United States* 1 (April 1833), 65-79; 1 (June 1833), 235-243; 1 (July 1833), 269-280; 1 (Aug. 1833), 353-362.

17. Brig. Gen. John M. McCalla to James Barbour, Sept. 18, 1826, *ASPMA*, Doc. 334, III, 418.

18. See, for example, Act of July 1, 1819, June sess., 1819, *Laws of the State of New Hampshire*, 195, RSUS, Session Laws, New Hampshire, reel 2. Maine provided for fines of twenty dollars to fifty dollars for towns negligent in providing arms and equipment to privates.

19. Brig. Gen. John M. McCalla to James Barbour, Sept. 18, 1826, *ASPMA*, Doc. 334, III, 418; Daniel Elmer to James Barbour, Aug. 14, 1826, ibid., III, 452. These reports confirm the study of Michael A. Bellesiles, "The Origins of Gun

Culture in the United States, 1760-1865," *JAH* 83 (Sept. 1996), 425-455, esp. 428-438, which shows a relatively disarmed America during this period.

20. Report of House committee, Jan. 17, 1817, 14th Cong., 2d sess., *ASPMA*, Doc. 152, I, 664. Huntington to Gov. Oliver Wolcott, Sept. 2, 1826, ibid., 408; Elmer to James Barbour, Aug. 14, 1826, ibid., 452.

21. Act of March 8, 1834, *Acts Passed at the Second Session of the Eleventh Legislature of the State of Louisiana* . . . , 143, 155-156, RSUS, Session Laws, Louisiana, reel 3; Act of March 19, 1835, *Acts Passed at the First Session of the Twelfth Legislature of the State of Louisiana* . . . , 128, ibid.; Act of Feb. 24, 1840, *Laws of a General Nature, Passed at the Twenty-fourth Session of the General Assembly of the State of Indiana* . . . , 23, RSUS, Session Laws, Indiana, reel 4; Act of Jan. 15, 1844, *General Laws of the State of Indiana, Passed at the Twenty-eighth Session of the General Assembly* . . . , 122, RSUS, Session Laws, Indiana, reel 5.

22. Joseph J. Holmes, "The Decline of the Pennsylvania Militia, 1815-1870," *WPHM* 57 (April 1974), 209. William H. Riker, *Soldiers of the States: The Role of the National Guard in American Democracy* (Washington, D.C., 1957), 30.

23. Act of July 5, 1834, June sess., 1834, *Laws of the State of New Hampshire*, 154-155, RSUS, Session Laws, New Hampshire, reel 2. Act of Nov. 6, 1834, Oct. 1834 sess., *Laws of Vermont* . . . , 12-13, RSUS, Session Laws, Vermont, reel 5; Act of March 28, 1837, *Public Acts of the State of Maine, Passed by the Seventeenth Legislature* . . . , 424, RSUS, Session Laws, Maine, reel 1; Act of Jan. 1840, Jan. 1840 sess., *Public Laws of the State of Rhode Island and Providence Plantation* . . . , 17, RSUS, Session Laws, Rhode Island, reel 10.

24. Annual Report of Adjutant General, Dec. 22, 1845, 5, RSUS, Executive Documents, Pennsylvania, reel 1.

25. Irwin to Gov. William F. Johnston, Dec. 28, 1848, 9, RSUS, Executive Documents, Pennsylvania, reel 2. Holmes, "Decline of the Pennsylvania Militia," 210-216.

26. Riker, *Soldiers of the States*, 22-27.

27. Examples of state reslutions include Vermont, Oct. 31, 1831; Connecticut, Jan. 4, 1832; and Indiana, Jan. 26, 1832, in *ASPMA*, Docs. 491, 492, 493, IV, 806, 807, 935. An example of state officer organizations is the resolution of the officers of Massachusetts, "Memorial of a Convention of Officers of Militia," ibid., Doc. 482, IV, 701-705. Report of the Secretary of War, Nov. 30, 1835, *Register of Debates*, 24th Cong., 1st sess. (appendix), 14-15. A typical debate encompassing most of these themes is in *Register of Debates*, 24th Cong., 1st sess. (House), 2267-2777.

28. Mahon, *Militia*, 41; Lena London, "The Militia Fine, 1830-1860," *MA* 15 (Fall 1951), 142. Riker, *Soldiers of the States*, 41; Paul Tincher Smith, "Militia of the United States from 1846 to 1860," *Indiana Magazine of History* 15 (1919), 44-47.

29. Bernardo and Bacon, *American Military Policy*, 184-189.

30. Message of Gov. Herny Rector, Nov. 15, 1860, RSUS, Collected Documents (D.11), 7, Arkansas, reel 1.

31. Holmes, "Decline of the Pennsylvania Militia," 200.

Bibliographical Essay

Historians of the War of 1812, surprisingly, have paid scant attention to the role of the militia. I have relied heavily, as the endnotes attest, upon primary sources for this study. (For a complete list of sources used, please see the endnotes as well.)

Primary Sources

This work is based heavily on the microfilm collection of early state records. In the 1940s the Library of Congress and the University of North Carolina organized a collection of the early records of the forty-eight states. The final compilation, the Records of the States of the United States, consists of approximately 2.75 million pages on 1,867 reels. The collection, housed in Washington, D.C., in the Library of Congress, is arranged into six classes: legislative records, statutory law, constitutional records, administrative records, and court records. The most useful for the purposes of my study was the collection of statutory law, which is divided into four parts: codes and compilations, session laws, special laws, and miscellany. Every state militia law passed in the four years before and during the War of 1812, as well as most of the laws from the War of 1812 to the 1850s, was examined and mined for information. The other useful collection was the administrative records, which are divided into five parts: executive department journals, governors' letterbooks and papers, secretaries' journals and papers, proceedings of extraordinary bodies, and miscellany, which were extremely valuable for understanding the numerous problems involving the militia that the state governors confronted.

A useful bibliography of the War of 1812 that is marred, however, by numerous typographical errors, is John C. Fredriksen, comp., *Free Trade and Sailors' Rights: A Bibliography of the War of 1812* (Westport, Conn., 1985). Primary sources consulted included Joseph Gales, ed.,

Annals of Congress of the United States . . . , 42 vols. (Washington, D.C., 1834-1856), the *American State Papers, Indian Affairs*, 2 vols. (Washington, D.C., 1832), and *American State Papers, Military Affairs*, 3 vols. (Washington, D.C., 1832). Department of War Papers available on microfilm and housed in the National Archives in Washington, D.C. (Record Group 107) that were most useful included: Letters Received by the Secretary of War, Registered Series and Irregular Series; Letters Sent by the Secretary of War Relating to Military Affairs; Letters Sent to the President by the Secretary of War; and Reports to Congress from the Secretary of War. Consulted on microfilm were the papers of Peter B. Porter (Buffalo and Erie Historical Society, Buffalo, N.Y.), Timothy Pickering (Massachusetts Historical Society, Boston, Mass.) and Daniel Webster (Dartmouth College, Hanover, N.H.). Also consulted in manuscript were the Papers of James Monroe (New York Public Library, New York City, N.Y., and Library of Congress, Washington, D.C.), John Armstrong (W.A. Chanler Collection, New York Historical Society, New York City, N.Y., and Rokeby Collection, Red Hook, New York), and J.F.H. Claiborne (Mississippi Department of Archives and History, Jackson, Miss.). Published collections of papers of participants in the war were very helpful, such as Logan Esarey, ed., *Messages and Letters of William Henry Harrison*, 2 vols. (Indianapolis, 1922); John S. Bassett, ed., *Correspondence of Andrew Jackson*, 6 vols. (Washington, D.C., 1926-1933); Harold D. Moser, ed., *The Papers of Andrew Jackson*, 5 vols. to date (Knoxville, 1980-); W. Edwin Hemphill et al., eds., *The Papers of John C. Calhoun*, 22 vols. to date (Columbia, S.C., 1959-); James F. Hopkins et al., eds., *The Papers of Henry Clay*, 11 vols. (Lexington, Ky., 1959-1992); Stanislaus M. Hamilton, ed., *The Writings of James Monroe*, 7 vols. (New York, 1901); Gaillard Hunt, ed., *The Writings of James Madison*, 9 vols. (New York, 1900-1910); Congressional Edition, *Letters and Other Writings of James Madison*, 4 vols. (Philadelphia, 1865); and Noble E. Cunningham, ed., *Circular Letters of Congressmen to Their Constituents, 1789-1829*, 3 vols. (Chapel Hill, N.C., 1978).

Newspapers were also a valuable source of information (and sometimes misinformation). *Niles' Register* (Baltimore), really a news magazine, complete with an index (although unreliable), proved to be the most useful. The *Washington National Intelligencer*, the semiofficial Republican Party newspaper, proved to be a reliable source on the war. Many other newspapers were consulted on specific aspects of the war, including: the *Philadelphia Aurora, United States' Gazette* (Philadelphia), *Albany Argus, Maryland Gazette* (Annapolis, Md.), *Charleston* (S.C.) *Courier, Hartford Courant* (Connecticut), *Lexington* (Ky.) *Gazette, Richmond*

Enquirer, New York Evening Post, Nashville Gazette (Tennessee), *Scioto Gazette* (Chillicothe, Ohio), and *Pittsburgh Gazette.*

Secondary Sources

There is no book dealing specifically with the militia in the War of 1812. A few general histories of the militia touch on the war. The most recent work is John K. Mahon, *History of the Militia and the National Guard* (New York, 1983), which deals with the war in one chapter. Even more general treatment is given the war in William H. Riker, *Soldier of the States: The Role of the National Guard in American Democracy* (Washington, D.C., 1957), and Jim Dan Hill, *The Minute Man in Peace and War: A History of the National Guard* (Harrisburg, Pa., 1964). See also Emory Upton, *The Military Policy of the United States* (1904, reprinted New York, 1968).

A good background on the militia before the War of 1812 may be found in many works, such as John K. Mahon, *The American Militia: Decade of Decision, 1789-1800* (Gainesville, Fla., 1960); Lawrence D. Cress, *Citizens in Arms: The Army and Militia in American Society to the War of 1812* (Chapel Hill, N.C., 1981); Richard H. Kohn, *Eagle and Sword: The Beginnings of the Military Establishment in America* (New York, 1975); Theodore J. Crackel, *Mr. Jefferson's Army: Political and Social Reform of the Military Establishment, 1801-1809* (New York, 1987); C. Joseph Bernardo and Eugene H. Bacon, *American Military Policy: Its Development Since 1775* (Harrisburg, Pa., 1955); and Leonard D. White, *The Jeffersonians: A Study in Administrative History, 1801-1829* (New York, 1951).

General information on the militia during the War of 1812 may be found in virtually any work on the war. Although he devotes little space to the conduct of the militia during the war, Donald R. Hickey, *The War of 1812: A Forgotten Conflict* (Urbana, Ill., 1989), is a superb study of the War of 1812 and should remain the standard work on the war for many years to come. Other excellent accounts of the war include J.C.A. Stagg, *Mr. Madison's War: Politics, Diplomacy, and Warfare in the Early Republic, 1783-1830* (Princeton, 1983); John K. Mahon, *War of 1812* (Gainesville, Fla., 1972); Reginald Horsman, *The War of 1812* (New York, 1969); Harry L. Coles, *The War of 1812* (Chicago, 1965); Glenn Tucker, *Poltroons and Patriots: A Popular Account of the War of 1812*, 2 vols. (Indianapolis, Ind., 1954); James R. Jacobs and Glenn Tucker, *The War of 1812: A Compact History* (New York, 1969); Benson J. Lossing, *The Pictorial Field-Book of the War of 1812* (New York, 1868), and C. Edward Skeen, *John Armstrong: A Biography* (Syracuse, N.Y.,

1981). Although his work is most useful for diplomatic and political history, Henry Adams, *History of the United States During the Administrations of Jefferson and Madison*, 9 vols. (New York, 1889-1891), is also valuable for the military history of the War of 1812.

State studies with useful information on the militia during the war include Sarah McCulloh Lemmon, *Frustrated Patriots: North Carolina and the War of 1812* (Chapel Hill, N.C., 1973), which is very good. James Wallace Hammack, Jr., *Kentucky and the Second American Revolution: The War of 1812* (Lexington, Ky., 1976), is a useful source on Kentucky's role. Jean Martin Flynn, *The Militia in Antebellum South Carolina Society* (Columbia, S.C, 1991), is helpful for the post–War of 1812 militia in that state. Two regional studies of the war have good information. Allan S. Everest, *The War of 1812 in the Champlain Valley* (Syracuse, N.Y., 1981), does not focus on the militia, but Frank L. Owsley, Jr., *Struggle for the Gulf Borderlands: The Creek War and the Battle of New Orleans, 1812-1815* (Gainesville, Fla., 1981), does, because the militia was heavily used in the southern theater.

Two articles that broadly address the war include Robert L. Kerby, "The Militia System and the State Militias in the War of 1812," *Indiana Magazine of History* 73 (1977), 102-124, and John K. Mahon, "The Principal Causes for the Failure of the United States Militia System During the War of 1812," *Indiana Military History Journal* 4 (1979), 15-21.

Militia organization and activity in the Northwest is found in contemporary accounts, such as Robert B. McAfee, *History of the Late War in the Western Country . . .* (Lexington, Ky., 1816); Elias Darnell, *A Journal, Containing an Accurate and Interesting Account of the Hardships, Sufferings, Battles, Defeat & Captivity of those Heroic Kentucky Volunteers & Regulars Commanded by General Winchester in the Years 1812-1813 . . .* (Frankfort, Ky., 1814); Samuel R. Brown, *Views of the Campaigns of the North-Western Army, &c . . .* (Burlington, Vt., 1814); James Grant Forbes, *Report on the Trial of Brig. General William Hull; Commanding the Northwestern Army of the United States . . .* (New York, 1814); and William Hull, *Defence of Brig. General W. Hull . . . with an Address to the Citizens of the United States, written by himself* (Boston, Mass., 1814). More recent accounts of the militia in the Northwest include, "The Conduct of Militia at Tippecanoe: Elihu Stout's Controversy with Colonel John P. Boyd, January 1812," *Indiana Magazine of History* 51 (Sept. 1955): 237-250; "Journal of the Northwestern Campaign of 1812-1813 under Major General W.H. Harrison; by E.D. Wood," in George W. Cullum, *Campaigns of the War of 1812-1815 . . .* (New York, 1879); John H. Niebaum, "The Pittsburgh Blues," *Western Pennsylvania Historical Magazine* 4 (1921), 110-122, 175-185, 259-270; 5 (1922), 244-250; E.D. Cruikshank, ed., *Documents Relating to the Invasion of Canada and the Surrender of Detroit, 1812* (Welland, Ont., 1912); James T. Doyle, *The Organization and Operational Administration of the Ohio Militia in the War of 1812* (Columbus, Ohio, 1958); Emanuel Hallaman, *The British Invasions of Ohio— 1813* (Columbus, Ohio, 1958); Paul LeRoy, *Some Social Aspects on the Life and Organization of the Soldier in the War of 1812* (Columbus, Ohio, 1958); Perry LeRoy, *The Weakness of Discipline and Its Consequent Results in the Northwest During the War of 1812* (Columbus, Ohio, 1958); Paul John Woehrmann, *The American Invasion of Western Upper Canada, September-October 1813* (Columbus, Ohio, 1962); and Alec R. Gilpin, *The War of 1812 in the Old Northwest* (East Lansing, Mich., 1958). Freeman Cleaves, *Old Tippecanoe* (New York, 1939), is an adequate biography, but a new study of William Henry Harrison's role in the War of 1812 is needed.

Any study of the militia along the Niagara frontier must begin with the extremely valuable Ernest A. Cruikshank, ed., *Documentary History of the Campaign on the Niagara Frontier,* 9 vols. (Welland, Ont., 1908), reprint, 4 vols. (New York, 1971). An interesting study of events along the northern frontier from the Canadian perspective are two works by Pierre Berton, *The Invasion of Canada, 1812-1813* (Boston, Mass., 1980), and *Flames Across the Border: The Canadian-American Tragedy, 1813-1814* (Boston, Mass., 1981). Also helpful in understanding New England's dispute over militia with the federal government during the War of 1812 is Donald R. Hickey, "New England's Defense Problem and the Genesis of the Hartford Convention," *New England Quarterly* 50 (1977), 587-604.

The Bladensburg debacle is covered adequately in the standard histories of the War of 1812. The most balanced specialized account is Walter Lord, *The Dawn's Early Light* (New York, 1971). Older accounts are John S. Williams, *History of the Invasion and Capture of Washington by the British* (New York, 1857), and Edward Duncan Ingraham, *A Sketch of the Events which Preceded the Capture of Washington by the British . . .* (Philadelphia, 1849).

Militia involvement in the Southern theater and New Orleans may be found in biographies of Andrew Jackson, such as Robert V. Remini, *Andrew Jackson and the Course of American Empire, 1767-1821* (New York, 1977), and Marquis James, *Andrew Jackson: The Border Captain* (New York, 1933). See also Robin Reilly, *The British at the Gates: The New Orleans Campaign in the War of 1812* (New York, 1974); Wilburt S. Brown, *The Amphibious Campaign for West Florida and Louisiana, 1814-1815* (University, Ala., 1969); and two useful works by contemporaries, A. Lacarriere Latour, *Historical Memoir of the War in West Florida and*

Louisiana in 1814-15 (Philadelphia, 1816), and George R. Gleig, *The Campaigns of the British Army at Washington and New Orleans* (Philadelphia, 1827). John William Ward, *Andrew Jackson: Symbol for an Age* (New York, 1955), details how the Battle of New Orleans enhanced the reputations of Jackson and the militia. A defense of the militia's conduct on the west bank during the Battle of New Orleans is "General David Morgan's Defense of the Conduct of the Louisiana Militia in the Battle on the Left Side of the River, January 8, 1815," *Louisiana Historical Quarterly* 9 (1926), 16-29.

Index

Tompkins, Daniel D., 72, 98, 102, 107, 109, 110, 111, 112, 113, 122; calls for reform of New York militia (1812), 101; assigns McClure to command militia, 108; recommends volunteer force, 117-18; calls for a state army, 151
Toulmin, Harry, 160
Treaty of Ghent, 31
Trimble, Allen, 83
Trimble, William A., 56
Troup, George M., 22, 25, 26, 28, 34, 37, 38, 164, 175
Tunkers (Dunkers). *See* "conscientiously scrupulous"
Tupper, Edward, 59
Turner, James, 128

Uniform Militia Act (1792), 6, 7, 8, 21, 48, 76
United States v. Peters, 143

Van Horne, Archibald, 13
Van Horne, Thomas, 81, 82
Van Ness, John P., 130, 133
Van Rensselaer, Solomon, 99
Van Rensselaer, Stephen, 28, 51, 98; and Battle of Queenston, 99-100
Varnum, Joseph, 11, 25, 33

Wadsworth, James, 113
Wadsworth, William, 98
"Wallace": critical of militia, 178
Ward, Artemas, Jr., 36
Washington, George, 7, 23, 156, 178; quoted, 4; calls for militia reform, 8
Wayne, Anthony, 7, 99
Weaver (Sgt.), of Va. volunteers: role in defense of Fort Stephenson, 91

Webster, Daniel, 26, 32, 36; speech against conscription bill, 35
Weekly Register (Baltimore), 63, 137
Wells, Samuel, 84
Whiskey Rebellion: militia in, 7
Whistler, John, 80
White, Hugh Lawson, 60
Widgery, William, 18
Wilkinson, James, 74, 157; takes command on Northern front, 108; moves down St. Lawrence and calls off assault on Montreal, 114-15
Willcocks, Joseph: killed at Fort Erie, 123
Williams, David R., 19, 20, 21, 23, 155
Winchester, James, 48, 54, 83, 172; dispute with Harrison over rank, 58-59; involvement in River Raisin incident, 84-85; placed in charge of defense of Mobile, 168
Winder, Levin, 58, 72, 130; seeks support of national government for defense, 126-27; complains of defense expenses, 144-45
Winder, William, 132, 133, 134, 135, 138; appointed command of Tenth Military District, 130; and Battle of Bladensburg, 136-137
Wood, Eleazer D., 54, 59-60, 85
Wool, John E., 99, 116
Worrell (Pennsylvania), 142
Worthington, Thomas, 56, 155; calls for a state army, 154

Yates, J.B., 123